Earthquake!
What, Where, and How to Prepare

Earthquake!
What, Where, and How to Prepare

Your essential preparedness guide for
earthquake risks and hazards in the U.S.

Christopher K. Cox

Preparedness is unique to each person and household. What is presented in this book is based on the personal preparedness efforts of the author, and those same efforts may not be applicable to you and your situation. While general preparedness is fairly universal, you should discuss your situation with a local preparedness expert who can better advise you on the risks in your area, and how your household situation can best prepare for those risks.

Additionally, any earthquake, preparedness, or other modifications to your home or other structure should be done using qualified experts in compliance with local ordinances and codes. You are responsible to become aware of, and adhere to, all ordinances/codes that may pertain to your preparedness, such as fuel storage regulations, food and/or water storage, home modifications, etc.

For better virtual preparedness—keeping your computer, digital identity, and personal information better protected—check out _Everyday Cybersecurity: A practical approach to understanding cybersecurity, security awareness, and protecting your personal information and identity_ by Christopher K. Cox, available on Amazon.

ISBN paperback # 978-1-7330186-2-3
ISBN ebook #978-1-7330186-3-0

Dedication

This book is dedicated to my sweet, patient, beautiful, and loving wife, Esther. Thank you for your continual love, support, and encouragement through the years. Thank you for encouraging preparedness in our home.

Acknowledgements

Without the support of others, this book would have likely languished as a draft under continuous revision.

Besides my wife, who encourages my writing and still asks about the sci-fi book draft I first introduced her to, I'm thankful for my children. They have been a source of motivation and inspiration. I hope this book helps them to become better prepared.

I'm also grateful to my parents. They instilled in me the desire to become better prepared and more self-reliant.

My brothers and sisters have also been examples and supportive, and I appreciate them.

Finally, a big thanks to Kaitlyn, my editor, who was willing to endure another book to edit and polish up.

Before we begin, thank you!

I appreciate you taking the time to read *Earthquake! What, Where, and How to Prepare.*

Before writing this book, I gave several presentations on earthquakes and preparedness. It was the lack of time at these presentations that motivated me to write this book. I have more information on earthquakes and preparedness than I can share in any single presentation, so writing became the means to assemble the best information together.

I've tried to present information as straightforward as possible to help you know what to prepare for. When I prepare for something, I want to know what to expect. Emergency preparedness is no different. Too many people have a vague awareness—based on news reports and Hollywood—of what earthquakes are, and too many people are either underprepared or not prepared.

If you want to become familiar with what earthquakes are without going into textbook details, where the risks are in the United States, and how to become better prepared, then this book is for you.

I apologize to those outside the U.S. because I haven't done as much research on earthquake risks specific to other countries. However, parts 1 and 3 are still relevant.

With over 160 sources, I've tried to include updated information to increase your knowledge and awareness and guide you to better preparedness.

I'm (slowly) building a website with much of the information from this book and other information. Visit it at www.Prep4Quake.com.

Please take a moment and leave a review on Amazon, or wherever you have obtained a copy of this book, so other readers can decide whether this book can help them.

Thank you.

Christopher K. Cox

Facebook https://www.facebook.com/christopherkcoxauthor
Instagram https://www.instagram.com/christopherkcoxauthor/

Contents

As the Earth Moves

When I was ten years old, my family moved to Santiago, Chile. It wasn't too long after we moved there that I experienced my first minor earthquakes. The first few earthquakes were a little unsettling, but it was kind of fun to feel the bed or floor briefly shake. None of the quakes were longer than a few seconds.

On Sunday, March 3, 1985, we were eating dinner when the table, chairs, and house started shaking. Because we were used to feeling little tremors, we weren't concerned. But the shaking got stronger. As it got more intense and didn't stop, my dad told us to get out of the house. We were living in an older rental home, and we didn't know how well it would hold up in a big earthquake.

As we exited the back door of our home, a long patio stretched out for about fifty feet, with grape vines covering much of the arbor. I remember seeing grapes falling from the vines as I went out the back door and along the patio.

On the back-right side of the backyard was an in-ground pool. The pool had a raised ledge a little more than a foot high. We usually only filled the pool to near ground level—well below the top of the ledge—so it wasn't too deep for us kids. As my family left the house, I saw three-foot waves cresting in the pool and sloshing over the ledges.

When the earth finally stopped shaking, our house was still standing. We did find new cracks and some of the chandeliers had shed a few glass crystals, but other than that, the damage was minor.

Where we lived was not near the earthquake's epicenter. The magnitude 7.8 earthquake had struck off the coastline of Chile—about 68 miles west of Santiago—between Valparaiso and San Antonio. The quake lasted about three minutes and twenty seconds and was felt throughout Chile and as far away as Buenos Aires, Argentina, and San Paolo, Brazil.

The earthquake killed 177 people, injured another 2,575, destroyed 66,000 buildings, and left 127,000 structures heavily damaged. One million people were displaced and 372,000 were left homeless. The damage was estimated at 1.8 billion dollars.

During our six years in Chile, we experienced numerous smaller quakes, but this was the largest. The experience was when my interest in earthquakes began. Since then, I have researched and studied earthquakes and been interested in new discoveries and how quakes might be predicted. A big advantage I have is I am not stuck in the mindset of the theories taught in school, many of which are being questioned now due to new evidences and discoveries.

About the same time, I became interested in earthquakes, I was also a Boy Scout. My parents were into preparedness, and, coupled with the Scouting motto "Be Prepared," I was becoming more preparedness aware.

As I grew older and became more preparedness minded, I became aware of how ill-prepared most people are. For many people, the only knowledge they have of earthquakes is what they have seen in news stories, in movies, or on TV. But they really don't know much about what an earthquake is, that there is much more involved than just the earth shaking, and they don't know about the other hazards directly related to earthquakes.

Most people aren't prepared and make excuses for why they aren't. Of those who say they're prepared, most seem to think a pre-made 72-hour kit, some water, and maybe some extra food is all they need to get through a disaster or other emergency.

I think it's interesting how many people talk of earthquakes and preparedness but have virtually no experience with earthquakes; some have little experience with any situation requiring actual preparedness.

When it comes to being prepared, it's good to have an idea what you're preparing for. Earthquake preparedness is too often discussed with little information about what earthquakes are and what hazards they can cause, besides the obvious ground shaking and buildings falling.

The lack of knowledge and a vague understanding of the potential hazards can be problematic. While there are a lot of general preparations, understanding what you are preparing for is valuable to becoming better prepared for any emergency. Once you understand the emergency, you know if your preparations are adequate or if you've overlooked something. A better understanding of earthquakes and their related hazards can result in better earthquake preparedness.

Using my own studies and preparations, I have given presentations on earthquakes and preparedness. After a few presentations, I decided I needed a way to provide more detailed information, without a time constraint. Additionally, it would be helpful if information could be easily reviewed and shared.

The result is this book, which is like my earthquake preparedness presentations in that there are three parts.

The first part is an overview of earthquakes, kind of like earthquakes 101. My hope is to demystify earthquakes a little by providing some understanding of what they are and what their associated hazards are. Earthquakes' shaking doesn't kill very many people. But falling debris, fires, floods, landslides, and many other hazards caused by the earth shaking are the bigger threats.

The second part covers some earthquake scenarios in the United States, most of which are based on estimated losses using the Federal Emergency Management Agency's HAZUS program.

Because I currently live in Utah, my presentations focus more on the Wasatch Fault and the hazards and losses of a large earthquake striking the Salt Lake Valley area. While I have a little more information for a Wasatch Fault earthquake scenario, part two also reviews a few other high-profile, earthquake-prone areas and loss scenarios for those locations.

While the specific fault information may be different for other parts of the country, much of the information is similar. Some areas have a few unique hazards, and a few places have better construction codes. However, with few exceptions, we as a country are woefully unprepared for major earthquakes.

The final part is about earthquake preparedness. This section will give examples of hazards or situations to expect if an earthquake strikes. For example, before my research, I didn't know I was living in an area with high liquefaction potential. I also didn't realize the earthquake scenario for a Salt Lake earthquake estimates that over 300,000 households (not people, but basically homes or residences) will likely be without potable water for 90 days after a large earthquake.

Knowing what might happen in an earthquake scenario can better help you know how to prepare. Therefore, I feel it is important to first discuss earthquakes and their associated hazards and then cover preparedness.

The good thing is earthquake preparedness is very cross-disaster applicable.

Unlike some preparations, which may focus on evacuation, earthquake preparedness covers short-term and long-term preparations and covers scenarios for both remaining in your home or evacuating to safety. Because of the myriad of hazards that can result from an earthquake, thorough earthquake preparedness can also help you become better prepared for most other disasters and emergency situations.

By no means is this book intended to include every possible preparation, nor is it a technical manual about earthquakes. In particular, please note that each person's locale and household situation is unique, and so your preparations will be different from mine.

If you have questions about what you should do, please consult a preparedness expert in your own community—someone who is familiar with the local hazards and risks. For example, if you live in the mountain or central states, you're not likely to be preparing for a tsunami as an earthquake hazard. However, living along a lake shore could still expose you to flooding, seiche, or subsidence risk. We'll discuss these hazards later.

In addition to considering your local hazards in your preparation, your preparation needs are also determined by your household. For me, I live in a single-family home with my wife, four young children, and a dog. Animals aren't usually accepted in an evacuation center. Children at different ages and stages have differing needs, which should be considered.

For those who are interested, in the appendix section I have included references for many of the facts presented throughout the book. There is also a list of many of the websites. My hope is this book will help you, or someone you know, to become better prepared for the inevitable events that will occur.

Part 1 – What: Earthquakes 101

Chapter 1
What Is an Earthquake?

Ask most people what an earthquake is, and they will respond with what they have seen on TV or in a movie. Most people simply say an earthquake is when the earth shakes back and forth, and buildings can fall down. While this is a good start, it's only a small part.

So, what causes the earth to quake?

It's the fault

What is an earthquake?

An earthquake is the sudden slip on a fault and the resultant radiated seismic energy and ground shaking. We will discuss a little more about what that means in a bit. Earthquakes can also be caused by volcanic or magmatic activity, or they can be caused by sudden stress changes in the earth. Most people think of the earth moving in a horizontal motion (side to side) during an earthquake, but the earth movement can be vertical, horizontal, or both.

A fault is where two tectonic plates meet. You can think of it as a fracture along which blocks of the earth's crust move relative to one another on that fault. The fault plane—the fracture that extends from the surface down through the crust—cuts down into the earth along the tectonic plates. It is on this fault plane where slipping can occur. This slipping on the fault, between the plates, is where the seismic rupture (the earthquake) begins.

In an earthquake, the point on the fault plane where this slipping is centered (where the rupture begins) is called the hypocenter, or focus, of the earthquake. Directly above the hypocenter (usually miles above), on the earth's surface, is the epicenter of the earthquake.

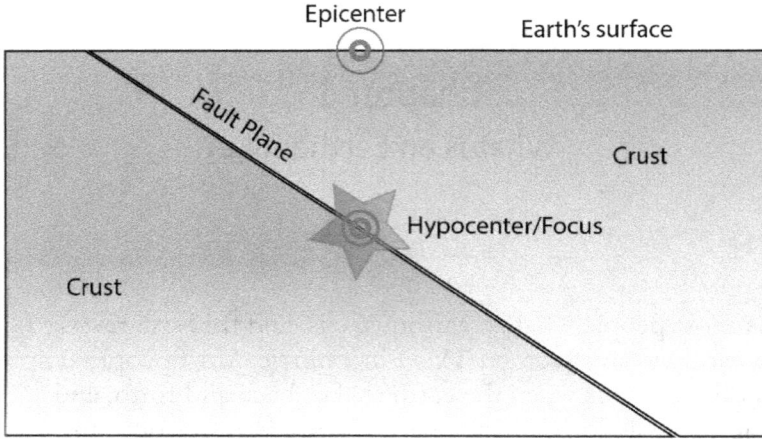

Figure 1: Crusts, fault, epicenter.

Types of faults

There are three general types of faults: strike-slip, normal, and reverse faults. Based on these three, other fault sub-types are defined, depending on characteristics such as which direction the plates move relative to an observation point. For simplicity, we will stick to the general types.

In a strike-slip fault, the blocks of crust are vertical, or almost vertical. When movement along the strike-slip fault occurs, the blocks of crust move sideways (horizontally) along the fault line.

The next two types of faults—normal and reverse faults—are both categorized as dip-slip faults, where the blocks of crust are inclined, and fault movement is mostly vertical. While these are both dip-slip faults, they are considered different based on how the blocks of crust move relative to each other.

These two faults reference the blocks of crust as one being above the inclined fault, and the other below the incline. The movement of the crust above the incline (on top) is what categorizes the fault as a normal or reverse fault.

Earth's surface

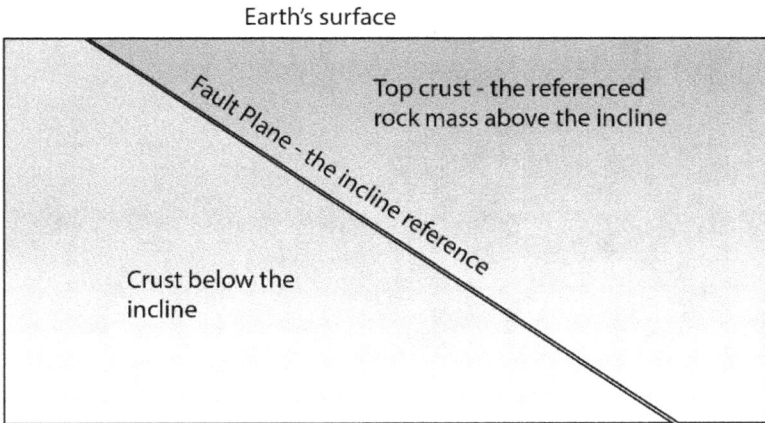

Figure 2: Dip-slip fault.

If the rock mass above the incline moves down, where the top crust drops along the incline, it is referred to as a normal fault.

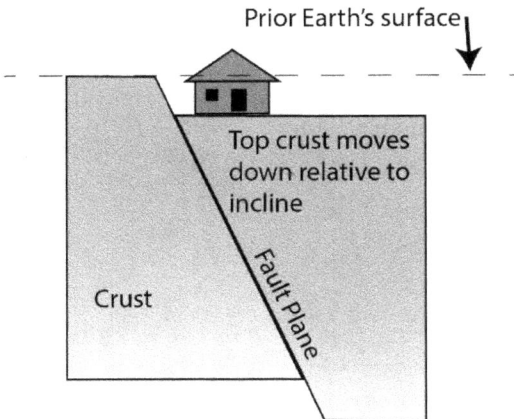

Figure 3: Normal fault.

The other type of dip-slip fault is a reverse fault. In the reverse fault, the top crust (the rock mass above the incline) moves upwards along the fault.

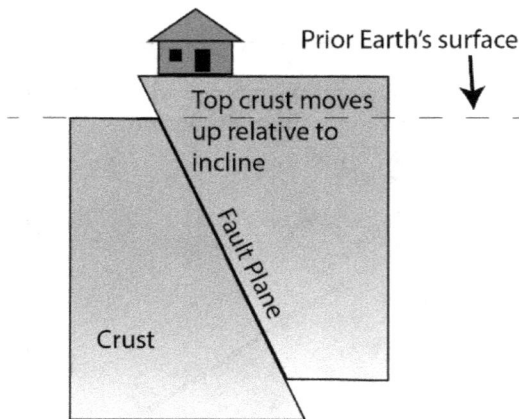

Figure 4: Reverse fault has a steep slope.

Various characteristics can further categorize a reverse fault as a thrust fault or a blind thrust fault. If a reverse fault has a dip of 45 degrees or less, it is called a thrust fault. In other words, a thrust fault has a much shallower slope than a typical reverse fault.

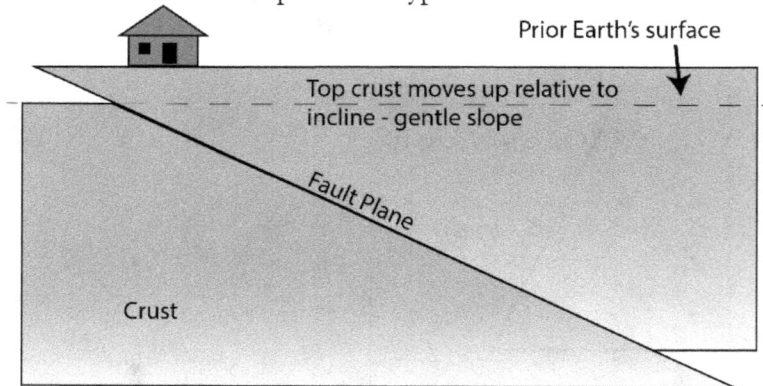

Figure 5: Thrust fault, with shallower slope than a reverse fault.

A thrust fault that has not ruptured to the surface, meaning there isn't any visible evidence of the fault on the earth's surface, is called a blind thrust fault. These are often faults that surprise us with an earthquake in an unexpected location.

On January 17, 1994, a hidden fault under the San Fernando Valley of the Los Angeles area was the origin of the magnitude 6.7 Northridge earthquake. This blind thrust fault shook the ground vertically and horizontally for 10 seconds and was strongly felt in a 30-mile (48 km) diameter area. Ground shaking was felt as far away as Las Vegas. The geology of the rupture sent most of the energy towards the northern mountains, but it still had enough to cause widespread destruction. The resulting death toll was 72, and about 9,000 were injured. There were 82,000 structures that were either damaged or destroyed. It took the area more than a year to mostly recover from the damage.

There are other types of faults as well, including oblique-slip faults, which have components of different slip styles.

Most earthquakes are single-fault ruptures, meaning there is only one fault that slips and causes the tremor. However, multi-fault earthquakes are possible. That means an earthquake on one fault can cause ruptures on other faults. It used to be believed that multi-fault earthquakes were only possible on nearby faults. However, as we'll discuss later, an earthquake on one fault can trigger another on a fault much further away than previously assumed.

Most earthquakes are, at least in part, described by the type of fault where the rupture occurred, such as a thrust fault. Many of the largest earthquakes are megathrust earthquakes.

Megathrust earthquakes happen where plate boundaries converge. This is where one crustal plate is forced under another in an area called a subduction zone. In the process of one plate going under the other, the top plate is pushed upwards, which is referred to as a thrust. Because these fault zones are usually quite large, the potential earthquakes can be extremely strong.

How are earthquakes measured

There are several measurement scales used for earthquakes. Among these are the Richter magnitude, surface-wave magnitude, body-wave magnitude, and moment magnitude scales. We will focus on the commonly used Richter and moment magnitude scales.

Richter scale

The most commonly known measurement is the Richter scale. It was created in 1935 by Charles F. Richter at the California Institute of Technology. The Richter scale measures the amplitude (size) of seismic waves. Basically, it measures an earthquake's size.

It uses a logarithmic scale, where each full step is 10 times greater than the one before. As an example, a magnitude 2.2 tremor would be 10 times bigger than a 1.2, and a 3.2 is 100 times bigger than the 1.2. Continuing up, a magnitude 4.2 quake is 1000 times bigger, and a 7.2 earthquake is one million times bigger than the 1.2 tremor.

Some of the biggest advantages of the Richter scale was its simplicity; it corresponded with observable damage, which made it useful for designing and building earthquake-resistant structures.

While the Richter scale is useful for measuring the size of an earthquake, there are some disadvantages. It is a local magnitude scale, which means it isn't very reliable for measurements taken from further than 370 miles away. The scale also has a limitation in its highest measurable magnitude, which means all large earthquakes tend to have magnitude 7. However, the Richter scale is still useful, particularly for small and medium earthquakes and in the local area of the earthquake. It is sometimes referred to as local magnitude (M_L) or Richter magnitude.

Moment magnitude scale

In the 1970s, the moment magnitude (denoted as M or M_W) scale was created to more accurately measure earthquakes. Two of its key goals were to accurately measure and characterize large earthquakes and to have improved accuracy in measuring earthquakes from a greater distance, or earthquakes that break faults over a large distance.

Like the Richter scale, the moment magnitude scale uses a logarithmic measure, meaning each step is measured as a multiple of the previous step. Where the Richter scale measures the amplitude (size) of the earthquake, the moment magnitude measures the amount of energy released by the earthquake.

Essentially, the scale measures how much energy it takes for each step up in size. Every 0.1 increase of the scale is equivalent to 1.4 times the energy released. This means a full step in the scale is 31.6 times greater than the previous step. A 6.2 magnitude earthquake releases 31.6 times more energy than a 5.2. A 7.2 magnitude has 1000 times more energy than the 5.2.

Because it is more difficult to compute, the moment magnitude is more commonly used for medium to large earthquakes. Although it is the preferred magnitude for reporting earthquakes, it is not normally used when calculating magnitudes of less than 3.5, which constitute most earthquakes.

Mercalli intensity scale

A problem with the magnitude scales is they measure the earthquakes size and energy released but they do not address the effects of the earthquake. A 7.2 earthquake can cause varying degrees of damage. The worst damage is at the epicenter. However, if the quake was extremely deep, then the amount of damage will be much less than if it was a shallow quake. Similarly, while those at the epicenter and in the immediate vicinity will receive the brunt of the destruction, those further away will receive lesser degrees of damage. Yet, for those at the epicenter and 50 miles away, it was the same earthquake. Geological conditions also influence the intensity of an earthquake.

The Mercalli intensity scale was created to measure the intensity and effects of an earthquake. The intensity is not completely determined by the magnitude. This scale attempts to quantify the effects on a scale from I, where it's not felt, to XII, which is total destruction. The values depend on distances from the epicenter, depth of the hypocenter, and data gathered from people who experienced the earthquake.

Originally developed in the late 1800s, the scale has undergone several modifications and is now known as the Modified Mercalli Scale (MM) or Modified Mercalli Intensity Scale (MMI).

Using various calculations and factors, including depth and distance, the Mercalli scale may often be employed in determining earthquake scenarios and what people may experience in certain earthquake conditions.

Table 1: Mercalli intensity scale (modified from table found at https://en.wikipedia.org/wiki/Mercalli_intensity_scale).

Scale	Effects
I. Not felt	Unlikely to be felt except by few if the conditions are right.
II. Weak	Only likely to be felt by a few people who aren't doing anything, especially those on the upper floors of buildings.
III. Weak	Most people indoors will feel the movement, particularly on the upper floors of buildings. However, most people won't correlate the movement to an earthquake, as it is like the vibrations felt from a passing truck. Some parked vehicles may rock slightly.
IV. Light	Most people indoors will feel it, and a few outside. During the night the movement may wake some people up. Windows, doors, and dishes will shake lightly. Parked vehicles will be noticeably rocked.

Scale	Effects
V. Moderate	Almost everyone will feel it, and many who are asleep will be woken up. The shaking can break windows, and unstable objects may fall.
VI. Strong	Everyone feels it, and it's enough to frighten many. The shaking can move furniture, damage plaster, and cause slight damage.
VII. Very strong	Poorly built or designed buildings will receive considerable damage. Well-built structures may receive slight to moderate damage. Buildings of better design and construction may only receive negligible damage.
VIII. Severe	Specially designed buildings receive slight damage, while considerable damage occurs in ordinary structures. Poorly built buildings will receive severe damage. Chimneys, factory stacks, monuments, and walls may fall. Heavy furniture may be overturned.
IX. Violent	Buildings may be shifted from foundations. Liquefaction can occur. Substantial damage to buildings as well as partial collapse can also occur. Specially designed buildings will receive considerable damage.
X. Extreme	Some well-built wood structures may survive, while most frame and masonry buildings and foundations will be destroyed. Railroad tracks will bend.
XI. Extreme	Few masonry structures survive. Bridges will be destroyed, and underground pipes will be out of service. Railroad tracks will get severely bent. Soft ground will cause land slips, and fissures will open.
XII. Extreme	This is total destruction. Ground waves may be seen. Objects may be thrown into the air.

Basically, the Mercalli intensity scale is used to measure how the earthquake was felt on the surface.

Depending on several factors, a really deep magnitude 7-range earthquake may cause little damage on the surface. However, a shallow 6.2 earthquake might result in extreme (X) shaking and destruction in the local area, similar to what might be expected by a high 7-range quake.

Frequency of earthquakes

There are millions of earthquakes measured around the world every year, although most are too small to be felt. Based on their magnitude (whether it's the Richter or Moment Magnitude scales), earthquakes are generally classified by their whole-number ranges. There are quakes with magnitudes less than 1.0, but they are basically omitted from most classifications.

Earthquakes in the magnitude 1.0–1.9 range are called microquakes. Millions occur around the world every year, but they are rarely ever felt.

Magnitude 2.0–2.9 earthquakes are very minor and only slightly felt by some people. These quakes don't cause any damage and can easily be mistaken for a large vehicle driving nearby. Over a million of these occur every year.

Earthquakes in the 3.0–3.9 range are considered minor earthquakes. Around the world, over 100,000 of these earthquakes occur every year. They are often felt by people but rarely cause damage. The shaking of objects is most noticeable. The cause of the movement could be mistaken for a construction vehicle operating nearby. The energy released by a low 3-range earthquake is equivalent to a large lightning bolt.

A light earthquake is in the magnitude 4.0–4.9 range. These earthquakes are more noticeable with the shaking of indoor objects and rattling noises. They are felt by most people in the affected area, but they cause little, if any, damage. In this range, most people realize what they felt was an earthquake. The most damage that occurs is usually objects falling off shelves or being knocked over. Worldwide, 10,000 to 15,000 of these earthquakes happen every year. A high magnitude 4 earthquake releases the same energy as an average (EF1) tornado.

The moderate earthquake category is in the 5.0–5.9 range. There are 1,000 to 1,500 of these earthquakes every year. These tremors cause damage to poorly constructed buildings but cause slight or no damage to other buildings. These tremors are felt by everyone in the affected area.

Magnitude 6.0–6.9 earthquakes are considered strong earthquakes. These large quakes can cause moderate damage to well-built structures; however, earthquake-resistant structures generally receive little to moderate damage. This magnitude of earthquake is felt throughout a much wider area, up to hundreds of miles away from the epicenter. In the epicenter, there is strong to violent shaking. Around the world, 100 to 150 strong earthquakes occur every year. A low 6-range earthquake releases the same amount of energy as the atomic bomb dropped on Hiroshima.

Major earthquakes are in the magnitude 7.0–7.9 range. These temblors cause damage to most buildings, with some structures partially or completely collapsing or receiving severe damage as a result. Major earthquakes are felt over significant distances and can cause damage over 100 miles away. Ten to 20 of these earthquakes occur around the world each year. A 7.0-magnitude rupture has the energy equivalent of more than 3.9 billion pounds (1.8 billion kilograms) of explosive. A high-magnitude 7 (7.8-7.9) earthquake has the same energy release as the 1980 volcanic eruption of Mount St. Helens.

Magnitude 8.0 and larger ruptures are considered great earthquakes. Magnitude 8.0–8.9 earthquakes cause major damage to buildings, destroy many structures, and cause moderate to heavy damage even to earthquake-resistant buildings. Normally only one magnitude 8.0–8.9 earthquake occurs each year. The world's largest nuclear test, performed by the Soviet Union in 1961, released the energy equivalent of a magnitude 8 earthquake, which is more than 123 billion pounds (56 billion kilograms) of explosive.

On average, one magnitude 9.0 or greater earthquake will occur somewhere around the world every 10 to 50 years. Extreme damage and shaking occurs over a very wide area, and near total destruction occurs in the immediate area. These great earthquakes cause permanent changes to the ground topography. The largest recorded earthquake was a magnitude 9.5 that struck near Valdivia, Chile, in 1960.

Table 2: Earthquake local magnitude, intensity, effects, and frequency.

M_L	Category	MM	Average Earthquake Effects	Estimated Annual Frequency
1.0–1.9	Micro	I	Microquakes are rarely felt but are recorded by seismographs.	Millions/year
2.0–2.9	Minor	I to II	Some people may slightly feel these, but no damage occurs to buildings.	1 million+/year

M_L	Category	MM	Average Earthquake Effects	Estimated Annual Frequency
3.0– 3.9	Minor	III to IV	Most people feel these, but they rarely cause damage. Objects can be seen shaking.	100,000+/ year
4.0– 4.9	Light	IV to VI	Shaking objects and rattling noises are seen and heard. Most people will feel these quakes when indoors, although the shaking is less noticeable outside. Usually causes very little damage to structures. Most damage is caused by objects falling off shelves or being knocked over.	10,000 to 15,000 / year
5.0– 5.9	Moderate	VI to VII	Poorly constructed buildings will receive varying degrees of damage. Little to no damage will be caused to other buildings. Everyone in the area feels these quakes.	1,000 to 1,500 / year
6.0– 6.9	Strong	VIII to X	Damage will increase to well-built structures, with slight to moderate damage to earthquake-resistant structures. Moderate to severe damage will occur on poorly constructed buildings. In the epicenter area, there is strong to violent shaking, and the earthquake can be felt hundreds of miles away.	100 to 150 / year
7.0– 7.9	Major	X to XII	Most buildings will receive at least partial damage, with poorly designed and built structures having severe damage or collapse.	10 to 20 / year

M_L	Category	MM	Average Earthquake Effects	Estimated Annual Frequency
8.0–8.9	Great	X to XII	Earthquake-resistant structures may receive moderate to heavy damage. Major damage will occur to other buildings, with many likely destroyed. These quakes are felt across large regions.	1 / year
9.0–	Great	X to XII	These quakes will cause complete or near-total destruction. Intense shaking and heavy damage across a large area will occur. Can cause permanent ground topography changes.	1 every 10 to 50 years

As previously mentioned, a major earthquake—those of magnitude 7.0 and higher—can cause damage 150 miles away and be felt much further.

As an example of an earthquake's far-reaching effects, on March 2, 2016, a 7.8 earthquake occurred southwest of Sumatra Indonesia. In Vietnam, 1,384 miles away from the epicenter, someone reported, "This is the first time I felt an earthquake. So scary!" A report from Singapore, 793 miles from the epicenter, another person reported, "The entire building was shaking and swaying beneath my feet." In Malaysia, 757 miles from the epicenter, it was reported, "At 13th floor, felt building was swaying left and right."[1]

Factors affecting earthquake intensity

When a fault ruptures, two main types of seismic waves are generated: body and surface waves. Body waves travel through the interior, or body, of the earth and are known as primary and secondary waves, or P waves and S waves. The P waves travel faster and are detected first. P waves are compressional waves and seldom

---

[1] These quotes are from people reporting the earthquake to the LastQuake application, which is produced by the Euro-Mediterranean Seismological Center. Since 2016, I've seen similar reports on the app of earthquakes being felt hundreds of miles away.

do much damage. They transmit through both solid and liquid materials.

The S waves move through the earth in a side-to-side motion and are slower than P waves. However, the S waves can cause more damage. S waves travel through only solid material. Some of the early warning systems being developed are trying to leverage the detection of P waves to give a 20–30 second heads up.

The second type of waves, surface waves, travel through the outer layers of the crust and are detected after the body waves. The two types of surface waves are Raleigh waves, which move in a rolling or circular motion like an ocean wave, and Love waves, which move horizontally with side-to-side motions.

The amount of potential damage seismic waves can cause is affected by several factors, including the depth of the fault rupture, the ground composition of the event area, and the shape, or geology, of the quake zone.

As an interesting side note, the frequency of seismic waves are usually less than 20 Hertz, which is lower than what most humans can detect. If a P wave manages to refract out of the surface and into the air, and has a higher frequency, it could be heard as a low rumble. However, most of the rumbling noise heard during an earthquake is the result of buildings and objects moving.

Depth
Generally speaking, the deeper the hypocenter (the point on the fault where the earthquake originates from below the epicenter), the less the earthquake's effects are felt on the surface. The magnitude of a deep earthquake may be large, but the seismic waves have further to travel before they reach the surface. As a result, seismic waves lose energy and destructive power. Deep earthquakes are often felt over a larger area, but they are less damaging. An earthquake is considered deep if its hypocenter is more than 186 miles (300 km) below the surface.

Shallow earthquakes have less distance for the seismic waves to travel, which means greater energy to shake things on the surface. Shallow depths are from the surface to about 40 miles (60 km) below.

Intermediate depths are considered from about 40 to 186 miles (60 to 300 km) below the surface.

Most earthquakes happen at depths less than 50 miles (80 km) from the surface.

Ground composition and geology

The ground composition and geology of the land are closely interrelated in how they can affect seismic waves. The shape, density, material, and other characteristics of the earth's crust and the surface each affect how the seismic waves travel and how long the waves last.

The shape of the underlying geology can have an amplifying or dissipating effect on seismic waves. For example, if a city is built over a geologic basin, then the basin can act like a bell ringing, where seismic waves are amplified and propagated resulting in increased shaking and duration.

Other topography, like mountains or rivers, can affect ground shaking. Softer sediments can amplify seismic waves, where hard rock will dampen the waves.

Rock and sediment layers, particularly along boundary layers where the differing materials have dissimilar elastic, compressional, and density properties, can reflect, refract, or even diffract and scatter seismic waves. These differing boundaries are often related to geology and topography of the area. Reflection is the abrupt change of the wave's direction. Refraction is the change in the wave as it passes through different materials, such as through loose soil versus hard rock. Diffraction occurs when the wave spreads around obstacles.

Foreshocks and aftershocks

When learning about earthquake basics, it is also useful to know what foreshocks and aftershocks are and what to expect from them.

Sometimes a large earthquake is preceded by smaller quakes. If the smaller earthquakes occur within hours, days, or even weeks before a large earthquake (the mainshock), they are known as foreshocks.

Sometimes there are small, infrequent, earthquakes that happen in the same area several weeks or months before a larger one. While these are not considered foreshocks, they may be considered pre-shocks.

Many earthquakes occurring within a relatively short distance of each other is called an earthquake swarm. Swarms do not necessarily indicate the coming of a larger earthquake. However, in some cases, they do. On April 23, 2017, there was a report of a significant earthquake swarm off the coast of Chile near Valparaiso. The next day, a magnitude 6.9 earthquake struck the same area.

The best way to react to any small earthquake is to get prepared, or check your preparations, for a larger one. Most of the time, small quakes do not precede a larger one. But, that's *most* of the time. Unfortunately, we don't know when a small tremor is a foreshock until after a mainshock event occurs.

The earthquakes and tremors that occur *after* a large earthquake are called aftershocks. The magnitude of aftershock earthquakes can be as high as the original earthquake. Aftershocks can occur immediately after the main quake and can continue happening days, weeks, months, and even years afterward. Hundreds and even thousands of aftershocks can follow a major earthquake, although only a small percentage will be large enough to cause significant additional damage.

It is not uncommon for aftershocks to end up causing more damage than the main earthquake. This is usually because the main quake will significantly weaken structures, and the aftershocks may finish the job. Because of the danger of aftershocks, people are often advised to not enter damaged structures after an earthquake until the building has been determined safe to enter.

An example of an earthquake and its aftershocks causing devastating damage was on August 24, 2016, when a magnitude 6.2 earthquake struck near the town of Amatrice, Italy. It left 300 people dead, 2,500 lost their homes, and 1,800 aftershocks occurred within five days.

Later that year, on October 30, a magnitude 6.6 earthquake struck the same region. It was preceded by a magnitude 5.5 earthquake on October 26.

The resulting damage, which was extensive, of these earthquakes in Italy was because the people were not used to big earthquakes. Many of their buildings, particularly the older ones, were not built to withstand significant seismic activity. Most of the damaged and destroyed buildings were constructed of unreinforced masonry.

Interestingly, the larger October quake caused no deaths. This was attributed to the warnings given as result of the foreshock that occurred a few days earlier, and many people were not in their homes and buildings at the time of the bigger earthquake.

As for how long aftershocks can follow, the longest I've heard of was in a May 2019 article on KSL.com titled "Aftershocks from 1959 earthquake sent tremors through Yellowstone in 2018." The article references a study of aftershocks from the 1959 magnitude 7.3 earthquake, near Yellowstone, known as the Hebgen Lake earthquake. In the original 1959 earthquake, 28 people died, and in some places the ground dropped 20 feet. The study identified more than 3,000 earthquakes, localized in the Maple Creek area, that occurred from June 2017 to March 2018. Earthquake swarms like this are common in the Yellowstone area and often result in numerous claims that a major disaster is about to strike, like a super volcano eruption.

This particular swarm, in 2017 through 2018, had more tremors and lasted longer than usual. As part of the study in determining the cause of the swarm, the researchers divided the tremors into subgroups. They ruled out magma or other activity as causing the northern cluster of quakes. After using formulas for predicting how many aftershocks should follow a quake, they discovered the Hebgen Lake quake was short the projected number of aftershocks. When the northern cluster of quakes were factored in to the Hebgen Lake event, it evened out aftershock expectations to what would be expected.

As for the southern cluster of tremors during the identified time period, the researchers determined they were likely caused by magma moving.

The Ring of Fire

As we conclude this chapter, we should briefly discuss the Ring of Fire as it is often brought up in conjunction with earthquakes. The Ring of Fire is a 25,000-mile (40,233 km) horseshoe shape around the Pacific Ocean. It wraps around from New Zealand, up along Indonesia, Philippines, Japan, the east coast of Russia, across to Alaska, down the west coast of Canada and the United States, to Mexico, along Central America, to Ecuador, Bolivia, Peru, and Chile.

The Ring of Fire is where 90% of the world's earthquakes occur, and 81% of the largest earthquakes rupture in this area.

The Ring of Fire is home to 75% (452) of the world's active volcanoes, ten percent of which are in Japan. This is relevant since quake activity can be caused by volcanic and magmatic action. Many of the active volcanoes in the United States are within, or near, the Ring of Fire. Mount St. Helens is included among these volcanoes, along with more than 30 other volcanoes that have erupted in the past 10,000 years.

In the United States, the Cascadia Subduction Zone extends 680 miles from Northern California up the coast to Vancouver Island, British Columbia. It is projected to be able to produce magnitude 9.0 or larger earthquakes. This zone is in the Ring of Fire.

Additionally, the San Andreas Fault in Southern California is also part of the Ring of Fire.

While the Ring of Fire may not directly be a factor in what an earthquake is, it can be a consideration in your preparations.

If you're interested in greater detail about what earthquakes are and the theories of how they are generated, there are other great resources some of which are listed in the website section of the appendix. However, a basic understanding of different kinds of faults, what earthquakes are and how they are measured, foreshocks and aftershocks, and various factors that can contribute to earthquake intensity is enough to move into the next chapters.

Chapter 2
Earthquake-Related Hazards

The most obvious hazards of earthquakes are the earth shaking and damage to buildings. The earth shaking as part of the main earthquake can cause objects to fall and injure (or kill) you.

Although there are several earthquake-related hazards during and after a mainshock earthquake, the single biggest risk most people face is damage to buildings, and more specifically entering an unsafe building. Most people expect damaged and collapsed buildings after an earthquake, although the full extent of the damage from a large earthquake can be hard to comprehend unless you see the aftermath in person; videos and images don't adequately capture the destruction.

Entering buildings damaged by earthquakes can increase the risk of injury or death, particularly if an aftershock strikes and causes the already damaged structure to partially or fully collapse. You should be wary around any damaged structure or building that has not been identified as safe.

Besides these obvious hazards, an earthquake can create various other hazards. Some are obvious, while others may not be so evident.

Aftershocks

Although they could technically be argued as separate earthquakes with their own related hazards, aftershocks are hazards. There may not be any warning before the main earthquake, but afterward, you can expect aftershocks.

Think of it this way: aftershocks are earthquakes you can expect, and, to some extent, plan for. When they strike and how intense may not be known, but some can be almost as large as the mainshock.

Aftershocks should be expected especially within the following days and weeks, which is when the biggest aftershocks generally occur. Aftershocks' intensity decreases over time.

Seiches

A seiche is a standing wave of water that moves back and forth across a semi- or fully enclosed body of water. On a small scale, the sloshing movement of waves across a pool or bathtub is a seiche. These same wave movements can be found in bays and lakes.

Seiches are typically caused by strong winds and rapid air pressure changes that push water back and forth. This oscillation can continue for hours or days. The time period between the high and low parts of the seiche can be several hours apart, which can make some people mistake the seiche on a large body of water for a tidal flow. Earthquakes can cause seiches thousands of miles away.

A seiche is what I witnessed in our pool during the 1985 earthquake in Chile. Thankfully, our pool was far enough away from our house it didn't cause any flooding. However, a pool sloshing its water out could certainly cause some water damage if it gets into a basement.

There is geological evidence that seismically generated seiches of up to 32 feet struck the shores around Lake Tahoe in California/Nevada in prehistoric times.

If you live in an earthquake risk area and are near a large body of water, flooding from a seiche may be a hazard you haven't considered but should prepare for.

Dam failures

If you live downstream from a dam, its failure after an earthquake should be a big concern for you. While many dams are built to a high seismic rating, many are not.

The only way to discover a dam's seismic rating is to investigate, as you probably won't find it stamped anywhere on the dam structure itself. There may be some plans in place in case of a failure, but most of the time these contingencies are based more on minor failures and not a catastrophic, complete failure, which could cause widespread flooding devastation.

Unfortunately, it seems that most authorities on dams overrate the integrity of the dam's superstructure and don't give much credence to the possibility of complete failure. While it's true that dams rarely suffer a complete failure, there have been unexpected failures.

While not caused by a seismic event, the Teton Dam collapse on June 5, 1976, was completely unexpected. The dam had been completed less than a year earlier and was filling, almost to its capacity, when the failure occurred.

The key takeaway is that the failure was not the result of the dam structure itself, which was an earthen dam, but was most likely due to the failure in the dam's abutments, allowing water to seep around and eventually cause the dam's collapse.

Similarly, a dam may have an earthquake rating, but what about where the dam joins the ground at either end, the abutments? What happens if those fail? Or, could a landslide into the reservoir cause a seiche of significant size to wash over the dam?

So, while a dam failure may be a remote possibility, if you live downstream it should be one of your considerations for emergency preparedness. Should the unthinkable happen, you may not have much warning to evacuate, especially if the electricity and communication systems are down as a result of the earthquake.

Damaged infrastructure

Damaged buildings are what most people expect in the aftermath of a strong earthquake, but roads, bridges, the water supply, the electrical grid, railways, airports, and other structures and facilities that support our modern life are all at risk.

If an earthquake damages transportation infrastructure, it will increase response time for aid, especially in the hardest hit areas.

If the electrical grid goes down, so does the option to use any device that requires power from the grid. In the summer, this means air conditioning probably won't be an option, although batteries, solar power, and alternative sources of electricity could provide needed power for some devices.

After the Northridge earthquake, about two million people were without power. Simply put, expect the power to be out, at least for a few days, after an earthquake.

Most backup power systems, such as those used for facilities like hospitals, care centers, or even data centers, are not designed to run more than a few days, usually due to the lack of fuel storage. What happens to patients or the elderly who are dependent on electrically powered equipment? What happens when vital computer systems cannot be used to monitor critical health conditions, or to access vital patient records for medication and other health information?

A damaged electrical grid is usually more quickly repaired than another, more critical infrastructure system: the water supply.

We take our utilities—water, electric, gas—for granted and easily overlook them. But what happens if the water system is damaged from an earthquake and it takes three months (or more) before it gets fully repaired?

How will you get water? Not just for drinking but for cooking, cleaning, and hygiene purposes as well. Most people don't store emergency food, and even less have considered adequate water storage. Those who do have an emergency water supply might have a couple weeks' worth, maybe as much as a month. But, what about three months' worth? We'll discuss more about these considerations in Earthquake Preparedness section of the book.

In chapter 10, we'll look at a few earthquake scenarios that have been developed in conjunction with the Federal Emergency Management Agency. Some of the most eye-opening factors have to do with anticipated infrastructure damage. Those who believe a 72-hour kit will suffice may end up getting a rude wake-up after a large earthquake.

Fires

Fires can break out in the aftermath of an earthquake. Damaged fuel tanks or leaking gas pipes can contribute to the fire danger. Fallen electrical lines and damaged transformers are only a couple of potential spark producers that can ignite fires.

Some fires could be ignited by stoves tipping over or a flammable object igniting on a stove left on during an earthquake. Gas stoves, water heaters, furnaces, and other appliances can also pose an increased fire risk if the gas isn't shut off completely.

To make matters worse, water availability, specifically through the municipality's water supply, may be limited or non-existent due to water main damage, making the suppression of fires more difficult.

But land is not the only place fires could occur. Interestingly, following a magnitude 7.8 earthquake in the Sea of Japan on July 12, 1993, there were reports of "several boats in the port spontaneously burst into flames, and winds from the tsunami drove the blaze inland, to devastating effect" (Weisberger, The Weird Reason 'Tsunami Fires' Broke Out After Japan Earthquake, 2018).

According to researchers, the bubbles and foaming in the ocean that were reported during the 1993 earthquake, and in the 2011 Tōhoku earthquake, were likely methane gas released from the ocean floor during the rupture. The subsequent tsunami would have stirred up the gas, bringing it to the surface. The methane gas was probably ignited electrostatically. Tests have found that certain conditions could generate the needed electrostatic charge, which could ignite a fire.

Post-quake fires were also reported after the 1994 Northridge quake. There were reports of places where water was running through the streets from broken water mains, while fire was roaring at the same place—on the water—due to a break in a gas main.

Flooding

Earthquake-induced tsunamis, seiches, and dam failures can all lead to flooding. Earthquakes can damage dikes and levees along rivers and waterways, which can then flood nearby areas. Often the areas along rivers and natural waterways are the natural flood plains, but our modern civilization has contained the water flow.

The threat of flooding is a big concern for those in the risk area for a large New Madrid earthquake, which we'll discuss more in chapter 10.

If a water main breaks in or near your home during an earthquake, you may face flooding.

Landslides and rockfalls

The shaking of the earth can easily destabilize cliffs and steep slopes. Water-saturated slopes, from rain or snowmelt, can further weaken slopes. Additionally, lots of loose, unconsolidated, or fractured rocks can make the problem worse.

Besides the possibility of rocks falling, or the side of hill sliding down and causing damage, injury, or death, tsunami waves and seiches can be generated by landslides falling into a body of water.

Landslides can also cause a river to dam up, flooding the area upstream of the obstruction and then creating more flooding hazards if the unstable dam fails.

Earthquake Lake (also known as Quake Lake) in Yellowstone was created from the 1959 Hebgen Lake earthquake. This magnitude 7.5 rupture caused a landslide that blocked most of the flow of the Madison River. Within about a month, the river had filled an area six miles long and up to 190 feet (57 m) deep. Because there wasn't a natural outlet for the water, the U.S. Army Corp of Engineers constructed a spillway to help minimize the threat of the water breaching the top of the landslide and potentially causing the failure of the natural dam.

Liquefaction

When soil is saturated, or partially saturated, it can act like a liquid when it is sufficiently shaken by an earthquake. Loose sand- and silt-based soils are most susceptible.

As the earth shakes, the soil loses its strength and stiffness and begins to behave more like a liquid, where anything on the surface could sink or move. Even the liquefaction of buried layers of soil can cause these problems.

Effects of liquefaction include:

- loss of the soil's ability to support structures;
- lateral spreading, as the ground over a buried liquefied layer could slide down a gentle slope;
- sand boils that can be ejected from a buried liquefied layer, forming sand volcanoes, with nearby ground settling and fracturing;
- flow failures can occur down steep slopes, resulting in a large displacement of material, much like a landslide;
- ground oscillation, which happens when the surface layer is shaken back and forth over a buried liquefied layer, resulting in the possible deformation of the surface;
- flotation may occur as light objects buried in the ground, such as pipelines and sewers, can float to the surface when surrounded by liquefied soil; and
- settlement can occur when the liquified ground surface settles or subsides after the shaking stops and the ground becomes firm again, which is particularly bothersome if your car, or other object, had sunk into the ground.

Liquefaction is more likely to occur in prolonged periods of ground shaking. However, there is no definite time minimum of how long the ground must shake before liquefaction occurs. Ground composition, saturation, and other conditions can all play a role in how quickly, or slowly, liquefaction occurs.

The United States Geological Survey (USGS) has various earthquake hazards maps, including liquefaction maps. The USGS, various state agencies, universities, and other organizations have identified areas at greatest risk of liquefaction. Many liquefaction potential maps are available online, if you're interested in knowing what your risk is.

Release of hazardous materials

Just as an earthquake can knock down buildings or cause landslides, the shaking can knock over or damage hazardous material storage tanks or containers. Hazardous material transportation vehicles could have an accident as a result of an earthquake. Many manufacturing and other facilities use various hazardous materials throughout their processes, and a tremor could cause the release of these materials through damaged or destroyed distribution or storage systems.

The potential list and description of hazardous materials, and their associated health and environmental hazards, would easily be their own set of books, so I won't even try to enumerate them. However, these materials include flammable liquids, solids, and gases as well as explosive material, corrosive materials, and toxic substances. Some substances are reactive to water and can create toxic or corrosive gases. Hazardous materials even include infectious substances and radioactive materials.

Here is a small list of possible failures that could lead to the release of hazardous materials:

- structural and storage container failures,
- open-topped containers sloshing material,
- falling containers or shelves,
- tanks falling or overturning, and
- pipeline breaks in both under- and above-ground lines.

Damage can happen at industrial sites releasing material from ruptured containers of pipes. Smaller storage vessels, like drums, barrels, and sacks can be damaged by falling or having something fall on them.

Fires in the area of the hazardous material could release toxic or combustible products into the air.

Furthermore, consider how frequently hazardous materials are transported on our roads and railways. Most of the time, we don't know what is on the roads or railways unless there is an accident. What happens when one of these tankers is damaged? Depending on the substance, a small to very large area may need to be evacuated, and it can take many hours of cleanup to contain the material. In the event of an earthquake, damaged roads and railways can cause derailment, tipping, and even the collision of tankers transporting hazardous materials. The damaged roads and bridges will delay containment and cleanup and will increase the exposure risk.

In addition to the transportation of hazardous material, how many industrial, commercial, and other facilities in the area use chemicals and hazardous materials in their day-to-day processes? Most of the time the use of these materials is done safely, with minimal to no threat. But, what if an unforeseen event (earthquake) causes the release of hazardous material?

In the aftermath of an earthquake, emergency response personnel will be overwhelmed. Unless there is an obvious loss of containment, it may be hours or days before the release of hazardous materials is discovered.

The 1994 Northridge earthquake was classified as a moderate earthquake, with a magnitude of 6.7. The news media focused on the structural collapses, and there were a few hazmat incidents reported by the national media. However, a 1996 analysis, "Hazardous Materials Releases in the Northridge Earthquake: Implications for Seismic Risk Assessment," completed by Michael K. Lindell and Ronald W. Perry states, "many more [hazmat incidents] were identified later and responded to by federal, state, and local agencies" (Lindell & Perry, 2006).

Lindell and Perry's analysis reported the Los Angeles County Fire Department and Health Hazardous Materials Division identified 134 locations with hazmat problems and 60 emergency hazmat incidents. Of these incidents, 10 were classified as major.

Surface fault rupture

A fault rupture is a slip and resulting displacement along a fault. When that rupture extends to the earth's surface, where we can see it, it's called a surface rupture. These surface fault ruptures can be vertical or horizontal, and can happen in a small location or extend over a larger area. In many earthquake hazards, surface fault ruptures are identified as ground displacement.

The biggest problem with surface ruptures is when a building or other structure is over the rupture. California passed the Alquist-Priolo Earthquake Fault Zoning Act in 1972 to mitigate surface ruptures. The Act prevents the construction of human-occupied buildings on the surface of active faults.

Outside of California, many other earthquake hazard locations don't have statutes regulating development on faults with surface rupture potential. The main reason for the lack of regulations is usually a lack of historical evidence of earthquakes rupturing the surface. But, if you are planning to build, it may be a good idea to make sure you're not building on an active fault, just in case.

Tectonic subsidence

Subsidence is the lowering of the ground surface. Tectonic subsidence is the lowering of the ground as a result of an earthquake. It can be caused by the vertical movement on one side of a fault.

Tectonic subsidence may also occur when loose sediments lose their load-bearing strength (as in the case of liquefaction) and the ground settles or slumps downward. For example, if an underlying layer of sediment liquefies, the top layer could drop, even though objects on the surface may not actually sink into the ground.

One of the greatest dangers of tectonic subsidence is in low-lying areas near large bodies of water, such as coastal areas or lakeshores. If the area drops below the water level, permanent flooding may result.

Tsunami

A tsunami is a high sea wave. It can travel hundreds, even thousands, of miles across the ocean. While over deep water, they can be difficult to detect due to their large wavelengths, which can take 20 to 30 minutes for it to cycle and may only have a few feet of height. As the tsunami passes through shallower water, wave shoaling compresses the wave, making it slower and taller.

Tsunamis can be caused by vertical displacement of the seabed due to an earthquake. They can also be caused by a landslide crashing into the water, and that landslide could have been caused by an earthquake.

A December 2004 Indian Ocean earthquake of magnitude 9.1–9.3 caused tsunamis along the coasts of the Indian Ocean. The tsunami waves killed 230,000 to 280,000 people, with heights up to 100 feet. The earthquake was the third largest since recording started in 1900, and it caused one of the deadliest disasters in modern history. It was also the longest earthquake ever recorded on a seismograph, lasting from 8.3 to 10 minutes, depending on the location of the recording station.

A magnitude 9.0–9.1 earthquake off the coast of Tōhoku, Japan, on March 11, 2011, caused tsunami waves that reached 133 feet in Miyako. Some of the waves travelled six miles inland in the Sendai area. This earthquake was the fourth strongest since 1900.

While earthquakes of these magnitudes are historically rare, it is interesting that these two occurred a little more than six years apart.

The two largest earthquakes, a 9.4–9.6 in Valdivia, Chile, in 1960 and a 9.2 in Alaska in 1964, also caused tsunamis. The 1960 Great Chilean earthquake lasted about 10 minutes. It was a tsunami from this earthquake that struck Japan and motivated Japan's tsunami preparations.

When you consider the earthquake risks for your area, make sure you also identify other potential hazards and threats that an earthquake can cause. Identifying these other hazards—such as flooding, seiches, landslides, and liquefaction potential—can help you become better prepared.

Chapter 3
Notable Recent Earthquakes

The largest earthquake on record was a magnitude 9.4–9.6 that struck in Valdivia, Chile, in 1960. We need to keep in mind that lists of largest earthquakes are generally only reliable since the early 1900s, when the use of scientific measuring equipment began to be used and records were kept.

Large earthquakes since the 1700s can have magnitudes reasonably deduced based on reports of the earthquake. However, if nobody was around to feel or record it, did it really happen?

Joking aside, the reality is there have been many extremely large and destructive earthquakes that we don't have records for, or which were not adequately recorded. Except for digging trenches and examining the geologic record, we don't have much historical records for determining size and frequency.

The reality is we can only guess to the size and strength of ancient (pre-1900) earthquakes. It is also possible that erosion and other environmental factors have reduced or hidden evidence of large earthquakes.

In a list of the top 36 largest earthquakes in the world, the largest quake registered was as high as 9.6, with the bottom of the list being fifteen magnitude 8.5 earthquakes. The earliest quake listed was in 1575, and the most recent (as of this writing) was in 2012.

Of those quakes, one was listed in the sixteenth century, and three for the seventeenth century. Nine occurred in the eighteenth century. Seven happened in the nineteenth century. Ten were recorded through the twentieth century. In the twenty-first century we have already had six, and we haven't even gotten out of the second decade.

Table 3: Magnitude 8.5+ earthquakes from the 16th century to early 21st century.

Century	# of M8.5+ Earthquakes
16th (1500s)	1
17th (1600s)	3
18th (1700s)	9
19th (1800s)	7
20th (1900s)	10
21st (2000-2018)	6

There may not be accurate records for past megaquakes, but it would appear, at least over the last few centuries, that we are in an upward trajectory and can expect more megaquakes.

While many notable earthquakes have happened, several of which are mentioned in other chapters of this book, this chapter will examine a few of the more recent big earthquakes, and a few that were not as big but caused extensive damage. Several of these earthquakes have caused other hazards, such as tsunamis. Some of these events are making geologists and seismologists rethink commonly held assumptions.

2004 Indian Ocean

In my opinion, the 2004 Indian Ocean earthquake was the first big earthquake of the 21st century. It occurred on December 25, 2004, about 100 miles (161 km) off the west coast of Sumatra, Indonesia. As an undersea megathrust earthquake, it had a magnitude 9.1–9.3 and caused massive tsunamis that flooded coasts around the Indian Ocean.

The quake has the distinction of being the third largest ever recorded by a seismograph, and it was the longest ever observed, lasting from 8.3 to 10 minutes, depending on the station that was recording it.

While the earthquake itself didn't cause much damage, the tsunami waves up to 100 feet (30 m) high killed an estimated 227,898 people in 14 countries.

The quake was also believed to have triggered other earthquakes, including some in Alaska.

Some seismologists believe the 2002 Sumatra earthquake, which had a magnitude 7.3, may have been a foreshock (or pre-shock) even though it happened more than two years earlier.

An earthquake of this magnitude releases as much surface energy as 26 megatons of TNT, or about the equivalent of 1,500 of the atomic bombs that were dropped on Hiroshima.

However, while the surface energy was estimated at 26 megatons, the total energy (most of it underground) was estimated to be 9,600 gigatons of TNT.

The tsunami was estimated to have an energy equivalent of 5 megatons of TNT.

Scientists calculated that the amount of energy released altered the Earth's rotation, which may have shortened the day by 2.68 microseconds and caused a 1-inch (2.5 cm) wobble on the Earth's axis. However, it should be noted that tidal effects of the moon cause the length of the day to increase by 15 microseconds each year, so the effect on the earth's rotation is lost. Likewise, the naturally occurring Chandler wobble of the Earth, which can be up to 50 feet (15 m), quickly offsets any effect an earthquake may have on the Earth's axis.

A few months later, on March 28, 2005, a magnitude 8.7 rupture occurred at the southern end of the same fault that caused the earthquake in December. It's believed the December quake caused increased stress to build up, leading to the March rupture (Than, 2010), which was about 99 miles (60 km) southeast of the December event. Both quakes were on the same fault, just at different sections.

2008 Sichuan, China

On May 12, 2008, a magnitude 8.0 earthquake struck about 50 miles (80 km) west-northwest of Chengdu, China. The shaking lasted for two minutes and was felt 1,060 miles (1,700 km) away in Shanghai. The fault ruptured for 149 miles (240 km), and its hypocenter was 12 miles (19 km) deep.

Three minutes after the earthquake, shaking was felt in Hong Kong and Macau. Other countries as far away as Pakistan and Russia also felt minor tremors in the minutes following the large earthquake.

At the epicenter, in Wenchuan County, 80% of the buildings were destroyed.

The earthquake caused more than 200,000 landslides, and more than 800 of those landslides dammed water, creating "quake lakes" of various sizes. Of the lakes formed, 28 posed a danger to people living downstream. Several villages and roads were flooded as a result of the rising waters. One town was evacuated when an earthquake-created dam threatened to burst and send flood waters downstream.

More than 69,000 people were killed as a result of the earthquake. About a third of the causalities were estimated to be a result of the geohazards caused by the earthquake. Reported injuries were 374,176, and another 18,222 people were listed as missing. More than 4.8 million people were left homeless.

Telecommunications, including internet, were cut off, and it took the government months to get parts of the infrastructure operational.

An estimated 12.5 million animals, including a million pigs, were killed.

Economic losses were estimated to be more than $75 billion.

An intriguing factor to the earthquake may have been human involvement triggering the rupture.

In a 2009 *Science* article, authors Richard Kerr and Richard Stone suggested that the completion and rapid filling of the Zipingpu Dam may have helped trigger the fault. The dam is about 1,640 feet (500 m) from the fault and 3.4 miles (5.5 km) from the quake's epicenter. The dam was completed in December 2004, and over the next couple years, rapidly filled with 393 feet (120 m) of water.

From 2006 to 2008, there was time for the water to penetrate the crust to potentially weaken the fault. Additionally, there was a loss of water in the reservoir from December 2007 to May 2008, with the water level declining even more in the week prior to the earthquake.

According to the calculations made by geophysical researcher Christian Klose, the effect of the several hundred millions tons of water was "25 times that of years' worth of natural stress loading from tectonic motions….When the fault did finally rupture, it moved just the way the reservoir loading had encouraged it to" (Kerr & Stone, 2009).

2010 Haiti

While Haiti is seismically active, the country is unprepared for major disasters. When a magnitude 7.0 earthquake struck near Haiti's capital on January 12, 2010, the results were devastating. The quake collapsed or severely damaged an estimated 250,000 homes and 30,000 commercial structures. As many as three million people were affected by the earthquake.

The number of people killed as a result ranged from 100,000 to 160,000. With morgues completely overwhelmed, and thousands of bodies on the streets, the government turned to mass graves.

Even as just a 7.0-magnitude earthquake, the Mercalli intensity was still recorded as a IX, which is classified as "violent" (the maximum intensity rating on the Mercalli scale is a XII).

A May 2010 study suggested that the earthquake rupture process may have included slips on multiple blind thrust faults and not just a rupture on the Enriquillo-Plantain Garden strike-slip fault system that branches to the south in Haiti.

Infrastructure, including air, sea, and land transport facilities, communication systems, and all hospitals within the capital, was either severely damaged or destroyed.

A year later, only five percent of the rubble had been cleared, and more than a million people were still displaced. By 2012, two years later, 500,000 people were still homeless.

2010 Chile

On February 27, 2010, a magnitude 8.8 megathrust earthquake struck off the coast of central Chile. The city of Concepción in Chile experienced the worst shaking, with a Mercalli intensity at IX. Tremors were felt in cities as far away as Buenos Aires, Argentina, and Ica, in southern Peru, 1,500 miles (2,400 km) away.

A small tsunami caused damage in several coastal towns in southern Chile, with some minor damage as far away as San Diego, California. A small tsunami was reported on the coast of Japan, but it caused no structural damage.

Officially, the quake killed 525 people, with an additional 25 missing, and 370,000 homes were damaged.

Ninety minutes after the main shock, a magnitude 6.9 earthquake occurred about 186 miles (300 km) southwest.

Later that same day, a 6.3-magnitude quake struck near Salta, Argentina, although at 1,319 miles (2,123 km) away, it doesn't seem likely to have been triggered by the Concepción quake. Still, we don't know what happens under the earth and the coincidence makes one wonder.

In the following six months, a network of seismometers recorded 20,000 aftershocks.

The power of the Concepción earthquake was such that seismologists estimate the earth's axis was moved by about 3.14 inches (8 cm) and the length of the day was shortened by 1.26 microseconds. Precision GPS indicated that Concepción moved to the west 10 feet (3.04 meters), and Santiago (which is about 267 miles [430 km] north of Concepción) moved 9.4 inches (24 cm) west.

The location of this earthquake was a little to the north of where the 1960 magnitude 9.6 Valdivia earthquake occurred. Some scientists believe the 2010 quake may have been a result of increased stress built up on the fault because of the 1960 earthquake (Than, 2010).

2011 Tōhoku, Japan

The most powerful earthquake ever recorded in Japan, and the fourth most powerful in modern records, struck on March 11, 2011, off the coast of Tōhoku, Japan. The magnitude 9.0–9.1 megathrust earthquake had its epicenter about 46 miles (70 km) east of the Oshika Peninsula at a depth of 18 miles (29 km).

Like the 2010 Chile earthquake, the Great East Japan Earthquake shifted the Earth's axis an estimated 4 to 10 inches (10 to 25 cm) and shortened the day by 1.8 microseconds. The quake also moved the main island of Japan, Honshu, about 8 feet (2.4 m) to the east.

The most vivid images of this earthquake are from the resulting tsunami that rose up to 133 feet (40.5 m) in Miyako and rushed inland 6 miles (10 km) into the Sendai area. The death toll and destruction from the tsunami was greater than the earthquake.

Several cities had tsunami walls that had been built based on the heights of tsunamis scientifically proven to occur on a regular basis. The unexpected size of the tsunami caught many people unprepared; they either believed the tsunami walls would protect them or thought they were on sufficiently high ground.

Tsunami waves were sent across the Pacific Ocean, striking coastal regions from Alaska to Chile. In most locations outside of Japan, the wave heights were low, with a 6.6-foot (2 m) wave hitting the Chilean coast.

The most infamous damage caused by the earthquake was the meltdowns of three reactors at the Fukushima Daiichi Nuclear Power Plant Complex. Evacuations occurred within a 12-mile (20 km) radius of the power plant.

The World Bank estimated the economic cost of the devastation at $235 billion.

In the five years following the 2011 earthquake, the Japanese Meteorological Agency reported 9 aftershocks over magnitude 7.0, 118 over magnitude 6.0, and 869 at magnitude 5.0 or greater.

In the aftermath of the earthquake, 4.4 million households were without electricity and 1.5 million households were without water. The Japanese National Police Agency confirmed 15,896 deaths, 6,157 injured, and 2,537 missing as a result of the quake. Extensive damage occurred, with 45,700 buildings completely destroyed and another 144,300 damaged from the earthquake and tsunami.

Ten days after the earthquake, the number of households without electricity dropped to 242,927.

In 2015, four years later, 228,863 people were still displaced.

Something to keep in mind: Japan is one of the most seismically prepared countries in the world.

2015 Illapel, Chile

On September 16, 2015, a magnitude 8.3 megathrust quake shook off the coast of Chile about 29 miles (46 km) from Illapel. The shaking lasted for over three minutes.

This quake was considered one of the most complex to be studied, as twenty seconds before the main shock, a magnitude 7.2 foreshock hit the area.

An earthquake-induced tsunami, with 15-foot (4.5 m) waves, caused flooding and heavy damage to at least 500 structures in the coastal region of the earthquake.

Because the quake happened in a less populated area, the casualties were lower. Earthquake preparedness, an improved tsunami warning system, and strict seismic building codes all contributed to only 15 deaths reported.

2016 Quito, Ecuador

The April 16, 2016, magnitude 7.8 earthquake in Ecuador was not large enough to be a megathrust, but Ecuador is over the Nasca Plate Subduction Zone. An 8.8-magnitude megathrust earthquake in 1906 ruptured the surface for about 249 miles (400 km) northeast of the 2016 rupture.

A magnitude 4.8 foreshock occurred 11 minutes before the main rupture, and 55 aftershocks occurred in the following 24 hours.

The earthquake's epicenter was in a sparsely populated area about 110 miles (170 km) from the capital city, Quito. However, there were more than 16,600 people injured in the earthquake, and 676 lost their lives. Had a megathrust event occurred, and been closer to Quito, the loss of life and devastation would have been much greater.

Some believe that a large earthquake such as this would delay the occurrence of a bigger quake. But, could this one be considered a foreshock of a much larger one, much like the 2002 Sumatra earthquake being considered a foreshock of the larger 2004 Indian Ocean rupture a little more than two years later?

2016 Italy

Two destructive earthquakes struck Italy in 2016. Both were much smaller than the others mentioned. The reason these are notable earthquakes is because of the damage caused. Italy does not experience earthquakes like countries around the Ring of Fire, so the country is ill-prepared for earthquakes.

The first earthquake was a magnitude 6.2, striking on August 24, 2016. Normally this magnitude may not cause as much damage, but the hypocenter of the earthquake was shallow, at a depth of about 3.1 miles (5 km).

By August 30, at least 2,500 aftershocks had been recorded. Official reports put the death toll at 297 and the number of people injured at 365.

The town of Amatrice, nearest the epicenter, received severe damage. Most of the damaged or destroyed buildings were not built or renovated according to an anti-seismic law passed in 1974. Many of those buildings were constructed with unreinforced masonry.

In October, three more strong earthquakes hit the area. A magnitude 5.5 occurred on October 26, followed by a 6.1 earthquake a couple hours later. These two quakes were about 20 miles (30 km) northwest of the August rupture. The day's first quake caused many to leave buildings and go to safer locations, which resulted in fewer injuries. Only one person died, having suffered a heart attack.

On October 30, a larger, 6.5-magnitude earthquake struck the region. Like the one in August, this quake was shallow and caused substantial damage to structures. More churches and historical buildings were destroyed. Except for two who died from heart attacks during the quake, there were no deaths as a result of this larger earthquake.

The biggest lesson from the Italy quakes is the importance of leaving potentially hazardous buildings immediately after an earthquake. Until the structure is safe, there may be danger of collapse in the event of an aftershock.

The other lesson pertains to those who live in areas that are not seismically active but that have an earthquake risk. Many older buildings may be particularly vulnerable. Unless they are built or renovated to seismic standards, those communities will likely experience what Italy did.

2016 Kaikōura, New Zealand

Two minutes after midnight on November 14, 2016, "one of the most complex earthquakes every recorded" (Hamling, et al., 2017) struck the northeastern South Island of New Zealand with a magnitude 7.8 earthquake.

The earthquake was a series of ruptures along multiple faults. The hypocenter was at a depth of approximately 9 miles (15 km), with its epicenter 37 miles (60 km) south-west of Kaikōura and 9 miles (15 km) from Culverden. Beginning at the hypocenter, faults continued to rupture northward over a 124-mile (200 km) range at a pace of 1.25 miles (2 km) per second. The shaking lasted for about two minutes.

Tsunami waves struck coastal areas over the next several hours, with the highest waves peaking close to 23 feet (7 m) at Goose Bay in New Zealand.

The earthquake caused coastal deformation that varied from a drop of 8 feet (2.5 m) to a rise of over 21 feet (6.5 m) along more than 68 miles (110 km) of coastline (Clark, et al., 2017).

Between 80,000 to 100,000 landslides occurred as a result of the earthquake. There were also 150 landslide dams (where the landslide blocks the flow of a stream or river), although most posed little risk.

As a result of the earthquake, major transportation routes were cut off as roads and bridges were damaged or destroyed, and railways cut off. Docks in some ports were also damaged, which prevented shipping.

Buildings were damaged, with several too severely damaged to repair.

There were 7,000 customers who lost electrical power after the earthquake, but within a day the number without power was down to 2,000. Five days later, only 340 were still without power.

Most of the water mains were restored in less than a week, but the water supply was limited. Water was cut off for several days. However, the sewage system was severely damaged.

Amazingly only two deaths occurred.

According to the geological hazard information for New Zealand, in the first year following the earthquake, more than 20,000 aftershocks were recorded, with an additional 2,552 from November 14, 2017, to May 14, 2018. Only 167 of those aftershocks were a magnitude 3 or higher, with only three breaking magnitude 6.0 or greater.

This quake caused a stir among seismologists because the rupture of multiple faults did not follow any of the models, basically suggesting that the theories need to be reworked.

2017 Mexico

Two large earthquakes struck Mexico in September 2017. The first was a magnitude 8.6 on September 7, which struck about 54 miles (87 km) off the coast of southern Mexico. The second quake hit on September 19 at a magnitude 7.1.

The September 7 quake was the second strongest in Mexico's recorded history and was the strongest of 2017. The quake affected about 1.5 million people and damaged 41,000 homes. In the hour following the quake, 12 aftershocks were recorded, and by September 14 (a week later) at least 1,806 aftershocks had been recorded, with magnitudes up to 6.1.

The epicenter was 400 miles (650 km) from Mexico City, but it still caused a power outage in the capital city that affected 1.8 million people. If the quake had been closer to a more populated area, deaths and destruction would likely have been much greater. As it was, 98 people died as a result of the earthquake.

The earthquake on September 19 was inland, about 34 miles (55 km) south of Puebla and caused extensive damage to the states of Puebla and Moreles as well as to the greater Mexico City area. It caused the collapse of more than 40 buildings, killed 370 people, and injured more than 6,000.

Interestingly, this earthquake happened on the 32nd anniversary of the 1985 Mexico City earthquake (which was a magnitude 8.0 megathrust earthquake) that killed around 10,000 people. A commemoration and national earthquake drill had happened only two hours prior to the 2017 earthquake.

Because of the proximity in dates and geography, it has been debated whether the September 19 quake was an aftershock of, or triggered by, the September 7 quake. Most seismologists dismiss the idea of the September 19 quake being an aftershock because of the 400-mile (650 km) distance between the two epicenters.

Some theories speculate whether large earthquakes can transfer stress to nearby faults. However, it is commonly accepted that this transfer of static stress, called Coulomb stress transfer, can only happen up to a distance of four times the length of the original earthquake rupture. The stress transfer theory in the case of these two earthquakes would suggest a transfer of static stress up to 249 miles (400 km) from the September 7 quake, so seismologists believe the September 19 quake being caused by the transfer of static stress was unlikely.

Another theory for the proximity in time and location of these quakes is dynamic triggering, where the seismic waves from one earthquake can trigger another fault. The theory suggests that triggered events can happen over greater distances than static stress transfer, but the triggered ruptures happen within hours or a few days. The 12-day gap between the two earthquakes falls out of the scope of the dynamic triggering theory.

Chapter 4
Unexpected Discoveries

Science is mostly theories. There are very few absolute facts, even though most of the time we, and scientists, may act like we know all the facts. The reality is, many theories are accepted as fact, but experimentation and observation may not yet have given evidence to question the theory.

Our understanding in the various sciences changes with time and new experimentation and observations. Sometimes generally accepted "facts" need to be re-evaluated when new evidence contradicts the expectation or isn't supported by current theories. Geology and seismology are no different.

However, unlike in many other sciences where scientists may be able to explore and experiment within their realm, in the earth sciences, scientists have more difficulties conclusively knowing what is happening below the surface of the earth. Certainly, various instrumentation and systems are used to gain a better understanding of what's happening under our feet. However, until we can go 20, 50, 100 or more miles below the surface of the earth, theories are still just our best guesses. Identifying earthquake "facts" is a continual process of observation, evaluation, analysis, and re-evaluation.

Over the last several years, unexpected discoveries and observations have caused rethinking about earthquakes and the assumptions surrounding earthquakes.

Multiple fault ruptures

The Kaikōura earthquake in New Zealand in 2016 caused ripples among the earthquake community. A March 2017 article states, "This complex earthquake defies many conventional assumptions about the degree to which earthquake ruptures are controlled by fault segmentation, and should motivate re-thinking of these issues in seismic hazard models" (Hamling, et al., 2017).

Prior to the Kaikōura earthquake, it was assumed that a large earthquake could trigger additional nearby faults, causing additional and nearly simultaneous earthquakes. It was previously believed that diverse fault orientations and distances between faults would limit the potential of an earthquake, causing other faults to rupture. In the article's discussion and conclusion section, the authors state:

> The Mw 7.8 Kaikōura earthquake clearly demonstrates that fault systems can undergo ruptures involving slip along numerous faults with diverse orientations, slip directions and degree of mechanical linkages. Geometric complexities have been suggested as a major control on the termination of a rupture. The exceptional rupture complexity during the Kaikōura earthquake, including apparent step overs of 15-20 km, would not have been considered as a plausible scenario in seismic hazard models. Moreover, the complex nature and lengthy propagation of the rupture hampered accurate early magnitude determination and would have posed issues for conventional earthquake early warning systems…. Regardless of the rupture mechanism, considering the incompleteness of many global fault databases, which typically only show surface faults, these observations highlight the need to account for larger jumps in hazard models which may be accommodated by unmapped faults or dynamic triggering."

Additionally, the authors state, "While the unprecedented, complex, multi-fault rupture observed in the Kaikōura earthquake may in part be related to the geometrically complex nature of the faults in this region, this event emphasizes the importance of re-evaluating how rupture scenarios are defined for seismic hazard models in plate boundary zones worldwide."

What was most remarkable and unexpected was the number of ruptured faults. Initially, a surprising five faults had been identified as having ruptured. But, as the aftermath was studied, the number increased to 12 and then to at least 21 faults discovered to have ruptured (Daly, 2017).

Ruptures can trigger other ruptures further away

In the numerous studies following the 2016 Kaikōura, New Zealand, earthquake, one of the most unexpected discoveries was that, unlike most earthquakes, not only did multiple faults rupture but the ruptures jumped much further than expected. Previously, ruptures were believed to be unable to jump large distances between fault segments. The long-held assumption was that fault jumping was limited to about 3.1 miles (5 km). In the Kaikōura earthquake, there were several jumps to separate faults. Several of these were due to hidden faults. However, several 9- to 12.5-mile gaps (15–20 km) between faults haven't been explained (Amos, 2017). The 9-mile to more than 12-mile (15-20 km) jumps in the Kaikōura earthquake were unprecedented. The rupture jumps were easily three or more times further than previously accepted as possible.

And if triggering a rupture nine miles away wasn't enough to confound conventional assumptions, a study published in the February 2016 issue of *Nature Geoscience* examined a 1997 earthquake in Pakistan that was revealed to be a magnitude 7.1 intracontinental earthquake. The earthquake was previously assumed to be a single rupture, but later analysis discovered it "was in fact an earthquake doublet: initial rupture on a shallow, blind reverse fault was followed just 19 s later by a second rupture on a separate reverse fault 50 km [31 miles] away. Slip on the second fault increased the total seismic moment by half, and doubled both the combined event duration and the area of maximum ground shaking" (Nissen, et al., 2016).

The results of the study "expose a flaw in earthquake rupture forecasts that disregard cascading, multiple-fault ruptures of this type" (Nissen, et al., 2016).

Seismologists need to rethink certain seismic hazard models, particularly those with the potential for multi-fault ruptures. Misunderstanding the multi-fault earthquake potential for areas such as Southern California will likely surprise everyone with the unexpected damage if multiple ruptures are triggered over an extensive area, as they were in the Kaikōura quake.

Current models artificially set the limit of multi-fault ruptures at 3.1 miles (5 km), which, based on recent findings, misses the possibilities of multiple faults rupturing at much greater distances.

Large earthquakes may trigger quakes on the opposite side of the planet

Most seismologists believe a large earthquake can only trigger another quake on a nearby fault. That triggering event is limited to about eight hours and to within the aftershock region.

However, an article published August 2, 2018, in *Nature Scientific Reports* analyzed seismic data from 1973 through 2016 and discovered that big earthquakes can trigger other quakes, including large ruptures, on the opposite side of the earth. As the article states,

"Scientists at Oregon State University looked at 44 years of seismic data and found clear evidence that temblors of magnitude 6.5 or larger trigger other quakes of magnitude 5.0 or larger" (Lundeberg, 2018).

The higher magnitude quakes were more likely to trigger another earthquake, usually within three days of the original, although there appeared to be minimal "systematic triggering" in the first 24 hours.

The "large earthquakes appear to be associated with an increase in the number of subsequent earthquakes up to three days later in time" (O'Malley, Mondal, Goldfinger, & Behrenfeld, 2018). The induced quake was also most likely to happen within 30 degrees of the point directly opposite (called an antipode) of the first quake, on the opposite side of the Earth. Evidence showed a minimum potential for impact near 90 degrees of the antipode.

Unexpected deformation patterns

One of the great things about the continual advances being made is learning that science may be wrong in some of its assumptions, which are too often presented as facts.

With the thousands of small earthquakes that happen along the San Andreas and San Jacinto faults in California, it was only recently detected that there is apparently "strange" and "unpredicted behavior" below the surface, and a recent study "suggests scientists have an incomplete understanding of the processes responsible for earthquakes in the region" (Dvorsky, 2018).

The San Andreas and San Jacinto faults are strike-slip faults, which means the movement is horizontal, with the plates sliding (slipping) past each other.

The surprise is that more than 6 miles (9.6 km) below the surface, previously undetected deformation patterns have a vertical movement instead of the expected horizontal slip.

It was assumed that the smaller faults in the region were locked, with no place to move, causing greater load pressure. The load pressure being placed on the two larger faults was calculated using the data from the thousands of smaller faults, and this would help scientists determine how much loading was occurring on the San Andreas and San Jacinto faults.

The problem is this assumed there was no creep in the smaller faults.

The 2018 study indicates creep is happening in the smaller faults, at a deep level. Because there is a different type of deformation happening at the smaller faults than on the large ground-rupturing ones, the study indicates that the data recorded by the small earthquakes should not be used to predict the loading of the San Andreas and San Jacinto faults (Cooke & Beyer, 2018).

While there is no definitive answer to when or how big an earthquake will strike, the real takeaway from the study is we don't really know what is happening below the surface.

Faults might open and shut

In some movies, earthquakes have been dramatically portrayed to open and close along the fault, where the ground opens up and swallows people, cars, and buildings. Geologists have long believed this to be complete fiction, and earthquake modeling programs were created with parameters that don't allow for faults to open and close. However, some major earthquakes in the past few years have broadened the possibilities and caused scientists to question long-held assumptions.

Robert Perkins reported on a study published in the journal *Nature* (Gabuchian, Rosakis, Bhat, Madariaga, & Kanamori, 2017) about the findings of a team researching the slips along thrust faults:

> "It has long been assumed that, at shallow depths, the plates would just slide against one another for a short distance, without opening.
>
> "However, researchers investigating the Tohoku earthquake found that not only did the fault slip at shallow depths, it did so by up to 50 meters in some places. That huge motion, which occurred just offshore, triggered a tsunami that caused damage to facilities along the coast of Japan, including at the Fukushima Daiichi Nuclear Power Plant.
>
> "…the team hypothesizes that the Tohoku earthquake rupture propagated up the fault and—once it neared the surface—caused one slab of rock to twist away from another, opening a gap and momentarily removing any friction between the two walls. This allowed the fault to slip 50 meters.
>
> "That opening of the fault was supposed to be impossible" (Perkins R. , 2017).

Most computer modeling of earthquakes has been programmed to not allow faults to separate, because it was thought to be impossible.

While trying to discover how the fault slipped occurred, the research team created a simulated thrust fault earthquake in a lab, using various materials, instead of relying solely on a computer model. Perkins reported:

> "The team was surprised to see that, as the rupture hit the surface, the fault twisted open and then snapped shut. Subsequent computer simulations—with models that were modified to remove the artificial rules against the fault opening—confirmed what the team observed experimentally: one slab can twist violently away from the other. This can happen both on land and on underwater thrust faults, meaning that this mechanism has the potential to change our understanding of how tsunamis are generated" (Perkins R. , 2017).

This discovery is one of my favorites. It not only shows the real likelihood of the earth swallowing buildings, but it waves a red flag of caution against assuming we "know" what will happen and can model things based on what we "know."

Earthquake modeling needs revisiting

New discoveries and flawed assumptions, such as a fault's inability to open and shut, prove the need for earthquake modeling to be reformed.

The surprises that cropped up in studying the Kaikōura earthquake certainly led many researchers to realize the need for rethinking assumptions. In a 2017 article about the Kaikōura earthquake, the research team concluded, "the exceptional nature of the Kaikōura event raises questions about how the risk of future quakes is assessed" (Amos, 2017). In addition, the researchers realized, "Some of the assumptions that go into building seismic models now need to be revisited."

Another of Kaikōura's surprises, which did not match previous assumptions, was the amount of "surface expression," which Amos described as "Giant fissures opened in the ground, highways were broken by metres-long offsets, beaches rose up from the sea, and railway lines were lifted high into the air."

Amos quotes Dr. Ian Hamling, of the New Zealand's geophysics research agency, talking about a section of along the Paptea Fault:

"You can call it bonkers; it's certainly a real puzzle…. It's a block of material of about 50 sq. km [about 19 square miles] that's been thrust up out of the ground by about 8m [26.25 ft] and then pushed south by 4-5m [13-16 ft].

"To try to model it in the traditional way is almost impossible; it's very hard to explain how you can get this thing to pop up in the manner that it has" (Amos, 2017).

Another theory that shows the need for reworking conventional earthquake modeling is a common theory formerly known as Reid's elastic rebound theory, which is based on the idea of fault "readiness." The concept, introduced in 1911, basically states that the probability of a large earthquake is lower on faults that have recently ruptured, and the likelihood increases the longer it's been since a big rupture, as tectonic forces build up. However, applying it as a model for earthquake forecasting has "proved challenging" (U.S. Department of the Interior, U.S. Geological Survey, 2015).

New research developments and the many unexpected discoveries have made it apparent that while current earthquake modeling programs are better than nothing, earthquake modeling and even forecasting could be improved by removing some artificial constraints that are based on nothing more than commonly held assumptions.

Chapter 5
Earthquake Prediction

Unfortunately, we can't predict when or where a large earthquake will strike. This doesn't mean people haven't tried; some have even had minor success. But nobody has had 100 percent accuracy in predicting earthquakes. Even a high percentage of successful predictions doesn't happen.

I've found one site that has a prediction model that is about 70–80 percent accurate at predicting an area that will likely have a large earthquake. However, the model usually identifies 10 to 15 percent of the major faults as being on alert at a single time, so it isn't precise enough to cover a single location. Still, it's better to know if you're in an area that has a higher immediate chance of an earthquake, even if it doesn't strike.

There are factors, several of which we've already discussed, that may contribute to large earthquakes. Potential factors that contribute to earthquake forecasting are still being tested and analyzed by some researchers. Some of the studies have had impressive predictive qualities, although the prediction of the exact magnitude and location of earthquake is still elusive.

Foreshocks and swarms

Earlier in the book, we discussed how foreshocks can be indicators of an impending earthquake. While not always the case, foreshocks are often stronger than expected (minor to moderate category) and are unusual or unexpected earthquakes that occur in or near a high earthquake risk area.

An earthquake swarm can also indicate an impending, large earthquake.

But foreshocks and swarms don't come with a "prepare for a bigger one" warning. Identifying when in the future the bigger earthquake will rupture is difficult. Usually quakes identified as a foreshock happen within a few days preceding the main shock. The reality of foreshocks and swarms is, it's hard to definitively state an earthquake is a foreshock until after a larger earthquake strikes.

What if the earthquake is big but not as big as expected? Some people believe that an earthquake of a higher magnitude will release stress on the fault and delay the occurrence of a larger earthquake. This is the fault "readiness" or elastic rebound theory mentioned at the end of chapter 4.

Others claim that an earthquake of lesser magnitude than expected can increase strain on the fault, or nearby faults, and may even lead to a bigger than expected earthquake. This view is kind of like balancing a large weight on multiple points of contact. When one point breaks away, it increases the stress on the other points. Eventually, with enough points broken, a large rupture occurs.

Since it's all theory—that is, we can't go down into the earth and observe or test our ideas—the truth is probably "it depends." There are probably earthquake zones that fall into both sides, and there may be faults ready to rupture with built up pressure. The problem is, we don't know which faults are which.

Personally, I think for some faults, a significant quake will release pressure, but in other fault locations, a significant quake may increase the stresses at the fault. This doesn't mean a larger than normal earthquake should be expected anytime; it just means we don't know.

The months and years after a large earthquake strikes can be particularly dangerous because people in the affected area may become casual about earthquake preparedness, believing another Big One won't happen in their lifetime. The safest option is to always be prepared for a large earthquake, even if the fault just experienced a big quake.

Geomagnetic influences

The common element among earthquake lights, solar influences, meteorological factors, and even changes in animal behavior is electromagnetic abnormalities.

Over 50 studies I have collected (and many more studies exist on the subject) indicate a strong relationship between seismic activity, particularly with large earthquakes, and factors that affect the Earth's electromagnetics, particularly within the lithosphere (the upper mantle and crust of our planet) and ionosphere, which extends from about 50 to 600 miles (80 to 1,000 km) above the earth's surface.

In one study, researchers reviewed ultra-low-frequency (ULF) magnetic variations recorded before the 2011 Tōhoku earthquake.

The results verified "the existence of criticality in the ULF magnetic fields a few days to one week before the occurrence of the main shock" and "only the ULF data of the nearest, to the epicenter of the EQ, geomagnetic observatory presented criticality" (Contoyiannis, Potirakis, Eftaxias, Hayakawa, & Schekotov, 2016).

Related to the same 2011 earthquake, another report analyzed the disturbance in the ionosphere prior to the earthquake. Despite strong magnetic disturbance during the time period before the large earthquake, the research found a "special disturbance" limited to the earthquake area (Oyama, et al., 2019).

Another study examined ionospheric disturbances associated with 16 earthquakes of magnitude 8.0 or larger that occurred from 2000 to 2012. Of those, 10 had ionospheric abnormalities that were observable one to five days before the earthquake. The report also cited another study, where "seismo-ionospheric precursors were detected 1–5 days prior to 20 major earthquakes in Taiwan" (Liu, et al., 2019).

Several researchers looked over geomagnetic variations beginning 11 years before the 2011 Tōhoku earthquake. They found a few variations, including a couple within two months before the tremor, that warrant further study (Rokityansky, Babak, Terehyns, & Hayakawa, 2019).

Most of this research on geomagnetic influences has been published within the last few years, so it's still very new. Many academics (particularly in the U.S.) still question its validity, despite the scores of studies. For some reason, it seems that most scientists want to isolate activity and either forget, or don't believe, external factors can have a role. Some research is coming from within the U.S. circles of academia, but many in the various scientific fields seem reluctant to consider alternatives to the closely held theories of many decades. Most of the interest in the U.S. comes from amateur researchers.

Remarkably, scientists outside of the United States appear to show greater interest in understanding how the lithosphere, atmosphere, and ionosphere interact and produce various anomalies before large earthquakes.

For me, the question is not whether earthquakes have an electro-magnetic component but how and why external factors, such as the sun, have such a big influence on Earth's seismicity.

Regarding planetary effects, if gravity isn't a likely option, could there be an electromagnetic coupling factor that might increase earthquake risk during certain planetary alignments? Personally, I have not reviewed any scientific articles studying this possibility.

The good news is there are some promising forecasting tools being developed using what has been discovered. While the forecasts cannot determine the exact location of, or how big, an earthquake will be, they can narrow the most likely areas that will need to be warned.

When you consider that a weather forecast is seldom 100% accurate, if you could identify the most likely 15% or less of the fault areas most at risk on a daily basis and have a 70% accuracy in predicting magnitude 7.0 and greater earthquakes, would that be helpful?

One of the websites I frequent has such a model that it has been using since the end of 2016. Since its inception, it usually has less than 10% of the world's faults on alert. Of the 28 large earthquakes (magnitude 6.9 and greater) since the model started being used, 20 of those quakes were within areas that the model had identified as an alert zone. That's better than 70% prediction success. The site is at https://quakewatch.net/predictioncenter/, but the information is used in a mobile app and is also published on the Twitter feed at https://twitter.com/TheRealS0s.

As more research and testing of new models happen, it will be intriguing to see how much better earthquake prediction will become over the next several years.

Earthquake lights

Another potential earthquake predictor that should be noted is earthquake lights (EQL), phenomena that are sometimes reported in conjunction with an earthquake. EQL can take the form of balls of light, steady glowing lights, sheet lightning, bluish flames appearing to come out of the ground, or flashes of light like lightning except they come from the ground. Usually the EQL is seen before or at the time of the earthquake, near the epicenter.

Because of the rarity of the event, and insufficient evidence to formulate a conclusion, some geophysicists doubt whether EQL exist, as some of the sightings have been attributed to such things as power lines shaking and arcing.

However, with the increasing number of security cameras running around the world, more evidence of attributed EQL have been reported, and some geophysicists believe the phenomena to be plausible.

Various theories hypothesize how EQL may be caused. A 2014 study determined that the electrical process causing the EQL may be from the stressing of certain types of rocks, causing them to store small electric charges (Theriault, St-Laurent, Freund, & Derr, 2014). A seismic wave may cause this electrical charge to be released, and these "charges can combine and form a kind of plasma-like state, which can travel at very high velocities and burst out at the surface to make electric discharges in the air" (Howard, 2014).

While EQL may be an indicator of an impending earthquake, they're not a very useful predictor. Less than one half of one percent of earthquakes are estimated to have conditions where an EQL may occur.

Planetary influences

Some people believe that the likelihood of a big earthquake can be increased by various planetary alignments. While there may be some correlation, the idea that the gravitational pull from the various planets contributes to increased earthquake risk is unlikely.

However, while it's uncertain whether gravitational forces from other planets play much of a role, a 2016 study in *Nature Geoscience* reported that "tectonic tremors deep within subduction zones are highly sensitive to tidal stress levels, with tremor rate increasing at an exponential rate with rising tidal stress" (Ide, Yabe, & Tanaka, 2016). The study also concluded that the "slow deformation and the possibility of earthquakes at subduction plate boundaries may be enhanced during periods of large tidal stress" and "large earthquakes are more probable during periods of high tidal stress."

It should be noted that since lunar and solar eclipses do not cause any unique tidal effects, they do not increase earthquake risk. It may be that gravitational or other forces acting on tidal flows could have an effect where the gravitational pull on its own has none.

Atmospheric and meteorological factors

Some studies suggest that the likelihood of large earthquakes can increase with certain meteorological conditions. Specifically, areas of extreme low pressure, such as large storm centers (like a hurricane), may reduce the pressure on the earth's crust in the area below and near the low-pressure centers. This reduction in pressure could increase the likelihood of an earthquake in the general area of the low pressure.

A recent instance of a hurricane and an earthquake seeming to affect one another was on September 7, 2017, when Hurricane Katia was barreling into Mexico, along the western Gulf of Mexico. That same day, a magnitude 8.2 quake struck just south of Mexico. Most would dismiss these two events as coincidental. However, multiple hurricanes in the Gulf from August through September could have plausibly caused a transfer of fault stresses in the region.

There are several research studies on air temperature, thermal infrared, air pressure, and relative humidity anomalies prior to big earthquakes. We won't go into any of them in depth, but the studies seem to imply a correlation between various atmospheric conditions and large earthquakes.

One of the more recent articles examined atmospheric anomalies that were associated with three magnitude 6.0 and greater earthquakes in Pakistan and Iran from 2010 to 2017. The researchers conclude, "Evidences suggest that abnormal atmospheric anomalies occur within one month before the main shock" (Shah, Tariq, & Naqvi, 2019).

In several studies, atmospheric factors are considered part of the earth's electro-magnetic field, which will be discussed in another section about earthquake prediction.

Changes in animal behavior

If you have read many articles about earthquakes, you will likely encounter those who claim that animals can sense electro-magnetic changes in the earth preceding an earthquake. They claim there is a significant increase in missing pets just prior to an earthquake, presumably because the animals are either more confused or trying to find a safer place. In any case, it is difficult to determine if animal behavior can predict earthquakes, as a baseline for "normal" behavior would need to be set. And, if you are using the behavior of pets, you would need to find out who monitors missing pets and get on their notification list for when there is an uptick in missing furry friends.

In 2015, a study was published titled "Changes in animal activity prior to a major (M = 7) earthquake in the Peruvian Andes." The study reviewed the changes in animal and bird behavior, as recorded by motion-activated cameras at the Yanachaga National Park in Peru, over a 30-day period. The conclusion was there was significantly lower activity in the three weeks prior to the earthquake when compared to periods of lower seismic activity. There was also changes in the Earth's ionosphere during that time, which could indicate a possible electromagnetic connection in the very low frequency range (Grant, Raulin, & Freund, 2015).

Another study, published in late 2018, examined the vocalizations of dogs as a possible precursor to earthquakes. The author found, through the study of unusual behavior and vocalizations, that dogs may be able to detect physical anomalies linked to the earth's magnetic field and earthquakes several hours before a local earthquake. There is also some evidence that uncharacteristic behaviors and vocalizations 40 to 70 seconds before an earthquake indicate an ability of the dog to detect the fast-moving p waves (de Liso, 2018).

Solar factors

To understand how something works, it is common to try to isolate it as much as possible. While this may yield greater understanding of the subject being studied, we run the risk of missing the effect of external factors.

For a long time, mainstream science rejected the idea that the sun could have any effect on the earth in producing large earthquakes. But the sun affects the earth in dramatic ways. The uneven heating of the earth's surface greatly influences weather patterns. Electromagnetically charged particles streaming from the sun—93 million miles (150 million km) away—cause the aurora borealis and aurora australis near the polar regions, as these charged particles interact with the earth's magnetosphere.

These particles also interact with the earth's ionosphere in other areas and can cause geomagnetic disturbances. When large solar storms occur on the sun, geomagnetic activity often increases. Scientists use the Kp index (also known as the planetary index) to measure the amount of geomagnetic disruption, with 0 being calm and 9 being the highest amount of disruption.

If a solar storm explodes a large amount of these particles at earth—called a coronal mass ejection or CME—regions on our planet may experience electrical disruptions or failure. An exceptionally large CME could effectively knock out our power grid.

With so many studies linking magnetic fields and ionospheric anomalies to seismic activity, and since the sun is known to affect our planet's magnetic field, is it really a stretch for the sun to be able to influence large earthquakes on the earth?

Some studies have tried to connect earthquakes with sunspots, solar flaring, and other space weather. More recent studies have looked at the sun's interplanetary magnetic fields and how they may be affecting the geomagnetism and large magnitude earthquakes on our planet.

A recent study in 2018, titled "Geomagnetic Kp Index and Earthquakes," found that "the stronger the earthquake is, more closely the Kp surge is associated" (Urata, Duma, & Freund, 2018).

A study in 2015 performed an analysis of the magnetism of solar polar fields (SPF) and large magnitude earthquakes over a 38-year period. The analysis indicated a "significant relationship between SFP and Earth's largest seismic events" (Davidson, U-Yen, & Holloman, Relationship Between M8+ Earthquake Occurences and the Solar Polar Magnetic Fields, 2015). The study suggests "the extremes in magnetism of the polar fields, and the polarity reversals, may be modulating the largest earthquakes on the planet" and "electromagnetic triggers of tectonic stress are a worthwhile mechanism to consider."

There are even more studies, many just in the last few years, that are finding strong correlations between large earthquakes and changes in the earth's global electric circuit.

It will be fascinating to see how earthquake predictions evolve over the next several years as solar, atmospheric, and other factors are considered in additional research.

Phone apps—early warning and notifications

Although not a true earthquake prediction identifying when and where an earthquake will hit, an earthquake early warning system using mobile phones and sensors is being experimented with.

Several phone apps are either available or in development whose main goal is to provide an early warning of an earthquake. Many of these apps are based on an earthquake early warning system called ShakeAlert®, which is being developed and tested by the United States Geological Survey (USGS) and several state and university partners. The warning is based on the early detection of fast-moving P-waves before the more damaging, and slower, S-waves arrive.

The ShakeAlert system is primarily for the west coast of the United States, and these early warning apps may give you a 20–60 second warning. But you can do a lot to better protect yourself with a 20-second or more warning than with no warning. Even 20 seconds can allow a complex medical operation to stop, sensitive industrial processes to halt, allow elevators to move to the nearest floor, and provide time for schools and public areas to issue alerts so people have a chance to move into a safer position.

Although the USGS's ShakeAlert system has been in development since 2006 and funding cuts have delayed the project, the West Coast ShakeAlert Earthquake Early Warning System began its phase 1 testing in California, Oregon, and Washington in the fall of 2018.

Version 2.0 went live and included two new messages. The first, original message is an Event Message, and the additional messages include a Contour Message and Map Grid Message. The Event Message includes information about the earthquake source, location, magnitude, and uncertainty. The Contour and Grid Map messages include a nested eight-point polygon map and a twelve-mile (20 km) spacing grid map of the projected affected area.

Phase 1 was rolled out to several commercial and institutional users, and the system will eventually be phased into a full public alerting system. Technical improvement and increased sensors are being deployed, with initial target areas being Los Angeles, the Bay Area, and the Seattle metro region.

In January 2019, about 50 percent of the sensor system was completed. As the speed and scale for mass alerting becomes available for more effective warnings, the system will be rolled out for broader public alerting of magnitude 5.0 and higher events, along with public education about the system. More information about the system can be found at https://www.shakealert.org/.

On January 3, 2019, Los Angeles Mayor Eric Garcetti announced the release of ShakeAlertLA, which only works for L.A. County (Hurley, 2019).

When ShakeAlertLA was rolled out, there was a lot of discussion about where to set the notification threshold. The decision was to notify users if the detected tremor was at least a magnitude 5.0 and expected to produce "light" shaking (level IV on the Modified Mercalli Intensity Scale) for those in Los Angeles.

On July 4 and 5, 2019, magnitude 6.4 and 7.1 earthquakes hit Ridgecrest, about 122 miles (200 km) north-northeast of Los Angeles. ShakeAlert generated a message 6.9 seconds after the first shaking, but users in Los Angeles didn't receive any alert. The reason was that while the magnitude met the notification requirements, the predicted shaking for Los Angeles did not.

In Ridgecrest, the shaking intensity was a level VIII, which is considered severe and can cause damage to ordinary structures and considerable damage to poorly built ones. However, the Los Angeles area was not expected to have more than a level III, and most of the county didn't experience much more than window blinds swaying or pools sloshing (Baumgaertner, 2019).

Even though the system performed as it was expected to, the public backlash in not receiving the earthquake notification caused officials to lower the threshold to magnitude 4.5 or greater with an intensity level of III or more. The fear is that this lower notification might make people complacent if they receive too many alerts.

A similar product called QuakeAlert can also provide early warnings. Developed by Early Warning Labs, who has partnered with the USGS, this app also uses the P-waves to predict where the damaging S-waves are likely to strike. The app's cloud server "calculates the individual alerts for all users with personalized time to shaking and intensity" (Early Warning Labs, 2019).

With this information, QuakeAlert provides an expected arrival time of the earthquake, its expected intensity, your estimated distance from the epicenter, the magnitude of the quake, and suggested safety measures to take.

As this book was being reviewed for publishing, I received an email from Early Warning Labs that the QuakeAlertUSA app is now available for Android and iOS devices. A message in the email from Josh Bashioum, the CEO and founder, said the delays were "due to political factors" beyond the company's control. The app is still in beta testing.: https://earlywarninglabs.com/.

A third company, SkyAlert, is developing a similar early warning product. The technology has been "evolving for years in Mexico" (Perry T. S., 2019). The company is designing the system to not only provide emergency notifications but also to be used with various internet-connected (Internet of Things, or IoT) devices. The SkyAlert system has been integrated with the USGS ShakeAlert warning system.

Other companies and organizations are also developing early warning tools and applications. However, most are geared towards companies, as app-based products targeting individual users "aren't going to bring in enough dollars to support a business" (Perry T. S., 2019). One exception is the UC Berkeley Seismology Lab, which has developed, and is continuing to develop, a free app called MyShake for Android devices and MyQuake for Apple iOS users. Information on the app can be found at http://earthquakes.berkeley.edu/myquake/.

A big difference between the UC Berkeley project and others is that MyShake doesn't rely on expensive, specialized equipment for detecting earth tremors. Instead, it uses a sophisticated computer system (an artificial neural network) to collect, compare, and analyze motion sensors from smartphones. The MyShake system then determines whether the data matches the model of an earthquake or gets filtered out as normal phone movement. Testing has shown that smartphones can be used to detect earthquakes as small as magnitude 5 and within nearly 4 miles (10 km) of the epicenter. The app also gives notifications of earthquakes reported by the USGS.

UC Berkeley is also piloting the ShakeAlert program and looking to integrate it into the MyShake system, which would provide users with early warning notifications.

As for phone apps that just notify you when an earthquake happens, there are a lot. I personally use two. (I don't hold any financial interest in any app. These are just what I have on my phone.)

The first one I use is called LASTQUAKE, and it's the official earthquakes app of the European-Mediterranean Seismological Centre (EMSC). There are times when I've seen it report earthquakes much earlier than the USGS website.

While LASTQUAKE is a free app, the other app I use is not. Called the Disaster Prediction App, it is based on a couple of studies on solar influence on the earth. One part of the app is for space weather risks, such as if we ever get a solar flare and related coronal mass ejection headed our way.

The other part of the app is for earthquakes. It gives earthquake alerts (usually a few minutes slower than LASTQUAKE when it reports an earthquake) and provides a daily alert map for higher risk areas.

Part 2 – Where Are the Threats in the U.S.?

Chapter 6
Earthquake Threats in the United States

Of all the notable earthquakes we have discussed, none were in North America. However, that doesn't mean there isn't a high risk in the United States.

From a list of the top 36 largest earthquakes recorded (in Appendix B), only four occurred in the United States, with three of those in Alaska. The only non-Alaska quake was the Cascadia rupture on January 26, 1700, that had an estimated magnitude range of 8.7 to 9.2. The rupture of the New Madrid Fault in Missouri on December 16, 1811, didn't even make the list, with its mere 8.1 magnitude.

While North America hasn't put in high-ranking earthquake numbers, the earth hasn't been quiet.

Since the January 26, 1700, Cascadia earthquake, more than 40 earthquakes of magnitude 6.5 or higher have rocked different areas of the United States. Seven of those happened in the 1800s. A whopping 24 occurred in the 1900s. Of those 24 in the twentieth century, the first three decades saw only one 6.5 or larger earthquakes per decade. The 1930s didn't have any. Then three happened in the '40s, four more in the '50s, and three in each of the decades from the '60s to '80s. Five more happened in the '90s.

From 2000 to July 5, 2019, there were ten quakes with a magnitude of 6.5 or higher. Of those ten, four quakes occurred in the first decade of the twenty-first century, shaking areas of Alaska and California. Nine-and-a-half years into the second decade, there have already been six more.

Table 4: Number of magnitude 6.5+ earthquakes per decade in the United States.

Decade	# of M 6.5+ Earthquakes
1900–1909	1
1910–1919	1
1920–1929	1
1930–1939	0
1940–1949	3
1950–1959	4
1960–1969	3
1970–1979	3
1980–1989	3
1990–1999	5
2000–2009	4
2010–2019	6

Some of these earthquakes in the United States were magnitude 7.0 and larger. The earliest recorded quakes at those higher magnitudes were one in the 1700s and four in the 1800s. It's very likely there have been more, but we don't have any record of them.

In more recent history, the 1900s saw 14 of these large earthquakes, with one in each of the first two decades, and none in the '20s and '30s. There was one in the '40s (a monstrous 8.6 in Alaska), four in the '50s (including another 8.6 in Alaska), two in the '60s (one was a devasting 9.2 in Alaska), and another two in the '70s. Only one magnitude 7.0 or larger happened in the '80s, and another two happened in the '90s.

In the twenty-first century, the first decade saw only one magnitude 7.0 or larger earthquake: a 7.9-magnitude quake in Alaska. The first nine-and-a-half years of the second decade, however, have had five quakes with a magnitude 7.0 or greater, with four of those in Alaska.

Table 5: Number of magnitude 7.0 or larger earthquakes per time period. (Note that the 18th and 19th centuries have their own rows, while the 20th and 21st centuries are divided into decades.)

Time Period	# of M 7.0+ Earthquakes
1700–1799	1
1800–1899	4
1900–1909	1
1910–1919	1
1920–1929	0
1930–1939	0
1940–1949	1
1950–1959	4
1960–1969	2
1970–1979	2
1980–1989	1
1990–1999	2
2000–2009	1
2010–2019	5

If you didn't notice, Alaska is the most earthquake-prone state. However, earthquakes in the Last Frontier State seldom make the news, as there isn't the damage and destruction that would make them newsworthy.

Looking at the numbers, the frequency of large earthquakes appears to be increasing.

When we look more closely at regions, big earthquakes are overdue in each region, with "big" being a magnitude 7.0 or greater rupture.

As mentioned in chapter 4, a big earthquake in one area could trigger earthquakes in another. This triggering could come within a very short time following the first earthquake. Or, the first earthquake could result in increasing stresses on other faults and increase the chances of a big earthquake happening sooner on those faults.

Earthquake risks in the U.S.

In 2014, the U.S. Geological Survey (USGS) released a report that found that 42 of the 50 states have a reasonable chance of experiencing a damaging earthquake over the next 50 years. With the report, they released an updated hazard risk map. The following image is the Simplified 2018 long-term risk map for earthquakes in the United States over the next 50 years. It's mostly the same as 2014, though several risk areas have been expanded. There are more recent short-term risk hazard maps, but as of this writing, the 2018 is the most recent long-term map. As indicated by the colored legend, pink, red, and orange have the higher risk for earthquake damage.

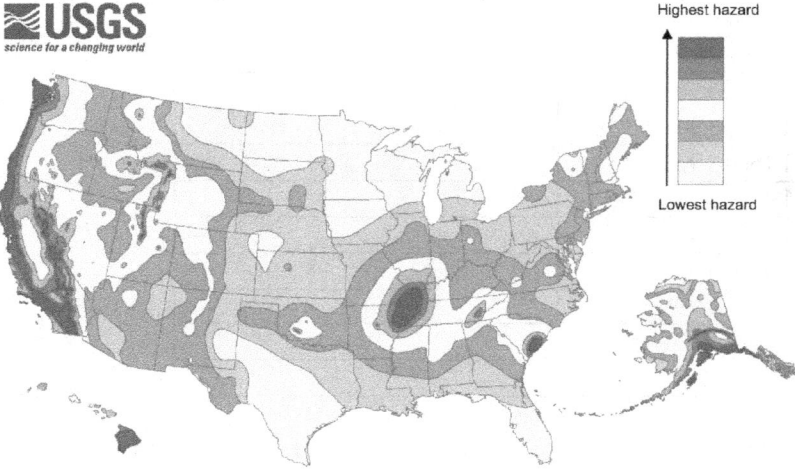

Figure 6: USGS Simplified 2018 Long-term Hazard Map. Retrieved from https://www.usgs.gov/media/images/2018-long-term-national-seismic-hazard-map - Public domain.

It's easy to see from the map that the West Coast states, Alaska, and Hawaii are high-risk earthquake locations. What about the other states?

Eight states, according to their risk assessment, don't have significant earthquake hazard levels. These states are Florida, Iowa, Kansas, Louisiana, Michigan, Minnesota, North Dakota, and Wisconsin. Florida and North Dakota have the least number of earthquakes in the U.S. From the map, you can see it's not that these eight states have no risk; it's just not a "significant" risk. The more probable risk factor is from a large earthquake happening in a nearby state. With shaking and other earthquake-related effects affecting areas hundreds of miles from the epicenter, just about every state has the potential to experience earthquake-related damage.

Risk by region in the U.S.

As mentioned, most of the United States has at least some earthquake risk. A few states have little risk, and several have very high risk. In the next chapter, we'll dig a bit into the 16 states with the higher risks. For now, we'll look at regional risk.

Western U.S. risks

The entire west coast is high risk for earthquakes. The Insurance Information Institute lists the ten costliest earthquakes in the United States from 1906 through 2018. Of those, six were in California (Insurance Information Institute, 2019).

Two other quakes on that list were also on the western end of North America. One quake was a magnitude 6.8 rupture that struck Nisqually, Washington, on February 28, 2001. The other was a magnitude 7.1 that shook Anchorage, Alaska, on November 30, 2018.

Of the remaining two costliest earthquakes in the U.S., one was a 6.7 rupture on October 15, 2006, in Kiholo Bay, Hawaii. The other was a much smaller, magnitude 5.8 tremor that rocked the Piedmont region of Virginia on August 23, 2011.

Returning to the west coast, the USGS estimates there is a 60 percent probability that a magnitude 6.7 or greater earthquake will strike the Los Angeles area within the next 30 years. Probabilities for magnitude 7 and 7.5 ruptures are at 46 and 31 percent, respectively.

Table 6: Thirty-year probability of earthquakes striking the Los Angeles area.

Magnitude	Probability
6.7	60%
7	46%
7.5	31%

For the San Francisco area, the USGS projects a 72 percent probability of a magnitude 6.7 or higher hitting the region. They project a 51 percent chance of a magnitude 7 tremor and only a 20 percent probability of a 7.5 or larger rupture.

Table 7: Thirty-year probability of earthquakes striking the San Francisco area.

Magnitude	Probability
6.7	72%
7	51%
7.5	20%

The largest earthquake to strike the U.S. was a 9.2 tremblor that hit Alaska in 1964. Damage from the quake and resulting tsunami was estimated to cost more than $500 million. But, while it was the largest, it didn't come with the biggest price tag.

The January 17, 1994, Northridge California, earthquake was the costliest, with insured losses estimated at $26.373 billion in 2018 dollars (Insurance Information Institute, 2019). Incidentally, "the Northridge earthquake occurred on a previously unrecognized fault" (Field & and members of 2014 WGCEP, 2015).

Incidentally, if the 1906 magnitude 7.9 earthquake in San Francisco were to happen today, insured loses would probably exceed $105 billion (Insurance Information Institute, 2018).

Regarding the major faults in California, geophysicist Glenn Biasi and paleoseismologist Katherine Scharer analyzed seismic records going back 1,000 years on the five major faults in California: the northern San Andreas Fault, the Hayward Fault, the southern San Andreas Fault, the San Jacinto Fault, and the southernmost San Andreas Fault. Altogether, the faults span from north of San Francisco to the Mexican border. What they found is while a single fault might have a 100-year quiet period, the fact that all five have been quiet for over 100 years is unprecedented. Their research showed an average of three or four ground-rupturing quakes each century. Neither the 1989 Loma Prieta quake in the Bay Area nor the 1994 Northridge earthquake were ground rupturing. Why the faults are quieter than average isn't known. One possibility is there is something unknown "synchronizing the activity across these five major faults" (Pappas, California's Eerie 'Earthquake Pause' Is Unprecedented, 2019).

Another possibility is that the faults were affected by the higher-than-average number of earthquakes from 1800 to 1900, where there were six ground-rupturing earthquakes. Those six plus two more in the early 1900s—the 7.9-magnitude 1906 Great San Francisco

Earthquake and a 6.7-magnitude earthquake on the San Jacinto Fault in 1918—may have released more seismic tension. It is possible that the faults need more time to build up stress.

Moving north, the Cascadia Fault, known also as the Cascadia Subduction Zone, had its last major earthquake in 1700, with a magnitude range of 8.7 to 9.2. Research presented at the May 2018 annual meeting of the Seismological Society of America suggests that the time frame between the megathrust events in the Cascadia Subduction Zone may be 200 years shorter that previously reported.

The geologic record suggests megathrust earthquakes, along with tsunamis, occur about every 500 years. However, new research indicates that the southern part of the fault zone may only have a 300-year frequency (Weisberger, The Next Cascadian Megaquake May Be Sooner Than You Think, 2018). With the revised estimate, and since the last megaquake was in 1700, the next one may be due soon.

Central U.S. risks

The biggest threat to the Central U.S. is from the New Madrid Fault Zone. It stretches along the central Mississippi valley, extending from northeastern Arkansas to southeastern Missouri, out to western Tennessee, then Kentucky, and up to Illinois.

On December 16, 1811, residents of the small town of New Madrid, Missouri, were awakened by the roar and violent shaking of a large earthquake. It was the first of three large quakes, estimated to be between magnitude 7.5 and 8.0, that shook the area over two months, the last large one striking February 7, 1812. Some sources estimate the highest magnitudes to be 8.7 to 9.2.

Residents of the area reported cracks opening, the ground rolling in visible waves, and large areas of ground rising or sinking. Locations as far away as Charleston, South Carolina, and Washington, D.C. reported damage (CUSEC, n.d.). The quake "rang church bells in Boston, Massachusetts, 1,000 miles away" (Insurance Information Institute, 2018). There were reports of the Mississippi River flooding and even running backwards in some locations (Arkansas Department of Emergency Management, 2019). Other accounts saw the river rise "like a great loaf of bread to the height of many feet" and fissures opening with geysers of sand, water, mud, and coal (Rusch, 2011).

Until a few decades ago, geologists assumed that the 1811-12 ruptures were one-time events. However, excavations of sand blows have revealed evidence of previous large earthquakes. Outside of the seismic zone, other faults have been discovered, including near Memphis, Tennessee, and Commerce, Missouri. All the discovered faults have evidence of having been active in the past few thousand to millions of years. As a result, scientists have warned that these quakes were not freak occurrences.

In 1811, the population in St. Louis was 5,700. Today, there are 11–12 million people in the St. Louis-Memphis region. With over 232,000 square miles of damage in the 1811-12 earthquakes, a similar event today would have catastrophic consequences.

Unlike on the west coast, earthquakes in central and eastern states are felt over much larger areas. This is due to the geology of the area, where the softer soils allow for the seismic waves to travel further.

East of the Rocky Mountains, the New Madrid Seismic Zone is the most seismically active area. Over the next 50 years, there is a 7–10 percent probability of a magnitude 7.0 or larger earthquake. The likelihood of a 6.0 or larger is between 28 and 46 percent (Arkansas Department of Emergency Management, 2019).

From seismic activity, geologists have also learned there are several thrust faults are in the area, from Marked Tree, Arkansas, to Cairo, Illinois. Unlike the west, where many faults are visible, faults in the central (and eastern) U.S. are buried deep. Since we do not know exactly where the faults are, they are categorized as seismic (or fault) zones. Besides the New Madrid zone, the Wabash Valley Seismic Zone can also produce damaging earthquakes.

North of the New Madrid Seismic Zone, in Southeastern Illinois and Southwestern Indiana, is the Wabash Valley Seismic Zone. This zone saw its most recent earthquake on April 18, 2008, when a magnitude 5.2 quake hit near Mt. Carmel, Illinois. It was felt in at least 16 states. There were no injuries or fatalities, but it demonstrated the area's earthquake risk. The zone also experienced a smaller, magnitude 4.6 quake several years earlier, on June 18, 2002, near Evansville, Indiana.

The Wabash Valley Seismic Zone is capable of magnitude 7.0 earthquakes. Geologists have found prehistoric evidence of liquefaction and sand dikes, and an estimated magnitude 7.1 earthquake created one formation. If a similar event happened today, there'd be widespread damage and destruction.

Eastern U.S. risks

Like the central U.S., the east has seismic zones. Some of these include the East Tennessee, Central Virginia, and Charleston/South Carolina seismic zones.

In 2011, a magnitude 5.8 earthquake struck central Virginia. It was an unexpected tremor, and the strongest to hit the eastern United States since 1897. People felt the quake from Florida to southeastern Canada and as far west as Wisconsin. Some estimated that almost a third of the U.S. population felt it. One reason it was felt over such a wide area is that the underlying ground structure—"the age, type, temperature and density of the rocks underlying the eastern United States"—transmits seismic waves more efficiently than in the western states (Perkins S. , Virginia earthquake wins by a landslide, 2012).

Analysis of the quake indicates that the eastern U.S. cities are at greater risk of being affected by earthquakes than previously estimated. Analysis of the quake also noted that "an unusually high fraction of the seismic energy radiating from [the 2011] quake was directed towards the northeast, where several major population centers lie, along the network of faults in the region" (Perkins S. , Virginia earthquake wins by a landslide, 2012).

The 2011 quake upended conventional assumptions because of the rockfalls and landslides that were triggered "across an unexpectedly large area" (Perkins S. , Virginia earthquake wins by a landslide, 2012). Previous studies estimated a quake of that size should trigger landslides up to only 37 miles (60 kilometers) away. But that quake set records by causing landslides at least 152 miles (245 km) away.

The largest recorded earthquake on the east coast was an estimated 6.9- to 7.3-magnitude tremor that occurred in 1886, striking Charleston, South Carolina, and killing at least 60.

In 1755, an estimated 6.0 quake hit Boston, and that same year, another magnitude 6.0 struck Cape Ann, Massachusetts.

A 5.0 in 1737 and 5.3 in 1884 struck near New York City. More recently, a 5.8 tremor rocked the northern part of New York in 1944.

While these magnitudes aren't really large earthquakes, they can cause significant damage, particularly to older buildings. In both Boston and New York City, many structures have been built with unreinforced masonry. While New York City is built mostly on bedrock, Boston has it worse, where much of the city is built on artificial fill, which can amplify seismic waves by as much as three times (Insurance Information Institute, 2018).

The issue with predicting earthquakes in the eastern U.S. is their rarity. Establishing a historical record is problematic, as our record goes back only about 400 years. Accurate measurements of earthquakes go back only about 100 years. So, our knowledge about east coast quakes comes from large events that were noticed, and recorded, by people in the area.

Unlike the west coast, there aren't active tectonic events such as subduction zones, collisions, or spreading in eastern North America. Where faults in California might have recurrences measured in decades or centuries, we don't know the intervals on the east. There may be thousands, hundreds of thousands, or even millions of years between major events (Klemetti, 2018).

What if a big earthquake, even in the mid-to-upper magnitude 6-range struck? Considering the aging infrastructure and many structures not built to be seismically resilient, there could potentially be enormous destruction.

Like many other parts of the country, residents on the east coast need to become better prepared. Many should be prepared for hurricanes (although most are not), and it's not much more work to become prepared for an earthquake.

Chapter 7
Top 16 Earthquake Risk States

We expect to see California, Alaska, Hawaii, Washington, and Oregon on the list of states with the highest earthquake risk. However, some of the other 11 high risk states might raise some eyebrows. These states are Arkansas, Idaho, Illinois, Kentucky, Missouri, Montana, Nevada, South Carolina, Tennessee, Utah, and Wyoming.

Let's look at some of the earthquake history and risks in the top 16 states, ordered by highest to lowest risk.

Alaska

Alaska is the most seismically active region in the United States. But the lower population means there isn't as much devastation to report.

That said, the second-largest earthquake ever recorded shook southern Alaska in 1964 with a magnitude of 9.2. In 2002, a magnitude 7.9 earthquake struck the Denali Fault in central Alaska. Another 7.9 hit on January 23, 2018, near Kodiak Island. Since 1899, six additional quakes in the magnitude 8 range have struck. Overall, Alaska has about 11 percent of the world's recorded earthquakes. Three of the eight largest earthquakes were in Alaska. Narrowing earthquakes to the United States, seven of the ten largest were in Alaska.

Southern Alaska is near the Alaska-Aleutian Megathrust Fault Zone, which is one of the most active and dangerous on Earth.

On average, since 1900, Alaska experiences a magnitude 8.0 or larger earthquake every 13 years. Table 8 shows how many earthquakes and their corresponding magnitudes the state experiences every year.

Table 8: Alaska earthquake magnitudes and number per year.

Magnitude range	Number of tremors
7.0–7.9	1
6.0–6.9	6
5.0–5.9	45
4.0–4.9	320

The good news is, with improved building codes since the 1964 earthquake, a relatively low population, and the lack of high-rise buildings, it is likely that large earthquakes in Alaska will have fewer fatalities than similar-size tremors in other locations.

California

For the contiguous United States, California has the highest earthquake risk. And, with its high population and large cities, the risk of damage from earthquakes is the highest.

California is overdue for a large earthquake, magnitude 7.0 or stronger. In the 1800s, 14 earthquakes of magnitude 6.0 or larger occurred. Since the 1906 Great Earthquake in San Francisco, there have been only three. According to a study on paleoseismic data, there has essentially been an earthquake drought since 1906 (Biasi & Scharer, 2019).

The San Andreas Fault is the most famous (or infamous) fault in California, but there are many others. In northern California, the Hayward Fault is the biggest threat. In 2015, the third Uniform California Earthquake Rupture Forecast (UCERF3) was developed to provide updated earthquake forecasting. Compared to the previous forecast, the likelihood of moderate earthquakes (magnitude 6.5 to 7.5) has gone down, but the probability of larger ones has gone up. Tables 9–11 summarize some of the probabilities.

Table 9: Likelihood of one or more earthquakes in a 30-year period, beginning 2014, for faults near San Francisco.

Fault	M6.7+	M7.5+	M8.0+
Northern San Andreas	6.4%	5.7%	2.1%
Calaveras	1.1%	—	—
Hayward	14.3%	3.6%	<0.1%

Table 10: Likelihood of one or more earthquakes in a 30-year period, beginning 2014, for faults near Los Angeles.

Fault	M6.7+	M7.5+	M8.0+
Southern San Andreas	19.0%	17.3%	6.8%
San Jacinto	5.0%	4.9%	2.7%
Elsinore	3.8%	1.0%	<0.1%

Combining smaller areas into larger regions, without considering specific faults, shows a more ominous earthquake probability.

Table 11: Likelihood for one or more earthquakes in a 30-year period, beginning 2014, for one or more earthquakes in all of California, by region.

Region	M5+	M6+	M6.7+	M7+	M7.5+	M8+
California as a whole	100%	100%	>99%	93%	48%	7%
Southern California	100%	100%	93%	75%	36%	7%
Northern California	100%	100%	95%	76%	28%	5%
San Francisco Region	100%	98%	72%	51%	20%	4%
Los Angeles Region	100%	96%	60%	46%	31%	7%

Simply stated, the UCERF3 documents estimate that California has a 93 percent probability of a magnitude 7.0 or larger earthquake by 2045. The San Andreas Fault system has the highest chances of a high-magnitude earthquake.

Looking more specifically at the Los Angeles area faults, a team of geophysicists at Caltech "created a new method for determining earthquake hazards by measuring how fast energy is building up on faults in a specific region, and then comparing that to how much is being released through fault creep and earthquakes" (Perkins R., Fast, Simple New Assessment of Earthquake Hazard, 2019).

With this new prediction method, the faults under central Los Angeles are predicted to have the strongest earthquakes in the magnitude 6.8 to 7.1 range. These quakes should strike about every 300 years on average. Previous estimates put the large quake average on the south San Andreas Fault at about every 150 years, with the last big one happening more than 300 years ago.

When assessing the risk for smaller earthquakes, the 10-year probability for a magnitude 6.0 or larger earthquake is about 9 percent, with the probability of a magnitude 6.5 or greater earthquake at about 2 percent.

Hawaii

By the numbers, Hawaii ranks third for having the most earthquakes in the U.S. However, given its small land mass, Hawaii is where you are more likely to experience an earthquake than in any other state.

Most of the seismic threat in Hawaii is directly related to volcanic activity. Earthquakes can happen before or during an eruption. They can also be caused by magma flow that doesn't erupt under the surface.

Large earthquakes in Hawaii that are not related to volcanic activity occur at irregular intervals.

A magnitude 6.9 earthquake shook Hawaii on May 4, 2018. Its epicenter was on the south side of Kilauea.

In April 2019, a magnitude 5.3 also rocked the island, although this tremor was caused by crustal movement and wasn't magma related.

The largest recorded earthquake in Hawaii, magnitude 7.9, occurred in 1868, when the island was far less populated. The earthquake caused a landslide that killed 31 people and a tsunami that took another 46 lives.

Nevada

After Hawaii, Nevada is the fourth most seismically active state, though some lists will rank Nevada as third. Near Las Vegas, the half-dozen faults have been mostly quiet for the past 1,000 years. However, they are capable of magnitude 7.0 ruptures.

Las Vegas, Carson City, and the Reno-Tahoe areas are all at high risk of large earthquakes, although tremors could strike anywhere in the state. A magnitude 7.0 or larger quake in the Reno/Sparks area could easily cause an excess of $1.9 billion of damage, and a rupture in the Stateline area near Tahoe could cause $590 million in damage.

At least 30 faults could potentially cause damage in the Reno and Carson City urban areas. The probability of at least one magnitude 6.5 tremor occurring in the next 50 years is between 50 and 60 percent.

The city of Fallon, in Churchill County, has a 20 to 25 percent probability of experiencing a magnitude 6.5 or larger in the next 50 years.

Faults around the Las Vegas area have a lower probability of a large magnitude tremor, but there is still a 10 to 20 percent chance of a magnitude 6.0 or larger striking the area within the next 50 years.

In 2008, a magnitude 6.0 tremor struck the small rural community of Wells. Of the 1,600 residences, 700 were damaged as a result of the earthquake. The area is still struggling to recover, as businesses closed and people left the area.

The Table 12 lists the biggest earthquakes in Nevada over the last century.

Table 12: Big Nevada earthquakes from 1915 to 2008.

Date	Location	Magnitude
October 2, 1915	Pleasant Valley	7.1
December 20, 1932	Cedar Mountain	7.2
January 30, 1934	Excelsior Mountains	6.5
July 6, 1954	Fallon-Stillwater area	6.6
August 23, 1954	Stillwater	6.8
December 16, 1954	Fairview Peak	7.1
December 16, 1954	Dixie Valley	6.8
February 21, 2008	Wells	6.0

Washington

Depending on the list, in the contiguous U.S., Washington has the second (or third) highest risk of earthquakes. While there are other earthquake risks, the state's biggest risk is a megathrust quake along the Cascadia Subduction Zone. Such an event will affect the millions who live in and around the Seattle area, along with those living in other areas around the Puget Sound and Pacific Northwest.

Besides the Cascadia Subduction Zone, there are two other major earthquake threats. The Seattle Fault, which is a complex of faults branching across the Seattle area, and a much larger fault zone north of Seattle called the South Whidbey Island Fault. The three fault zones can produce earthquakes with magnitudes of 7 to over 9 (Farley, 2018).

The magnitude 6.8 Nisqually quake in February 2001 was Washington's most recent big earthquake.

A magnitude 7.0 event on the Seattle Fault would not just shake the city and surrounding communities, but it would likely cause a tsunami in the Puget Sound that would inundate the waterfront area. The last rupture was about 1,000 years ago, and scientists have no idea when the next one might happen.

The South Whidbey Island Fault could produce a 7.5 rupture, although, like the Seattle Fault, scientists have not determined any average interval.

Wyoming

Earthquakes have occurred in every county of Wyoming. However, the most seismically active area is the northwest region, where Yellowstone National Park is located. Historical records indicate that earthquakes as strong a magnitude 6.5 are possible in most parts of the state. Several faults in western Wyoming are capable of magnitude 7.2 to 7.5 ruptures, including the Teton Fault, Star Valley Fault, Greys River Fault, Rock Creek Fault, and Bear River Fault. Recent studies have led researchers to conclude that many of these fault systems are past due for big quakes.

The largest recorded earthquake in Wyoming occurred on August 18, 1959, in Yellowstone National Park. It was a magnitude 6.5 event and was considered an aftershock of the magnitude 7.2 Hebgen Lake earthquake that struck southwestern Montana the night before.

Despite the headline grabbing attention of the threat of the Yellowstone supervolcano, or another volcanic eruption in the area, the reality is, a large earthquake poses a higher risk to the area.

Idaho

On the morning of October 28, 1983, a magnitude 6.9 earthquake shook Central Idaho at Borah Peak. It was the largest quake to strike Idaho in recent history. Like any major tremor, aftershocks rattled the area for months afterwards, including a 5.4 quake. Two children died as a result of falling masonry while they were walking to school. While 200 homes received minor to moderate damage, 39 houses and 11 commercial buildings had major damage.

In August 1959, the southeastern corner of the state experienced the magnitude 7.2 Hebgen Lake, Montana, earthquake.

The area near the city of Soda Springs, in southeastern Idaho, experienced an earthquake swarm in September 2017. The largest of the tremors was a moderate 5.3, but it was enough to make the few in the area wary of a bigger one. The nearby Eastern Bear Lake Fault could rupture in the future with a magnitude 7.3 earthquake, although the U.S. Geological Survey estimates a 63 percent chance of a magnitude 6.0 or larger earthquake to hit the area within 50 years.

Should a large earthquake hit a small, rural community, the area could potentially become isolated with the destruction of roads, bridges, cell and radio towers, and electrical power transmission lines.

Montana

A magnitude 7.2 earthquake, named the Hebgen Lake earthquake, struck southwestern Montana on August 17, 1959. The earthquake was the deadliest and strongest on record to strike Montana. The tremor killed 28 and caused a huge landslide that blocked the Madison River and created Quake Lake, which is five miles long and a third of a mile wide.

The second largest quake in Montana's recent history was a magnitude 6.2 that hit near Helena on October 18, 1935. A large aftershock of magnitude 6.0 struck on October 31. Those two quakes killed four people. Before the October 18 main shock, a small foreshock happened on October 3, and a more damaging 5.9 foreshock occurred on October 12.

Helena is at the northern end of the Intermountain Seismic Belt, which is an area of seismic risk that runs from northwestern Arizona through Utah and Idaho and into Montana. Near Helena is the Lewis and Clark Fault Zone, which typically has west-northwest trending faults.

If a magnitude 6.3 earthquake were to strike the Helena area today, it would likely result in over $500 million in property damage. North of the city, where the water table is high and alluvial soil is common, damage would likely result from liquefaction.

Utah

The Wasatch Fault Zone stretches about 240 miles from southern Idaho into northern Utah. While it is the longest fault zone in the area, it's not the only one. Other large fault zones in the area include the Oquirrh-Great Salt Lake, West Cache, Stansbury, and Eastern Bear Lake fault zones.

The Wasatch Fault is at the base of the mountain range that runs through the state. Along the urban corridor, this section of the mountains is referred to as the Wasatch Front. With many communities built along the foothills, a major seismic rupture could not only cause a lot of liquefaction damage in the lowlands but hundreds of rockslides that could cascade into neighborhoods.

Running north-south along the Wasatch Fault is the main transportation artery, Interstate-15. Interstate-80 runs east-west through the Salt Lake Valley. A large earthquake would virtually shut down most transportation into and through the area.

Throughout Utah, there are more than 200 active faults, and many of these can produce ruptures of magnitude 6.5 to 7.5. While the Wasatch Fault tends to receive the most attention, and it has the highest risk, Utah's high earthquake risk area extends from the Idaho border on the north down to the Arizona and Nevada borders. Over 95 percent of Utah's population live within this high-risk zone (Geologists and Engineers for Earthquake Safety, n.d.).

With nearly 80 percent of Utah's population living and working within fifteen miles of the Wasatch Fault and about 75 percent of the state's economy also in the same area, combined with a large number of buildings susceptible to earthquake damage, there is a very high risk of economic and property loss in the event of a large earthquake.

A 2016 report estimated the probability of a magnitude 6.75 or higher earthquake in the next 50 years at 43 percent, which is much higher than earthquake experts had expected. The Wasatch Fault itself has an 18 percent probability, with other fault zones adding the extra 25 percent risk (Working Group on Utah Earthquake Probabilities, 2016).

In the event of a 7.0-magnitude tremor, it's estimated that as many as 1 in 3 homes, about 76,000 single-family houses, in Salt Lake County are at risk of major damage or collapse. But residences aren't the only buildings at risk. In some of the older, historic districts, as many as 9 in 10 brick-and-mortar buildings are built with unreinforced masonry (URM) and are high risk (Knox & Thatcher, 2018). Throughout Utah, over 200,000 buildings are constructed with URM, and about 25 percent of the population work, go to school, or live in these buildings. As a comparison, California has about 25,000

URM buildings. These URMs pose a great hazard, and it's estimated that up to 90 percent of the deaths and injuries in Utah's next major earthquake will be from damaged or collapsed URMs (Geologists and Engineers for Earthquake Safety, n.d.).

In recent recorded history, the two largest earthquakes in Utah were a magnitude 6.6 in Hansel Valley in 1934, and a 6.5-magnitude quake in the town of Richfield in 1901. Two other quakes, although not as large, have occurred since then: a magnitude 5.7 earthquake hit Richmond in 1962, and a 5.8 shook St. George in 1992. These last two smaller-magnitude quakes actually caused more damage (Utah Geological Survey, 1997).

Oregon

Like Washington, the greatest threat to Oregon lies in the Cascadia Subduction Zone. A magnitude 9.0 Cascadia event would likely cause damage to 38 percent of the buildings in Portland. In this scenario, tens of thousands could be injured or killed, while more than 250,000 could experience long-term displacement. Building damages could range from $23.5 billion to $36.7 billion as a result of the event (Bauer, Burns, & Madin, 2018).

But a Cascadia earthquake may not even be the worst-case scenario. Stretching from Oregon City to Scappoose lies the 30-mile-long Portland Hills Fault. Estimates of a large quake striking that fault are less than the Cascadia Subduction Zone, but it would be more devastating. The Portland Hills Fault is estimated to have only had two large seismic events during the last 15,000 years. Still, if a large earthquake were to hit, its devastation could be far worse than a Cascadia rupture.

A magnitude 6.8 event on the Portland Hills Fault could cause more than $83 billion in building damages, which is more than double the high estimate of a 9.0 Cascadia rupture. The building loss ratio could be as high as 32 percent. The number of people displaced from the earthquake and its aftermath might be more than a quarter million of the population. The amount of debris generated from the quake may exceed 33 million tons. Depending on whether the earthquake occurs at night or in the day, total casualties could range from 29,000 to 63,000, respectively. Casualty estimates include everything from minor injuries to fatalities.

Like other places, the time of the year can be a factor in the effects of an earthquake. For example, when the soil is saturated, like during the winter months, the area is more prone to landslides and could result in worse damage than an earthquake in a dry summer. Similarly, earthquakes at night, when most people are home, are less likely to cause a lot of injury when compared to a day-quake where more people are out and about.

Another consideration to account for in gauging the effects of an Oregon earthquake is the high risk for liquefaction or landslides in certain areas, particularly if the soil is saturated. These areas would include a large portion of Portland's west side, some parts of the city's inner east side, and long stretches along the Columbia River.

For the central and northern Oregon coast, experts put the probability of a large earthquake between 15 and 20 percent in the next 50 years (Williams, 2018).

Arkansas

The biggest earthquake risk in Arkansas lies in the New Madrid Seismic Zone. The 19 counties in northeast Arkansas, those that stretch out from the Seismic Zone, are at greatest risk.

A magnitude 7.7 New Madrid earthquake would likely damage 162,000 buildings and 1,100 bridges. The number of casualties could be as high as 15,300, and direct economic losses might top $40 billion.

In 1976, a magnitude 5.0 earthquake struck Poinsett County, Arkansas.

Illinois

Southern Illinois is near two significant earthquake zones. The most notable is the New Madrid Seismic Zone, which poses a high risk to several states. The second fault zone is the Wabash Valley Seismic Zone, where a magnitude 5.2 earthquake shook the area in April 2008. Prior to that, a 5.3 quake caused some damage in 1968.

A large earthquake in the New Madrid Seismic Zone could have 6,300 casualties and possibly damage 45,000 buildings and 160 bridges. It could have a $44 billion economic impact on the state.

Kentucky

Kentucky is also at risk from the New Madrid Seismic Zone. A large 7.7-magnitude earthquake in the New Madrid Seismic Zone would likely cause a $53 billion economic loss for Kentucky. Among the losses would be damage to 68,400 buildings and 250 bridges. The number of casualties could be 6,900.

Within Kentucky's borders, the largest recorded earthquake was a magnitude 5.2 that hit on July 27, 1980 in Bath County. The shaking caused an estimated $3 million in damages in Maysville. A smaller 4.2-magnitude tremor shook Perry County in 2012.

Missouri

Missouri is another state that would be severely affected by a major earthquake in the New Madrid Seismic Zone. In fact, the seismic zone is named after the Mississippi River town of New Madrid, which was part of the Louisiana Territory when the 1811 earthquake hit and is now part of Missouri.

A repeat of the 1811 earthquake would likely damage 87,000 buildings and 1,000 bridges. There could be 14,100 casualties, and the state could face $49 billion in direct economic losses.

Because of the below-ground geology of the region, a major earthquake in the New Madrid Seismic Zone could cause destruction over an area 20 times larger than a similar quake in Southern California (Jackson County, n.d.). It's estimated that these major quakes occur probably every 200 to 300 years.

A study at the University of Illinois determined that a magnitude 7.7 New Madrid rupture would leave more than 7 million people in the region homeless and would leave large parts of St. Louis, Missouri, and Memphis, Tennessee, uninhabitable. The St. Charles County Division of Emergency Management puts the odds of another major New Madrid quake happening before 2040 at 25 percent (Jackson County, n.d.).

South Carolina

In the 2014 U.S. Geological Survey Hazards Map, Charleston, South Carolina has a high risk of a damaging earthquake within 50 years. The area was hit by a magnitude 7.0 (or higher) tremor in 1886. A smaller, 5.5-magnitude quake struck near the town of Union in 1913.

Like much of the Midwest and eastern United States, the frequency of large earthquakes in South Carolina is a best guess due to the lack of visible evidence. But increased research is improving estimates. Large ruptures are estimated to occur about every 200 to 250 years, with larger events, like the one in 1886, happening between 250 and 500 years. However, moderate tremors are likely much more frequent, with a probable frequency of about every 125 years.

According to a 2016 HAZUS report released as part of the South Carolina emergency management plan, if South Carolina were to experience a magnitude 7.3 earthquake, more than 4 percent of the buildings would be damaged beyond repair. Among those would be

13 hospitals, 30 fire stations, and two emergency operations centers. Of the 83,961 buildings that would likely experience complete damage, more than half would be single-family homes. The most vulnerable of the structures are unreinforced brick masonry buildings (Waters, 2018). More than 2,000 bridges would be at least moderately damaged.

Initially, an estimated 166,675 households would be without potable water. A week later, 94,500 would still be without water.

The HAZUS report estimates 213,063 households would be without power, and one month later, more than 53,000 would still be without electricity. Three months later, there would still be 1,341 households without power.

Nearly 94,000 households would be displaced, and 62,464 residents would likely need temporary shelter.

Depending on when the earthquake strikes, a midday tremor would likely result in 2,877 fatalities and leave another 1,553 with life-threatening injuries.

Tennessee

Wednesday, December 12, 2018, a small magnitude 4.4 earthquake shook eastern Tennessee. A 3.3 magnitude aftershock followed. While these were not quakes to worry about, they do provide the reminder that the state has earthquake risk.

Like other midwestern states, Tennessee's greatest earthquake risk is the New Madrid Seismic Zone. A repeat of the 1811 event would result in major economic losses and thousands of fatalities, including several thousand in Memphis. Like nearby states, tens of thousands of structures would be damaged in the event, and vital infrastructure, such as water supply, would be affected.

Some of the Tennessee-specific impacts of a magnitude 7.7 New Madrid earthquake include:

- 33,000 injuries
- 1,300 deaths
- 710,000 households without power
- 510,000 households without potable water
- 265,000 buildings damaged
- 107,000 buildings completely damaged
- 55 hospitals damaged and unable to provide service
- 250 fires stations and 125 police stations damaged and unable to provide service

- 40 airports damaged and not operational
- 1,000 bridges damaged, with 250 completely unusable
- 50 dams and 7 levees damaged
- 21 million tons of debris requiring 850,000 truckloads to remove

What isn't really mentioned in the analysis of a possible repeat of the 1811 New Madrid earthquake is how the quake could affect the Mississippi River. It is entirely possible that the series of levees could fail in one or more places, causing the river to invade the spaces civil engineers have tried to protect. Even worse is if the river were at or near flood stage. Water, especially large amounts of it, wants to flow through the path of least resistance. The result of a flood would not only affect Memphis but also have consequences in western Kentucky, southern Missouri, and parts of Arkansas.

Besides the New Madrid Seismic Zone, there is another risk for tremors in Tennessee. Near the eastern border of the state is the lesser-known Southern Appalachian Seismic Zone, which stretches from northeastern Alabama into southwest Virginia and east Tennessee. Most earthquakes in this seismic zone are small, with magnitude 4.6 tremors occurring in 1973 near Knoxville and in 2003 in nearby Fort Payne, Alabama. It's estimated the seismic zone can produce a magnitude 7.5 rupture, which would be as devastating as an earthquake in the New Madrid Seismic Zone.

Chapter 8
Top At-Risk Earthquake Cities in the U.S.

We've discussed regional areas and states with higher earthquake risk. Now we'll look at some cities.

Many of the major cities in the United States have an earthquake risk. While some are well known, such as those in California, others may be a bit of surprise. The earthquake risk is from both natural and induced causes.

Induced causes include those which are triggered by human activities, such as from oil and gas operations, where wastewater is injected into deep underground wells.

The cities listed here are not in any order based on risk.

Anchorage, Alaska

California usually takes the headlines for earthquakes in the U.S., but Alaska has the highest earthquake risk.

It's not uncommon to hear about a large earthquake in Alaska. However, since the population density is extremely low, few people are affected, making the event not very newsworthy.

Anchorage has a population of around 300,000. While not as large as some of the other cities mentioned, if an earthquake were to strike the city, considerable damage, injuries, and even fatalities would occur. Most of the negative effects may not come from the earthquake itself but as the result of an earthquake-caused tsunami.

Recent studies of the seafloor off the coast of Alaska, an area called the Shumagin Gap, indicates a subduction zone, with a detached section, similar to the one that caused the 2011 Tōhoku earthquake and tsunami (Osborne, 2017).

Charleston, South Carolina

If you look at the USGS earthquake hazard map, Charleston has a high risk for having a damaging earthquake within 50 years. As one of 16 states that has experienced a magnitude 6.0 or greater earthquake, South Carolina has "a relatively high likelihood" of another damaging quake (Rindge, 2014).

Charleston was struck by an estimated magnitude 7.0 earthquake in 1886, but evidence is difficult to find. The local faults—the Middleton Place-Summerville Seismic Zone—are buried under thick layers of sand and sediment, which keep the fault lines hidden, unlike the San Andreas Fault, where much of it can be seen on the surface. The seismologists know the faults are there, but it's harder to determine which are moving and at what rate.

As mentioned in Chapter 7, and evidenced by the 1886 earthquake, Charleston is within the target zone that has the potential for large earthquakes.

Dallas, Texas

While it's unlikely a true "Big One" will strike, the risk of a damaging earthquake in the Dallas-Fort Worth area is between 2 to 5 percent. With over 6.8 million people in the Dallas-Fort Worth-Arlington area, a lot of people would be at risk if an earthquake were to strike.

For now, the earthquakes are still in the lower-magnitude range, although these can still cause cracks in buildings and knock things over. However, as Rob Williams, the USGS coordinator for the earthquake program in central and eastern United States, stated, "The more small earthquakes you have, the more of a chance [there is] of having a bigger one" (Borenstein, 2016).

In July 2019, researchers at the University of Texas at Austin released a study that includes a map of more than 250 faults in the Dallas-Fort Worth area. Together, the faults total more than 1,800 miles of length under the region. The study found the faults to be stable, if left alone, but they are sensitive to changes.

Furthermore, a big part of the increasing seismicity risk in the region comes from induced earthquake risk. As oil and gas operations increased from 2008 to 2015, the seismic activity in the region also went up. As wastewater injection has slowed since 2015, seismic activity has significantly reduced.

The study found that because the fault system is sensitive and can potentially produce earthquakes, any future increase in deep wastewater disposal needs to be managed better.

Honolulu, Hawaii

Being a volcanic hotspot, Hawaii is a top earthquake risk. With the largest population of the islands, Honolulu is the highest risk.

An 1868 magnitude 7.9 earthquake in Honolulu killed 77 people with the resulting tsunami and landslide. With today's much larger population, a quake of that magnitude poses a greater threat. Since 1868, seven earthquakes of magnitude 6.1 and larger have hit the islands, including a 6.9 that struck in May 2018.

Los Angeles, California

With the nearby San Andreas Fault, stories and movies about the "Big One" laying waste to Southern California are a common theme. While the possibility of California dropping into the ocean may seem like science fiction, the USGS gives the Los Angeles area a 67% probability of at least one magnitude 6.7 or larger earthquake happening by 2037.

Expanding the area beyond Los Angeles, the probability of a magnitude 6.7 earthquake striking Southern California is 97% for that same time period. A magnitude 7.0 earthquake is an 82% probability. Even a magnitude 7.5 has a 37% chance of hitting the region (Field & Milner, Forecasting California's Earthquakes—What Can We Expect in the Next 30 Years?, 2008).

The magnitude 7.1 earthquake on July 5, 2019, certainly fits into the probability, and it has refueled anxieties and fears about a Big One on the San Andreas Fault.

Memphis, Tennessee

Memphis lies within the earthquake hazard risk area of the New Madrid Seismic Zone, which is why it is one of the top cities in the U.S. for earthquake risk. According to the USGS, a magnitude 6.0 or greater earthquake has a 25–40% probability of striking the area within the next fifty years.

New York City, New York

Some people are surprised that New York City has an earthquake risk. Although the area isn't as seismically active as Los Angeles, there are faults all over—or, more accurately, all under—the area. Historical evidence suggests a moderate quake of at least 5.0 should shake the area about every hundred years. The last one to strike was in 1884.

A 5.0 isn't going to cause epic destruction, but it'll do plenty of damage. Estimates for a 5.0 quake in New York City predict $39 billion worth of damage and over 30 million tons of debris (Miles, 2017). The already congested roads will become littered with rubble from brick and stone buildings, making it almost impossible for first responders to quickly reach those in need. Public transportation will be at a standstill.

Subway tunnels will also be hit. Traveling through soft riverbed mud and hard bedrock, the shaking will cause different segments to shake at differing rates. With parts of the tunnels—particularly the Steinway Tunnel, a 1.3-mile cast-iron tube deep below the East River—being built before earthquake codes, moderate shaking will likely cause major problems.

But while a 5.0 may be what the local faults are capable of, much more damage is possible. The Ramapo Fault stretches 185 miles, from Hudson Highlands through New Jersey and Pennsylvania, and it could produce a 7.0 earthquake. If a 7.0 were to strike, it'd do more damage than Superstorm Sandy or the tragic events of 9-11. This large earthquake would likely collapse, or severely damage, the 6,000 unreinforced masonry buildings in the New York City area.

In addition, potential disaster could result from the nearby Indian Point Energy Center, a nuclear power plant in Westchester County. The U.S. Nuclear Regulatory Commission (NRC) required extensive seismic evaluations to be performed at all U.S. nuclear plants following the Fukushima, Japan, disaster in 2011. A formal request was sent to the NRC that the Indian Point Energy Center be waived from the requirement, as it's slated to close in 2021. How well the nuclear plant would fare in a 7.0 earthquake is unclear. However, a nearby large natural gas pipeline may be more susceptible to damage and, possibly, explosion in the event of a large earthquake. Such an explosion could trigger a disaster at the power plant like Fukushima (Miles, 2017).

Oklahoma City, Oklahoma

The heartland of the United States isn't known for earthquakes, yet when you look at the USGS earthquake hazard maps, Oklahoma has a seismic target on it. Prior to about 2009, the state only experienced a few minor tremors every year. Since 2009, the state has a few almost every day. Much of the increased risk is blamed on induced seismicity, as a result of hydraulic fracking and wastewater injection. Fracking is the injection of high-pressure water, sand, and chemicals into deep rock, where the rock is broken up to release trapped gas and oil.

A seismicity risk report for 2017 stated, "The chance of damage in the next year [2017] from induced earthquakes is still similar to that of natural earthquakes in high-hazard areas of California" (Petersen, et al., 2017).

While the number of earthquakes has appeared to decrease over the last year, the risk is still significant. Oklahoma's capital city, Oklahoma City, has about 3 million people living in the area. Combined with many older unreinforced masonry structures, the risk for damage and injury is high as a result of the increased earthquake risk (Il, 2017).

The biggest earthquake recorded in the state was a magnitude 5.8 near Pawnee in September 2016. A 5.0 temblor occurred in November of that year as well.

From 2010 to April 2018, Oklahoma experienced 2,724 earthquakes of magnitude 3.0 or higher. The year 2015 had the most at 903. Prior to 2009, the normal average was one or two magnitude 3.0 or larger quakes per year. As more regulations were put into place, and many operations moved to shallower depths, the number of earthquakes has appeared to be decreasing (Pappas, Oklahoma Suffers Its 2,724th Earthquake Since 2010, 2018).

And Oklahoma isn't the only place where fracking has caused earthquakes. Texas, Kansas, Colorado, and Arkansas have experienced fracking-linked quakes. In March 2014, a fracking operation in eastern Ohio triggered a magnitude 3.0 earthquake. That quake was on a hidden fault. Before that tremor, no quakes had been recorded in that region (Oskin, Fracking Led to Ohio Earthquakes, 2015).

It's generally believed that deep fluid injection from fracking operations only enhances seismic activity limited to the area where the fluid is injected into the ground. However, researchers at Tufts University found evidence to support the hypothesis that deep wastewater injections may potentially cause damaging earthquakes further away. These injections can affect deeper and larger faults that are under greater stress and more susceptible to fluid-induced slipping (Silver, 2019).

The Figure 7 is from the U.S. Geological Survey on their induced earthquakes page. Over a 35-year period (1973 to 2008), 852 earthquakes of magnitude 3.0 or higher were recorded. The next nine years (2009 to 2018) saw a huge increase of 3,514 magnitude 3.0 or larger earthquakes. Most of those earthquakes appear to be induced by nearby fracking operations.

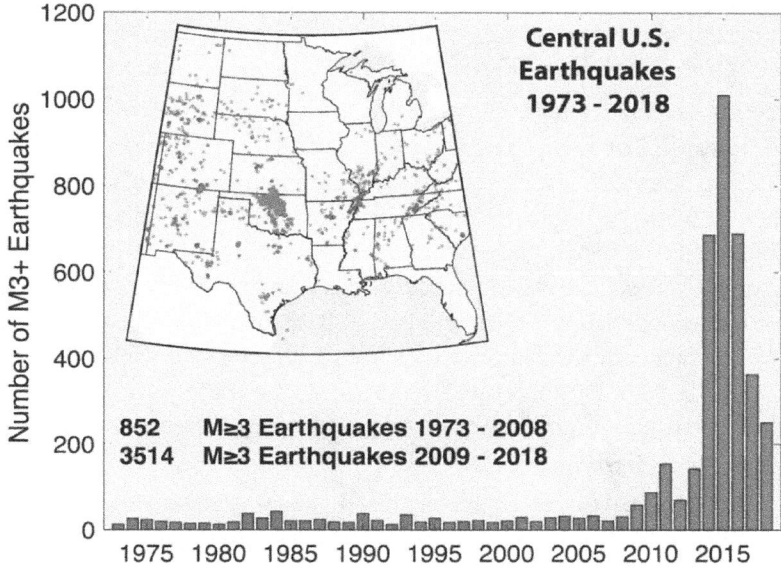

Figure 7: The long-term average is approximately 25 earthquakes of magnitude 3.0 or larger per year. In 2009, this rate increased. The chart shows the annual number of magnitude 3.0 or greater tremors. From USGS's website: https://earthquake.usgs.gov/research/induced/overview.php.

Portland, Oregon

While not at the same risk as Seattle, Portland is along the Cascadia Subduction Zone, and it is now estimated to have a 17 to 20 percent chance of an 8.0 earthquake over the next 50 years. Previously, its estimate was only a 12 percent chance (Meyer, A Major Earthquake in the Pacific Northwest Looks Even Likelier, 2016).

As mentioned in a chapter 7, Portland not only has the risk of the Cascadia Subduction Zone but the Portland Hills Fault, which runs under the city. While earthquake damages and losses from a Cascadia rupture are significant, an earthquake on the Portland Hills Fault could easily double the losses.

San Francisco, California

Overall, California has a greater than 99 percent probability of one or more magnitude 6.7 or larger earthquakes occurring by 2037. However, while the probability is greater for Southern California, Northern California's chances are 93 percent for a magnitude 6.7 earthquake during that time frame. A magnitude 7.0 has a 68 percent probability, while a 7.5 has only a 15 percent chance of occurring.

Focusing on the San Francisco area, the USGS gives the region a 63 percent chance of a magnitude 6.7 or larger happening by 2037 (Field & and members of 2014 WGCEP, 2015).

Salt Lake City, Utah

The capital of Utah, Salt Lake City, sits on one section of the 240-mile-long Wasatch Fault, and nearly 80 percent of Utah's population lives within fifteen miles of the fault. Earthquakes of magnitude 7.0 and larger have historically struck at some point along the fault about every 350 years. The last definitively large quake happened around 600 years ago, with another one possibly as recent as 400 years ago. In either case, the area is primed for another big one. Recent projections have estimated the likelihood of a magnitude 6.75 or higher earthquake over the next 50 years is 43 percent.

Seattle, Washington

California usually takes the spotlight when it comes to earthquake risks, but in recent years, the Cascadia Subduction Zone has been stealing some of the thunder.

With more than 4 million people in and around the Seattle area, a lot of scientists may be more worried about that metropolitan region than any other.

The odds of a big, magnitude 8.0 to 8.6 "Cascadia earthquake happening in the next fifty years are roughly one in three" (Schulz, 2015). But the Cascadia Subduction Zone can produce even megathrust earthquakes, from 8.7 to 9.2, and the chances of that happening are one in ten.

The frequency of a magnitude 6.0 or larger earthquake is about every 30 to 50 years. The frequency of a megathrust quake varies from 200 to 1,500 years. Lack of data for the Seattle Fault has left earthquake interval estimates to vary from 200 to 15,000 years.

For the Seattle Fault, the most recent earthquake was about 1,100 years ago. The fault is estimated to be able to produce a magnitude 7.5 event.

A large tremor on the Seattle Fault could cause 5,000 to 30,000 landslides in the region, depending on soil moisture conditions when the quake strikes. The quake could also produce a 16-foot tsunami that would strike within seconds and flood the area within five minutes. Over 1,100 unreinforced masonry buildings in the city would be subject to collapse. Like in other earthquake-risk areas, fires will break out, and many of the roads, bridges, and other infrastructure, including water and electricity, will be damaged (Seattle Emergency Management, 2019).

Tulsa, Oklahoma

Like Oklahoma's capital city, Tulsa has a population of more than 400,000 at risk of earthquakes.

As in other parts of Oklahoma, the earthquake risk is largely due to induced seismicity. A 2015 Stanford University study of earthquakes and wastewater injection showed a "clear relation" and that Oklahoma was "'almost certain' to have at least one damaging earthquake in the next five years, with heightened risks of a large quake probable to endure for a decade" (Jones C. , 2016). The reason the heightened risk is not expected to continue much beyond that is due to regulatory caps on how much wastewater can be injected back into the ground. The study noted the "state's 180-day moving average of magnitude-2.8 or greater quakes peaked at approximately 4.5 per day in summer 2015, tailing off to about 2.3 a day this fall [2016]."

Prior to 2009, the average number of magnitude 3.0 or greater earthquakes in the state was one per year. There were about 900 of these size quakes in 2015.

Washington, D.C.

In 2011, a magnitude 5.8 earthquake in the Virginia Seismic Zone damaged buildings and other structures in the D.C. area. It was estimated almost a third of the U.S. population felt the earthquake. The geology of the area causes an earthquake to be felt over a larger region, as has been previously mentioned. As a comparison, a 2010 magnitude 7.2 rupture in Baja California was felt over a similarly sized area as the 2011 Virginia quake (Perkins S. , Seismic Risk in Eastern U.S. May Be Higher Than Previously Thought, 2012).

While the USGS hazard map indicates a lower risk in the D.C. area, analysis of the 2011 Virginia quake "indicates that Washington DC and other affected population centers could be at a higher risk of major ground movement than previously recognized" (Perkins S. , Seismic Risk in Eastern U.S. May Be Higher Than Previously Thought, 2012).

An interesting finding came after the 2011 Virginia earthquake. Previously, scientists believed a magnitude 5.8 earthquake couldn't possibly trigger landslides further away than about 37 miles (60 km). But the quake caused rockfalls at least 152 miles (245 km) away— more than four times the distance scientists believed was possible (Perkins S. , 2012).

Wichita, Kansas

The risk of a damaging earthquake in northern Oklahoma and southern Kansas, where Wichita is located, was estimated in 2016 to be 10 to 17 percent. Because building codes in Wichita were not as earthquake resilient as those in California, a lower magnitude earthquake has the potential to cause comparable damage as a higher magnitude quake in the Bay Area of California. For further comparison, Los Angeles County has a 2 to 5 percent risk of a damaging earthquake (Lefler, 2016). Please note the risk of a "damaging earthquake" is not necessarily prediction of a high-magnitude quake in the Wichita area, just the potential for damage using the Modified Mercalli Intensity Scale.

As we've discussed, the thousands of small earthquakes striking northern Oklahoma and southern Kansas over the past several years have been blamed on wastewater from fracking operations being injected deep underground. Limits on locations and disposal amounts have been put into place in an attempt to reduce the earthquake hazard.

Chapter 9
Earthquake Scenarios

The U.S. Geological Survey (USGS) works with various federal, state, and local agencies and organizations to create earthquake scenarios for many of the highest-risk areas of the country. The catalog of scenarios, containing almost 800 ShakeMap scenarios, is found at https://earthquake.usgs.gov/scenarios/catalog/. Most of these scenarios are just rupture-related information for the potential event and don't contain actual loss estimations.

Many state agencies and local organizations have used these ShakeMap scenarios to estimate the potential effect an earthquake might have on an area.

In this chapter, we'll go over some of the projected information for a few of these scenarios. The overview of these few earthquake scenarios is intended only to point out some of the loss projections, not cover every aspect of the scenarios, as some of these scenarios are essentially books on their own. For example, the 2008 ShakeOut scenario for the San Andreas Fault is 312 pages long.

This chapter will focus on identifying the estimated damage to infrastructure and buildings as well as estimated casualties and injuries. Of particular interest are estimations of how long certain utilities, like water, may be unavailable.

For more detailed information, such as ground shaking and liquefaction potential maps, go to the USGS scenarios catalog or the related websites listed at the end of this book.

San Francisco Scenario

In 2006, an earthquake scenario designed to repeat the 1906 San Francisco earthquake was simulated among federal, state, and local California officials. The simulated earthquake had a magnitude of 7.9. As we review some of the estimated damages, remember this information is from 2006—nearly 13 years old (as of me writing this). Today, costs would be much higher, and losses may also be higher due to increased population and development.

In 2006 dollars, and based on assets at that time, the area had 1.1 trillion dollars' worth of building exposure:

- $780 billion in residential
- $204 billion in commercial
- $43 billion in industrial

Over 10.5 million people would be at risk, including 3.7 million households and 1.2 million people over 65 years old.

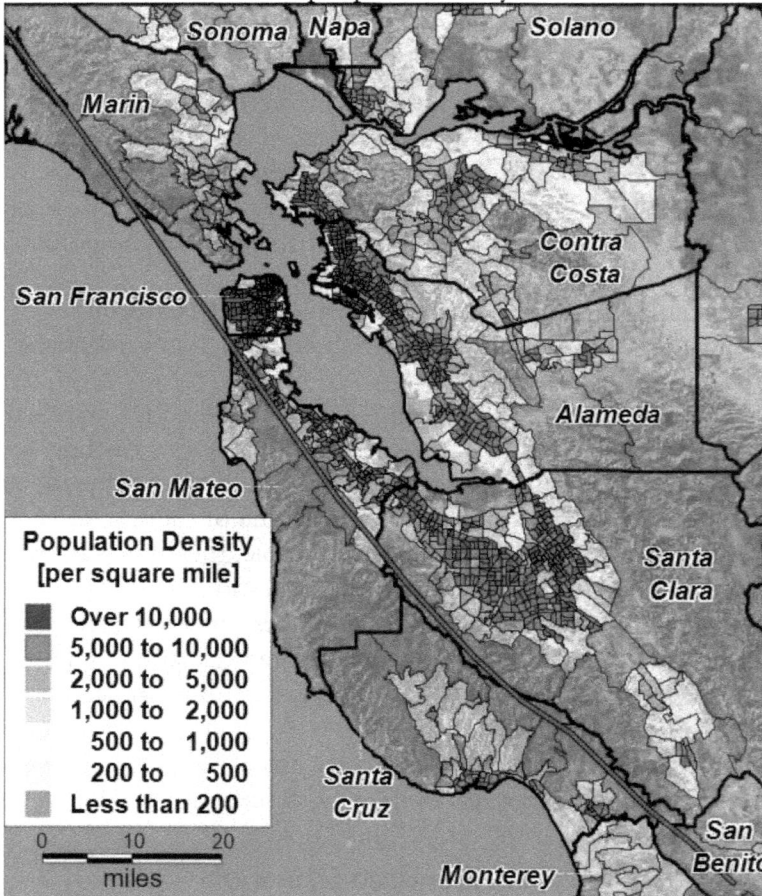

Figure 8: The population data of the San Francisco area in 2006.
https://www.fema.gov/media-library-data/20130726-1742-25045-9381/dl_sfeqlosses.pdf

The projected damage from the simulation included the following:

- Of the 3 million residences, over 100,000 could potentially be destroyed.

- 10,000 commercial facilities are expected to have extensive, or worse, damage.
- 1,300 bridges of the 6,900 in the nineteen-county area may be damaged enough to require repairs.
- 30 to 50 of the area's 120 hospitals may experience minor to major damage.
- 35 fire stations and 50 police stations may be seriously affected.
- 2 emergency operation centers would likely have significant damage.
- 400 of the 4,000 schools may be closed.
- 500 to 600 fires may ignite in the area, with about 100 fires in San Francisco.
- 25 to 40 million tons of debris would be generated.
- 200,000 to 300,000 households would be displaced.
- 60,000 to 120,000 people would require short-term shelter.

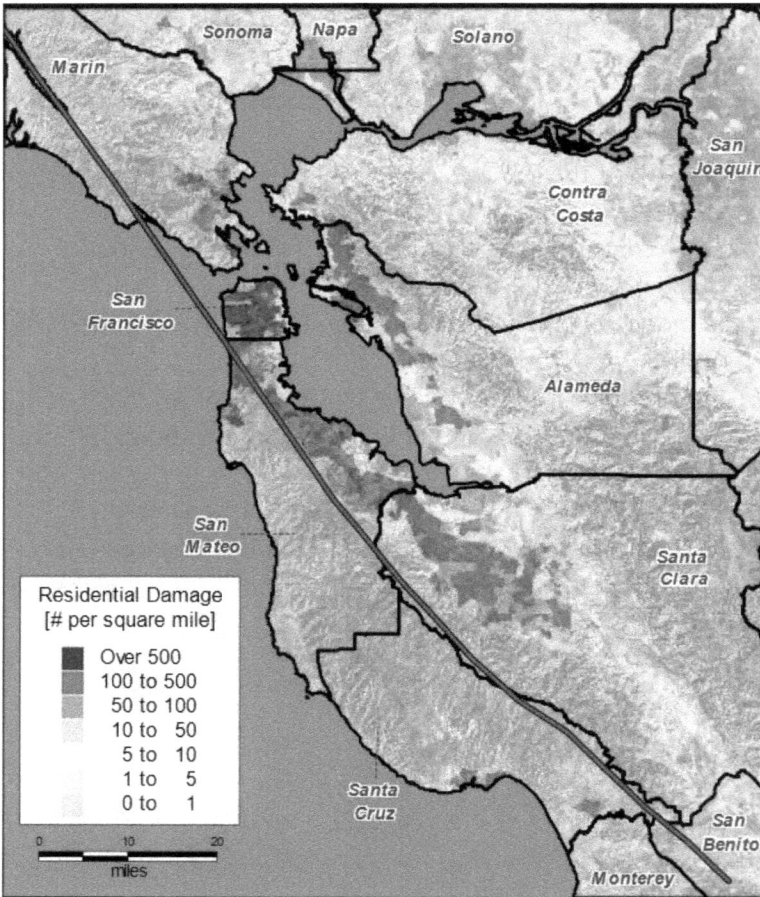

Figure 9: The projected residential damage from a simulated San Francisco earthquake. https://www.fema.gov/media-library-data/20130726-1742-25045-9381/dl_sfeqlosses.pdf

A daytime earthquake would likely cause 13,000 injuries requiring hospitalization and 3,400 deaths. A nighttime event would likely cause about 8,000 injuries and 1,800 deaths.

The economic impact would be over $120 billion in building losses, with 463,254 buildings damaged and 37,025 being a total loss. Direct and indirect losses would be in excess of $150 billion.

One day after the earthquake, 500,000 households would be without electricity, and over 1 million households without water.

San Andreas Fault Scenario

The State of California Department of Conservation has a 2008 earthquake scenario that was used for its ShakeOut drill in the event of an earthquake on the San Andreas Fault (2008 ShakeOut Scenario). The scenario projected about 2,000 deaths, 50,000 injuries, and $200 billion in damages. Like other scenarios, this doesn't include the lasting disruption those damages will cause. And, those numbers are just estimates from the main shock. Additional damaging aftershocks can increase those numbers.

In this scenario, the earthquake is a magnitude 7.8 that lasts about 55 seconds and occurs on the southern 186 miles (300 km) of the San Andreas Fault. Compared to the Northridge quake, which lasted only 7 seconds, shaking lasting this long will be terrifying to many who have never experienced more than a few seconds of ground movement.

> "A magnitude 7.8 is not the largest earthquake that the southern San Andreas Fault can produce, nor is the San Andreas the only fault to threaten the populated areas of southern California with very large earthquakes. However, those other faults have recurrence intervals (an estimate of the average time) between larger earthquakes that are considerably longer, measured in thousands of years. By contrast, the southern San Andreas Fault has generated earthquakes of ShakeOut size on average every 150 years—and on a portion of the fault that ruptures in the ShakeOut Scenario, the last earthquake happened more than 300 years ago" (Jones, et al., 2008).

Some of the expected consequences of the earthquake include the following:

- At least 10 million people would be within the heavy shaking areas.
- Only 1,800 casualties would be expected, due to strong building codes, but tens of thousands of injuries would also be expected.
- All unreinforced masonry buildings within fifteen miles of the San Andreas Fault would be destroyed.
- Hundreds of older buildings will have collapsed into heaps. Thousands of other buildings will be so damaged they'll eventually need to be torn down.

- The fault rupture would offset all infrastructure lines going into Southern California, including:
    o Interstate-15 at Cajon Pass
    o Interstate-10 at San Gorgonio Pass
    o Route 14
    o pipelines
    o power lines
    o roads
    o railways
    o telecommunications
    o aqueducts
- At least 1,600 large fires will likely start, and many small fires will also start, possibly flaring up into larger ones. The fires could double the death count.
- Two-thirds of the hospitals in Los Angeles, Orange, Riverside, and San Bernardino counties will be non-functional.
- 50,000 people will be trying to get to emergency rooms.
- The state highway system will mostly survive, due to seismic upgrades, but many bridges and overpasses under the control of cities and counties won't do as well.
- Many roads will be impassable due to damage, collapsed structures, or abandoned vehicles.
- The water distribution system will also not do well, and some buildings will be six months, or more, without water.
- Many of the buried water and sewer pipes will become cracked or broken with the earthquake. Initial cleanup in the newer, relatively undamaged buildings will likely need to be done without running water.
- Electricity will be out. Electric trains and elevators will likely not be functional. Non-working traffic lights will gridlock streets, with many drivers eventually deciding to make the long walk home.
- Phone systems will be unusable or overwhelmed by the number of attempted calls.
- Total economic impact and loss would exceed $213 billion.

In the months following the earthquake, damage repairs would be extensive. By about a month after the big one, electricity and water should be restored to most of those who had lost those utilities, particularly in areas with less damage. However, residents will likely need to continue to boil water due to possible contamination from cracks in the water system. It may take a year or longer before the entire system is considered safe.

A month after, tens of thousands of people will still be without permanent shelter. Many will also be without jobs due to damaged buildings. Many roads, freeways, and bridges will still be closed for repairs.

Six months after the quake, many small businesses will have closed, and their closure will contribute to the closure of other businesses.

Cascadia Subduction Zone Scenario

The last time the Cascadia Subduction Zone ruptured was on January 26, 1700. At least forty high-magnitude events have happened in the past 10,000 years. Seismologists estimate the likelihood of another major earthquake striking the zone in the next fifty years at 10 to 14 percent. The average for megaquake events is about every 350 years, so we are getting close to when the next Big One is due.

Simulating the ground motions of a magnitude 9.0 earthquake, researchers in the Pacific Northwest found that buildings under 24 stories, built to the current minimum seismic standards with reinforced concrete walls, might not fare well. The problem is with seismic waves passing through the soft and deep sediments in the basin below Seattle. The ground is likely to trap large-amplitude waves. The study suggests structures built to minimum seismic standards may have up to a 33 percent chance of collapse (Ham, 2019).

If a 9.0 megaquake strikes the Cascadia Subduction Zone, a 600-mile fault line along the West Coast, the residents of Grays Harbor and Pacific County would first be subjected to the severe shaking and then, about 15 to 20 minutes later, a massive wave rushing towards shore. The exposed outer coasts could see 20 to 60 feet of water, while the more sheltered Willapa Bay and Grays Harbor might only get 10 feet or less (Eungard, Forson, Walsh, Gica, & Arcas, 2018).

Strong shaking would be felt from lower British Columbia down into Northern California. Strong shaking implies you would not likely be able to remain standing.

For the Portland area, a report published in 2018 estimates damages to be much higher than previously estimated. A magnitude 9.0 rupture in the Cascadia Subduction Zone could cause more than $36 billion in building damages and displace more than 85 thousand people. A daytime earthquake could result in over 27 thousand casualties, while a nighttime event could have fewer than 10 thousand. With the possibility of creating more than 17 million tons of debris, it could take 400,000 to 680,000 25-ton dump trucks to clear it (Bauer, Burns, & Madin, 2018).

New Madrid Seismic Zone Scenario

In 1811–12, the region was sparsely populated. Today, it's home to millions. Unlike California, where tremors are more common and earthquake awareness has enforced higher building standards, many of the structures in the New Madrid Seismic Zone were not built to withstand violent shaking. A large quake in this area would directly affect several million people across eight states and indirectly affect millions more. The eight states in the most affected region are Alabama, Arkansas, Illinois, Indiana, Kentucky, Mississippi, Missouri, and Tennessee.

It is still unknown why the area is at risk for large earthquakes, since the New Madrid region is far from tectonic plate boundaries. It's been questioned whether "applying what has been learned from studies of places like the San Andreas fault in California to the New Madrid region" (U.S. Geological Survey, 2007) is even appropriate. During the last fifteen years, new discoveries have led to new estimates of the frequency of large earthquakes in the area. The latest probabilities of a large quake happening for a fifty-year period are

- magnitude 6.0 or larger, 25 to 40 percent and
- magnitude 7.5–8.0 (repeat of the 1811–12 events), 7 to 10 percent.

According to one source in "the chance of a magnitude 6 or 7 earthquake occurring within the next 50 years is roughly 90%" (Elnashai, Cleveland, Jefferson, & Harrald, 2008, p. 6).

To begin to make efforts for earthquake preparation in the region, the New Madrid Seismic Zone Catastrophic Planning Project was officially started in 2006. A magnitude 7.7 New Madrid earthquake scenario was developed by the Mid-America Earthquake Center,

George Washington University, Virginia Tech, in partnership with the USGS and the Association of CUSEC State Geologists. The basic scenario parameters were a magnitude 7.7 earthquake occurring at 2 a.m. on February 7 (the same as the 1811 event). Aftershocks in the magnitude 6.0 range would continue to be felt in the following days and weeks.

The Central United States Earthquake Consortium (CUSEC) released an after-action report with the following estimates of the earthquake's impact:

- 8 states and 7 million people directly affected
- 85,000 injuries
- 3,500 fatalities
- 2 million people displaced and seeking shelter
- 700,000 buildings damaged
- 300,000 buildings destroyed
- 3,600 bridges damaged
- 2.6 million households without electricity
- 1 million households without water
- 2 million 25-ton truckloads of debris
- $300 billion in economic cost (CUSEC, 2011)

As a comparison, Hurricane Katrina cost $88 billion and resulted in 2,500 deaths. A large earthquake in the New Madrid Seismic Zone would kill an additional 1,000 people and cost three times as much.

Like other large earthquakes, critical infrastructure will be heavily damaged and out of service, with the outages likely affecting an area much larger than the eight states directly affected. Many hospitals in the worst affected areas will not be able to care for patients, and current and new patients will have to be transported to other locations.

With transportation systems severely impaired, any mass evacuation would be unlikely. Airports, ports, and ferry services will be crippled or non-functioning. Road and bridges will be damaged or destroyed, making travel difficult. It will be extremely challenging for local emergency services and first responders to respond in the impacted regions, and it will be problematic for external aid and supplies to reach the hardest hit areas. Many schools that might normally be used as public shelters will be unusable after a large earthquake.

Utility services will be disrupted. Extensive damage to facilities and pipelines will affect hundreds of thousands of customers. Lack of utility service (particularly water and electricity) will make it difficult for many to stay in their homes, even if their homes are structurally safe.

The planning scenario used by CUSEC includes ten scenarios, with eight focused on the New Madrid Seismic Zone and two using the Wabash Valley Seismic Zone. The scenarios were designed to identify effects of plausible earthquakes in the eight states directly affected.

It should be noted that a repeat of the 1811–12 events, with three magnitude 7.0 to 8.0 earthquakes, cannot really be modelled, as current modelling tools are incapable of doing so. Three successive large earthquakes would likely cause more catastrophic effects.

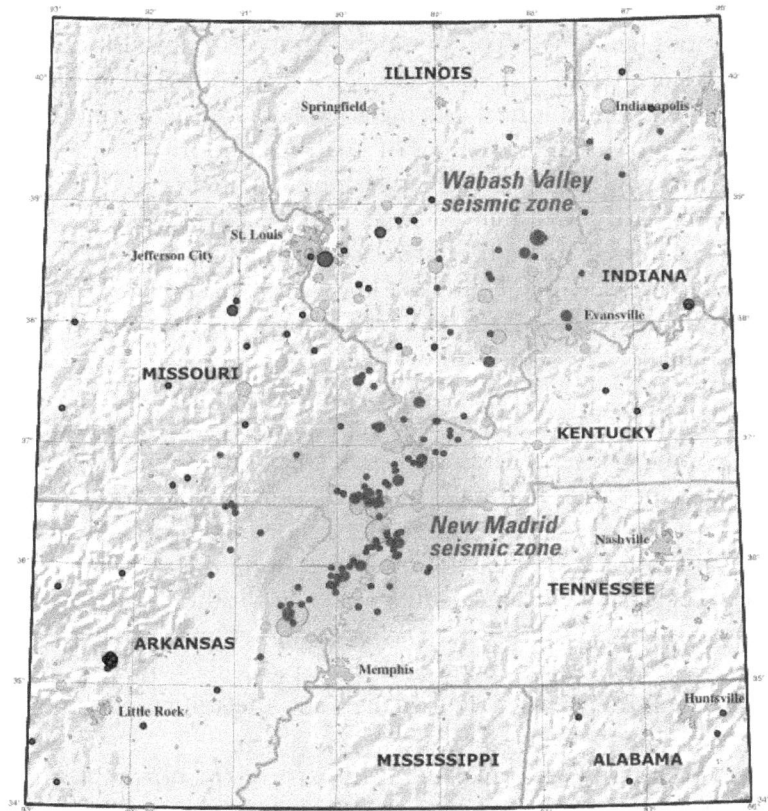

Figure 10: Map of New Madrid and Wabash Valley seismic zones. Red circles are M2.5+ quakes from 1974 to 2002. Green circles were prior to 1974. Larger circles are larger quakes. Image from USGS's "Earthquake Hazard in the Heart of the Homeland,"
https://pubs.usgs.gov/fs/2006/3125/pdf/FS06-3125_508.pdf.

Research has indicated at least two similar events to the 1811 New Madrid Earthquake, with one in about 1450 AD and the other in 900 AD. Additionally, over the past 5,000 years, other large earthquakes have occurred in the region surrounding the New Madrid Seismic Zone.

Wasatch Fault Scenario

First, a little background. I live in Utah, so this scenario is more applicable to me and my family. As a result, I've done more research and gotten more information for this scenario.

The Wasatch Fault runs along the Wasatch Front, a section of the Wasatch mountain range. The Wasatch Front spans a four-county area of northern Utah, from Brigham City in the north to Levan in the south. The population of this metropolitan area is nearing 3 million, and more than 75 percent of Utah's economy is found in this region. Utah's capital, Salt Lake City, is near the center of that stretch. The population of those four counties is like Cleveland and Pittsburgh, and well above that of New Orleans and Nashville metropolitan areas. While Utah isn't known for earthquakes, like California, there are more people living along a major fault line in Utah than in any other state, other than the Golden State (Pipkin, 2019).

However, Utah has a few unique geographic risks that could cause even more havoc than in other high-risk areas. The Great Salt Lake in Salt Lake County and Utah Lake in Utah County could both pose threats to nearby cities in the event of a major earthquake. Seiches could wash ashore, damaging communities along the shorelines of the lakes. Tectonic subsidence could lower or tilt the valley floor, causing water to rush onto what was once higher ground. Soil liquefaction could cause structures to sink, particularly in areas near the lakes where the water table is higher, and the soil composition is more susceptible to this hazard.

Unlike Southern California and even parts of the north, northern Utah—where the Wasatch Front is located—experiences winter weather. From November to March, freezing temperatures are common, with single digit lows likely, particularly in late December through January. Since the probability of an earthquake is the same throughout the year, there's just as good of a chance it could strike during the cold winter months.

It's practically a guarantee the power will be out after an earthquake. The question is, how long? Other utilities, including potable water, will also be out or severely crippled.

Earthquake scarps—tall ledges—can be found all along the valley from historical quakes. These scarps form when sections of the land along the fault drop or rise up (depending on your view) during an earthquake. The resulting scarps are, on average, three to nine feet high. Twenty-foot scarps are not uncommon. Some ancient scarps are about 130 feet high, which most experts believe were caused from repeated earthquakes. Many of the smaller ancient scarps have eroded, or modern construction has obscured their presence.

A magnitude 7.0 earthquake would certainly create new scarps across the valley. A possible thirty-mile scarp could form along the eastern side of the Salt Lake Valley, and a similar one is possible on the western side. One new scarp, and definitely two, would severely impact utilities and transportation. Other scarps from the various faults in the valley could cripple sections of the city, complicating immediate rescue efforts and hampering recovery.

Unlike California, too many of Utah's buildings are not earthquake ready. There are 150,000 buildings lacking any kind of earthquake retrofit. Especially concerning are more than 500 brick schools in the Salt Lake Valley that need reinforcement.

A deeper look at Utah's Wasatch Fault

The Wasatch Fault is a normal fault, where the Wasatch range mountain block of crust slips mostly vertical, relative to the western, valley side that has a downward movement. It is the "most studied...normal fault in the world" (Working Group on Utah Earthquake Probabilities, 2016, p. 6).

The fault runs for about 240 miles and has ten segments. The north end reaches towards Malad City, Idaho, and the southern-most segment extends to Fayette, Utah. Each segment is thought to rupture independent of the others. Because of the multiple segments, the term Wasatch Fault Zone is often used interchangeably with Wasatch Fault.

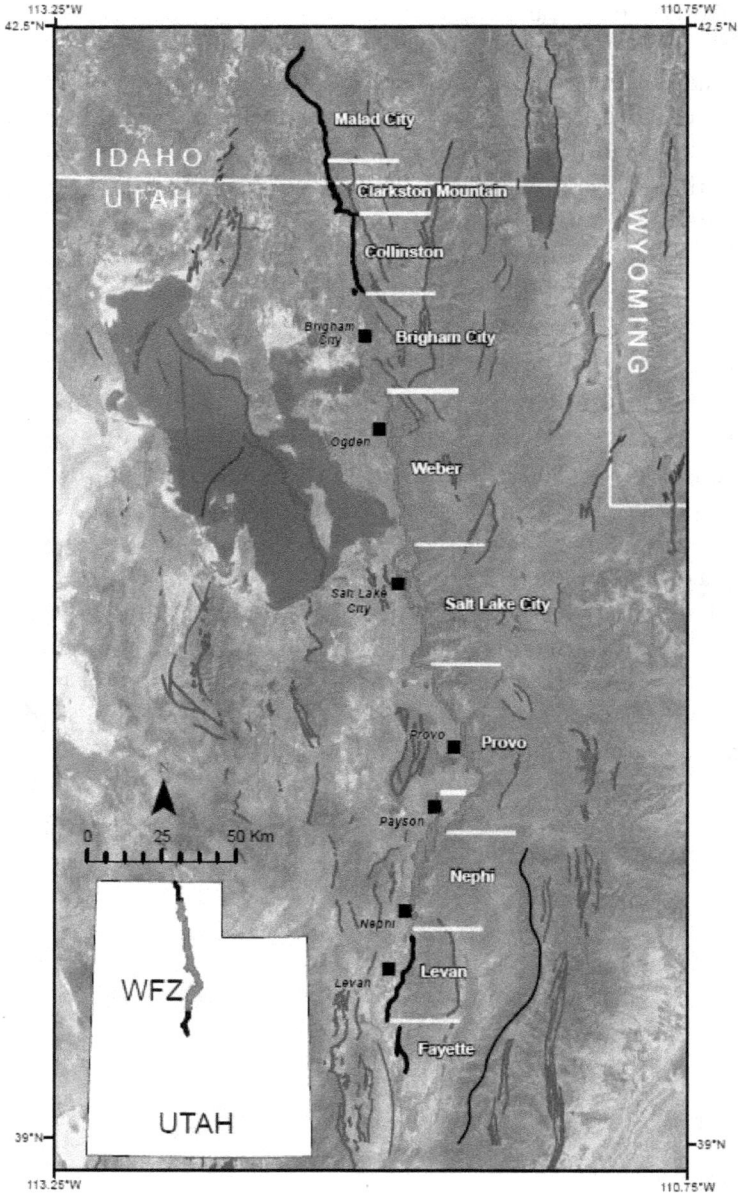

Figure 11: Segments of the Wasatch Fault. Central segments are in red. Other northern Utah faults are shown in dark gray. Image from the Utah Geological Survey document "Earthquake Probabilities for the Wasatch Front Region in Utah, Idaho, and Wyoming" (Working Group on Utah Earthquake Probabilities, 2016).

The Wasatch Fault is the most active fault of the seismically active area known as the Intermountain Seismic Belt, which extends from south from Montana to Arizona and west to Nevada.

The five central segments of the Wasatch Fault have had at least 22 surface-faulting earthquakes during the last 6,000 years. These central segments extend from Brigham City in the north to Nephi in the south. The Wasatch Front urban corridor, which includes the cities from Ogden to Salt Lake City to Provo, are in these segments. Another large earthquake hit the Levan segment, south of Nephi, about 1,300 years ago.

Collectively, the average recurrence interval (long-term average) of these large earthquakes is about once every 300 years. The last definitively large earthquake happened on the Provo segment about 600 years ago.

There are some discrepancies among sources about a large quake on the Nephi segment (just south of the Provo segment) that possibly occurred as recent as 400 years ago. Some carbon dating indicates it struck the area about 1,200 years ago. However, research in the last few years has once again revised that estimate to about 200 to 300 years ago. If anything, this just proves how much earthquake research is changing and revising what we think we know.

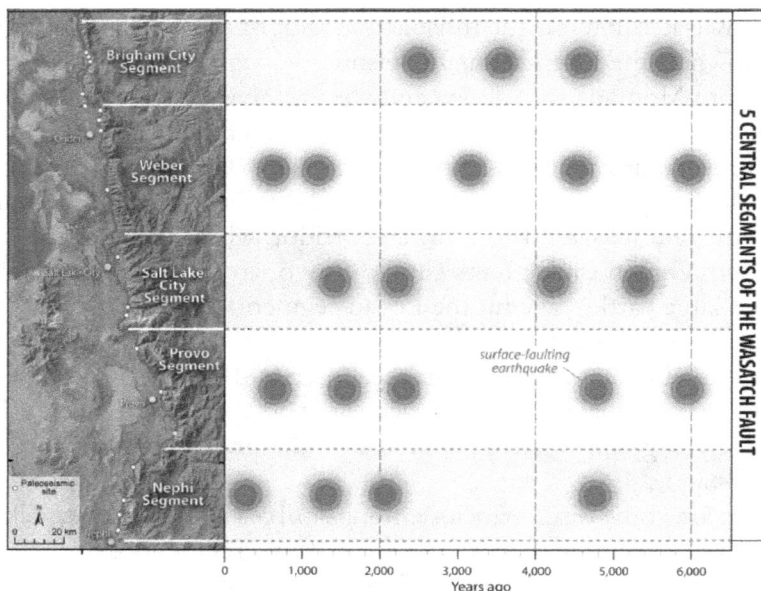

Figure 12: Past major earthquakes on the five central segments of the Wasatch Fault. Image from the Utah Geological Survey document "Earthquake Probabilities for the Wasatch Front Region in Utah, Idaho, and Wyoming" (Working Group on Utah Earthquake Probabilities, 2016).

Individually, each central segment has its own recurrence interval ranging from 700 to 2,700 years. The outlying, or distal, segments have recurrence intervals of about 10,000 years.

The largest earthquake potential for any of the segments along the Wasatch Fault is estimated to be a magnitude 7.5.

Based on the limited 6,000-year earthquake record, the next Big One is past due. It's been over 600 years since the rupture on the Provo segment, and possibly less than that since the last Nephi event. However, using the 300-year average, the area is past due for its next Big One. Where it will happen is unknown. Of the five central faults, the Brigham City segment has gone longest since any major activity, so it could be the most susceptible. However, if segment ruptures are regular, then the Salt Lake segment will be the next one hit.

Previous estimates put the likelihood of a large earthquake at 13 percent in the next 50 years, and 25 percent in the next 100 years. However, the Working Group of Utah Earthquake Probabilities (WGUEP) conducted a thorough analysis of the probability of large earthquakes along the Wasatch Front. They then produced a report in 2016, and the results were surprising.

The analysis factored in the various fault zones in the area. Previously, evidence of only 18 surface-rupturing quakes had been found along the central segments. Additional research identified at least 22 large earthquakes in the last 6,000 years in the segments from Brigham City to Nephi.

Another change based on the 2016 report was the estimated recurrence interval. Previously, the average interval between large earthquakes was estimated to be about every 350 years. The new interval is every 300 years. The average rupture intervals for individual central segments were also changed, ranging from 700 to 2,700 years. Earlier studies had recurrence intervals ranging from 1,200 to 2,600 years.

The study confirmed that both the Brigham City and Salt Lake segments have gone the longest without major earthquakes, which places the highest risk of large quakes on those segments.

During the past 6,000 years, large earthquakes on the Salt Lake segment have occurred about every 1,300 years. Over a 14,000-year period, large ruptures happen on average about every 1,500 years. The last Big One on the segment happened 1,400 years ago.

Overall, the Wasatch Front region has a 43 percent probability of experiencing a magnitude 6.75 or larger earthquake in the next 50 years. The chances of a magnitude 6.0 or larger are 57 percent. The Wasatch Fault itself is projected to have a probability of 18 percent for large earthquakes of magnitudes 6.0 and 6.75 or larger.

It should be noted that the probabilities are projecting one or more earthquakes of at least these magnitudes. That means there is a chance that there could be more than one Big One. So, even if a Big One occurs, don't get complacent thinking another can't happen in your lifetime.

It should also be noted that the percentages for individual fault zones are specifically for those zones. So, if one fault zone has a major rupture, the others still have their own probabilities of Big Ones.

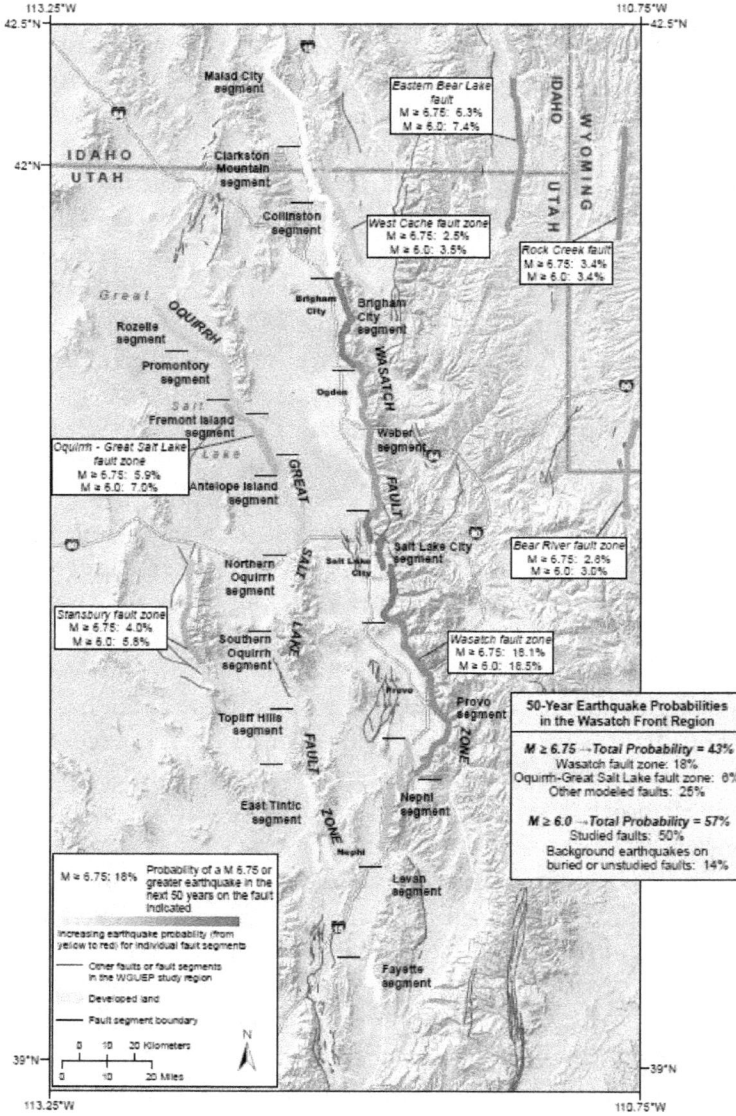

Figure 13: Probabilities of one or more earthquakes of magnitude 6.0 and greater from 2014 to 2063. Image from the Utah Geological Survey document "Earthquake Probabilities for the Wasatch Front Region in Utah, Idaho, and Wyoming" (Working Group on Utah Earthquake Probabilities, 2016).

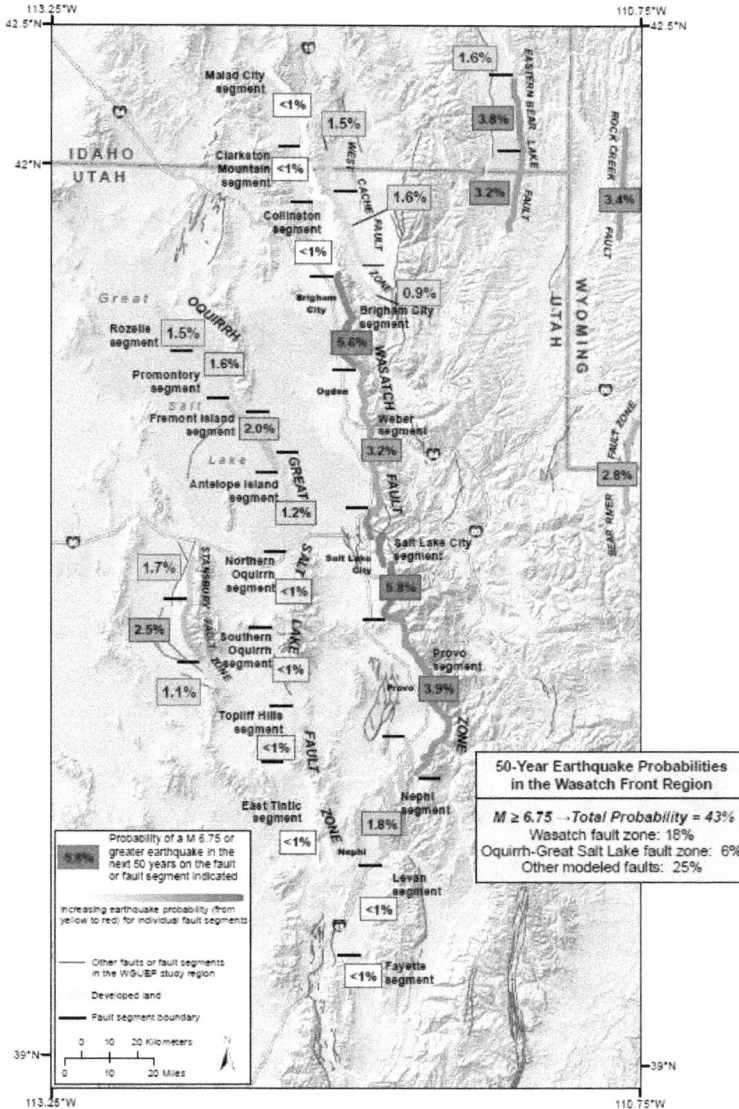

Figure 14: Probabilities of one or more earthquakes magnitude 6.75 or larger in the next 50 years. Image from the Utah Geological Survey document "Earthquake Probabilities for the Wasatch Front Region in Utah, Idaho, and Wyoming" (Working Group on Utah Earthquake Probabilities, 2016).

The Salt Lake City earthquake scenario

Although Federal Emergency Management Agency (FEMA) HAZUS earthquake scenarios have been created for both the Provo and Salt Lake segments, we'll focus on the Salt Lake segment. A 2008 FEMA study ranked Utah as 6th in the nation for relative earthquake risk. Salt Lake City was ranked 11th out of 43 metro areas. FEMA's Salt Lake HAZUS report was created in 2012 for a magnitude 7.0 earthquake. This ShakeMap scenario, as it is called, is the basis for the earthquake scenario analysis calculating hazards and losses.

In 2015, the Utah Chapter of the Earthquake Engineering Research Institute developed a "Scenario for a Magnitude 7.0 Earthquake on the Wasatch Fault—Salt Lake City Segment Hazards and Loss Estimates." This scenario incorporated the Salt Lake HAZUS data into its analysis.

Magnitude estimations of past earthquakes on the Salt Lake segment have projected normal magnitude large earthquakes to be 7.1, plus or minus 0.2. So, a 7.0 earthquake scenario is not a worst-case event.

The 2013 Real Gross Domestic Product (Real GDP) for Utah was valued at $131 billion. The urban corridor from Ogden to Salt Lake City to Provo accounted for 85 percent of Utah's Real GDP, and the Salt Lake City metro area was 54 percent of that.

A large earthquake is probably the single greatest threat to Utah's people and economy. As mentioned, the earthquake scenario is for a magnitude 7.0 rupture on the Salt Lake segment. The scenario is only for the main shock event and does not factor in aftershocks.

Using aftershock models, in the 30 days following the main shock, the area could reasonably expect three aftershocks of magnitude 6.0 or larger, thirteen aftershocks greater than 5.0 magnitude, and seventy-seven quakes at 4.0 or higher. The additional structural damage, injuries, and economic impact from the aftershocks are not calculated in the scenario. Additionally, these aftershocks will affect rescue and recovery efforts and further cause panic.

With a magnitude 7.0 earthquake on the Salt Lake segment, the entire valley and surrounding vicinities will experience strong to severe shaking, which corresponds to intensity levels ranging from VI to IX on the Mercalli Scale.

The Big One will certainly cause surface fault ruptures, liquefaction, landslides, and ground subsidence. Wet soil conditions would increase the number of landslides as well as the effects of liquefaction.

The loss estimations for the event are considered severe and include the following.

A short-term economic loss of over $33 billion, which includes $24.9 billion in losses in structural, non-structural, content, and inventory in direct building-related losses. Income-related losses would exceed $6.9 billion. Lifeline-related losses—which include damage to electric systems, water, gas and oil pipelines, as well as major transportation corridors like highways, bridges, airports, and railroads—would top $1.4 billion.

The event would displace 84,000 households, and 53,000 individuals would need shelter.

Like other scenarios, the time of day would impact the number of injuries and deaths. Fatalities are estimated to range from 2,000 to 2,500. The injured and those needing hospital care could range from 7,400 to 9,300. Unfortunately, the number of available hospital beds will likely be reduced from 4,790 to 3,200.

One challenge would be the need to evaluate the safety of over 300,000 structures in the following thirty days.

Unreinforced masonry (URM) buildings will receive the brunt of damage, with 61 percent (90,200 buildings) of those being moderately damaged to totally destroyed in the main shock. Many more will likely be further damaged or destroyed with strong aftershocks.

Another challenge would be in removing over 820,000 truckloads of debris, at 25 tons per truck. In total, 21 million tons of debris are likely.

Table 13: Some loss estimates for a magnitude 7.0 earthquake in Salt Lake City.

Loss	Estimate
Life threatening injuries	7,400–9,300
Fatalities	2,000–2,500
Displaced households	84,400
Displaced individuals	Over 263,300
Individuals needing temporary shelter	52,700
Building-related loss	$24.9 billion
Income loss	$6.9 billion
Lifeline/essential utility loss	$1.4 billion
Total short-term economic loss	$33.2 billion
Hospitals, at least moderately damaged	15 out of 32
Available hospital beds after earthquake	3,200
Bridges, moderately damaged or worse	595 out of 1,805
Tons of debris generated	21,000,000
Truckloads to remove (25 tons per truck)	821,600

Essential utility lifelines—like water, electricity, sewer, and gas—could be disrupted for days to months, with the areas hardest hit experiencing even longer outages. Being aware of this potential should really open one's eyes to preparedness needs.

Table 14: Electricity and water outage estimates for a Salt Lake City earthquake.

Households Without...	Day 1	Day 3	Day 7	Day 30	Day 90
Potable water	483,600	466,100	442,800	362,900	332,800
Electricity	444,600	251,200	105,900	27,300	800

With most electrical distribution systems being above ground, the power grid should be quickly restored.

However, of note is the number of households that are expected to not have potable water—even after three months. Immediately after the main shock, nearly a half-million households will be without water. Even after three months, the number of households without potable water is likely to still exceed 300,000. Even if your home survives with minimal impact, what are your plans if you don't have water for more than three months? In addition, while running water may be restored, it is likely to remain contaminated for many months due to cracks and leaks in the distribution system.

The impact on infrastructure will make life difficult. Bridges, highways, and local roads will be affected to varying degrees. The Salt Lake City International Airport could face issues with liquefaction as well as structural damage from the shaking.

Electrical and communication systems—including lines, distribution stations, and towers—as well as the natural gas lines, sewer pipes and treatment systems, and the water supply system will all be affected. It will be months before any resemblance to "normal" is restored, although parts of the area may take years to fully recover.

Disaster Response

Our country's emergency response system is primarily designed with the consideration that only one region is struck by a major natural disaster at a time, leaving other regions available to respond. For decades, this approach to natural disasters has worked moderately well. After all, what is the likelihood that more than one area or region would suffer major disasters at the same time or even in rapid succession?

The 2017 hurricane season revealed the weakness of this planning, when multiple hurricanes threatened and struck. While the damage could've been worse had the storms tracked differently into the mainland, it was still the costliest season on record.

Hurricane Harvey struck near the Houston area in late August, with record rainfall flooding the area.

In early September, Hurricane Irma struck several locations in the Caribbean, including Cuba, and then moved on to hit Florida.

Less than a month after Harvey, Hurricane Maria become the worst natural disaster to affect Puerto Rico and Dominica.

While not a part of the United States, Costa Rica was struck by Hurricane Nate in early October and became that nation's most costly natural disaster.

Hurricanes were not the only natural disasters around that same time in neighboring regions. On September 7, 2017, a magnitude 8.2 earthquake, with a Mercalli Intensity of IX, struck off the coast of southern Mexico. Less than two weeks later, on September 19, a magnitude 7.1 struck near the Mexico City area.

In just over a month's time, four major hurricanes and two earthquakes struck in and around a geographical area that is smaller than the size of the United States. This doesn't even include several smaller hurricanes that affected Central America and the Caribbean. And, it doesn't account for the likelihood of smaller disasters, like local floods, wildfires, and storms that can also affect an area.

What would happen if multiple major natural disasters strike more than one region of the United States?

While local and state emergency response time within the disaster zone is severely limited, it can take three or more days for emergency relief efforts from outside the affected area to get in and render assistance. The limitations of disaster relief in the event of a major natural disaster is a big reason 72-hour kits are not enough and is why you'll be seeing more of push for 96-hour (or longer) kits.

With each successive disaster, response time from outside of the affected area will increase. Available resources will diminish because the country's plan is based on other areas being available to provide aid.

One region cannot provide much assistance to another if it is also experiencing a major natural disaster. And, with much of the manufacturing, warehouse, and retail companies running just-in-time operations, there is little extra to spare when interstate transportation is affected.

Without going into any hypothetical sequence of events, just understand that if no other major disasters have happened, outside help will likely arrive within three to four days. However, if the disaster in your area happens after another disaster, the response time will increase, and the available resources will be much less.

Certainly a 72-hour kit will help you initially. But, that's only a drop of preparedness when you consider the possibility of recovery taking months or years.

An issue related to the lack of preparedness, aside from maybe a small kit, is the lack of preparedness of others. In the first few days following a disaster, most people are willing to help. Most of those who are prepared for an emergency are rarely actually prepared for anything lasting more than two or three days. Very few are prepared for anything that extends past three days.

After the stress of a few days of post-disaster recovery, those who aren't prepared will really start to panic when they realize help hasn't come or isn't as helpful as they expected. The norms and expectations of civil society start breaking down after about three days, and, without adequate law enforcement and government prevention, things can go from bad to worse.

The last thing you need is to expose yourself and your family to those who are not prepared, and who are looking for those who are. The idea of "fair" is gone. Even though they had their chance before the disaster to choose to become prepared, they chose not to. Maybe they spent their money on TVs, game systems, ATVs, or other fun things instead of getting a little better prepared first. Now, in the aftermath of the disaster, they will see your preparedness as being unfair and say that you should share. The problem is, too often their idea of sharing means taking everything from you and your family.

Many believe you should be able to defend your supplies. While I am not discounting that possibility, a better strategy would be to avoid possible confrontations by either being out of the situation— where you've evacuated to a bug out location—or keeping on the low-down by not apprising others of your preparedness. The best option in the latter case is to limit exposure to others. Even if you have self-defense options, you will not be able to hold out against an undoubtably larger force that may come after your supplies if it's discovered you have what they don't.

In short, you need to be able to respond to a disaster, and you are responsible for the preparedness of your family. If you rely on the government or another group to help, it's almost guaranteed you and your family will end up in a shelter, waiting in lines for a small amount of food and water, with only the clothes on your back and wishing you had done something to be better prepared.

Part 3 – How to Prepare: Earthquake Preparedness

Chapter 10
How to Prepare

The National Center for Disaster Preparedness at Columbia University published a 2015 study revealing that two-thirds of Americans are not prepared for an emergency. The center's director, Irwin Redlener, thinks the actual numbers are far lower. At presentations to groups of emergency preparedness specialists, he'll ask how many have personal or family emergency plans. Of the few who raise their hands, most of those have "half-baked" plans (Hampson, 2018).

While I haven't done any official polling, my own experience and observation is that most Americans see the importance in preparing for emergencies, but the majority have virtually no preparations. Of the few who claim to be prepared, most are underprepared. I believe those who are truly prepared for a disaster or emergency are less than ten percent of the population. There are various reasons—excuses—to not be prepared, but those are a topic to be discussed in another book.

For those who want to be prepared, all the possible disasters and scenarios to prepare for can feel overwhelming, so our tendency is to not do anything.

In my case, with small children and feeling overwhelmed trying to be a good husband and father, while also taking university classes (first for a bachelor's degree and then a master's) and working full time, it was easy to just put off preparations.

But I finally decided I needed to do something. Now, five years later, we're much better prepared for emergencies. And, our children are learning. We're not obsessed with "prepping," although preparation is a common topic of conversation and consideration. We don't want to be caught unaware and unprepared when a disaster strikes.

I've learned that preparation is a mind-set—not an obsession, but a regular evaluation of your situation and what might be needed in the event of an emergency. Preparing is not a "once-and-you're-done" action. There is no such thing as a preparation pill or kit that will solve all your preparedness needs. But it also doesn't need to consume your life. Becoming better prepared is making regular efforts, evaluations, and changes towards preparedness. Continual little efforts make a big change over time.

For us, it was not possible to become immediately prepared in getting all the equipment, supplies, food, and water we might need. But, with little purchases and actions over a few years, we are now better prepared for emergencies in our home, vehicles, and at work. And as kids get older and our situation changes over time, it's important to re-evaluate our preparedness regularly.

After reading the first two parts of this book, you should be aware that earthquakes involve a lot more than just the ground shaking and the potential for buildings and stuff to fall. Because earthquakes contribute to a wide variety of other potential hazards and disasters, the good news is a lot of your earthquake preparations easily cover other emergency situations as well.

I know the challenges of trying to become prepared amid the struggles and demands of life. Full-time work, classes—along with homework—at the university, four kids and their school and activities, and being active in our church keep us wondering what time we have left to do anything.

To start your own preparations, lists are helpful. I've included several, but they can also be overwhelming if we think we need to get everything right away. So, while I have full lists, I've also made modifications and evaluated what incremental steps might be taken. The last part of the book offers suggestions for how to get better prepared over time.

I have also pared down some preparedness efforts and lists into more "bite-sized" pieces. These efforts are pieced into things you could do within the next week, four weeks, three months, and over the next year.

Using these "what to do now" lists as guidelines, you can be on your way to becoming better prepared without trying to do everything at once.

Keep in mind that the preparedness information presented here is somewhat simplified and not intended to be comprehensive. Much of what will be shared are preparations I have made or preparations I am in the process of doing with my own family. The information is intended to help you begin or improve your own foundation of preparedness.

One more thing to remember about being prepared: In the event of a disaster, emergency, or other scenario, what you do in the first few minutes can substantially affect the outcome—even life or death—for you and your loved ones. Being prepared gives you options.

Before we discuss becoming better prepared, I think it's useful to touch on general emergency scenarios. These scenarios are shelter-in-place and different types of evacuation.

Shelter-in-place

When I'm faced with an emergency, I hope it's a shelter-in-place situation and that the place is my home. In a shelter-in-place, you stay put until conditions are safe to leave.

If a shelter-in-place restriction is in place, it is often because of a hazardous situation, such as an active shooter in the area, that will not necessarily worsen if you remain in your home.

This restriction can also happen in places other than your home. In an active shooter scenario, law enforcement may instruct all those in the affected area to remain in a lockdown, which is effectively sheltering-in-place. A lockdown is generally a temporary—hours at most—condition.

However, what if there were a hazardous materials condition that warranted a restriction to remain indoors at your place of employment or school for a day or longer? What preparations do you have to shelter-in-place?

While I don't expect a shelter-in-place restriction of any considerable length of time when I am at work, I do have some emergency items on hand. I have a get-home kit I keep in my backpack, and I have additional emergency food and water bottles in a drawer.

Long-term preparations are generally made under the assumption that you and your family will remain at a single place, usually your home or another location.

Evacuation

Some might consider an evacuation a "bug-out" situation. Personally, I consider a bug-out as leaving without an intent to return, at least not for a while. For me, bugging out usually assumes a breakdown in society, where you want to leave before things get bad, or before bad becomes worse. I generally consider a bug-out as completely voluntary (meaning the government is not going to tell you to do so).

While an earthquake or other serious emergency could potentially lead to a breakdown in society, the evacuation we will discuss is assuming you will be able to return to your home when it is safe. An evacuation is usually advised or mandated by the local government, emergency management, or law enforcement.

If an evacuation is expected, it is much better for you and your family to evacuate when, and to where, you choose. Being forced to evacuate quickly limits what supplies you can take. Being required to evacuate to a specified location also limits what resources you can bring and what you can do; it subjects you and your family to the requirements of the evacuation facility.

You should also be aware that most emergency or evacuation shelters/centers/facilities do not allow pets. This is for the health and safety of those in the shelter as well as for the animal. Pets brought to the center are usually taken to a designated animal shelter.

In the event of an evacuation, it's much better to be prepared to leave so that you can go where you can be comfortable, especially if you have pets you want to keep with you and not at an animal shelter.

While evacuations are not my first choice of action, if an evacuation is recommended or ordered, it's best to leave as quickly as possible. Delays in leaving will make it more difficult to leave, as roads will get more crowded. Few communities have good evacuation plans, and, in most places, evacuations can become messy, chaotic, and poorly managed and coordinated. The last thing I want is to be stuck on a road for hours (or days) trying to evacuate to safety. Leaving quickly in the event of an evacuation is where advance preparation is vital.

There are two general categories of evacuation: voluntary and mandatory. These are exactly as the names imply. Under a voluntary evacuation, residents are advised to evacuate, but there is no legal requirement to do so. You need to evaluate your own condition, preparedness, and other factors to determine if evacuating is the better option.

A mandatory evacuation means you are required to evacuate. Whether or not you choose to do so is still your choice. While law enforcement could become involved, the reality is, lives are at risk by staying and there probably won't be any help if the situation worsens.

Your safety and the safety of those in your care should be your primary goal. This is ultimately the reason for being prepared: to get safely through an unexpected situation.

In recent years, officials have become more cautious about issuing mandatory evacuations. Mandatory evacuations are only given for locations that are immediately threatened by an emergency or disaster situation. The logistics and time to evacuate a large population can endanger more people than allowing those not in the area of immediate threat to shelter-in-place. Issuing a recommended, or advised, evacuation notice to the surrounding areas that may be threatened provides a warning but leaves the choice up to those in the area.

Your preparation planning should identify evacuation options, including primary and alternative routes leaving the area, and where you will be evacuating to. Ideally, you'll have another place you can go, such as to a relative's or friend's home a few hours from the danger zone.

Mandatory and voluntary evacuations can further be categorized as either a rapid (emergency) or noticed evacuation.

Rapid

Under a rapid evacuation, you are basically told to leave immediately. Maybe winds shifted and a wildfire is suddenly consuming your neighbor's house and threatening yours. Maybe a dam broke and the flood is on its way. Rapid evacuations are usually mandatory, as there is substantial threat of injury or death.

I read a very direct warning to evacuate that occurred when Hurricane Harvey was threatening one area in Texas. KSBW-8 reported emergency management officials in Tyler County, in east Texas, warning of "imminent and deadly flooding" and "residents near the area must evacuate immediately" (Ramirez F. , 2017). Tyler County Judge Jacques Blanchette reportedly wrote on a Facebook post:

> "Anyone who chooses to not heed this directive cannot expect to be rescued and should write their social security numbers in permanent marker on their arm so their bodies can be identified. The loss of life and property is certain. GET OUT OR DIE!"

There have also been some emergency situations where residents were not ordered to leave, but they just had to understand and accept they were on their own and emergency assistance would not be immediately available.

Rapid evacuations can also be self-initiated, meaning you decide to evacuate without any official mandate or recommendation. Maybe you believe a situation is going to break down and you want to leave before things get worse.

Noticed

What I called a "noticed" evacuation is when you are given notice to evacuate. Often, these are voluntary evacuations. Depending on the risk, the evacuation may be mandatory. Noticed evacuations may have a short time, as in you have two hours to leave before the wildfire reaches your home. Or, they can be over a longer time frame, as in the case of a hurricane threatening to come on shore in the next two days.

In the case of a hurricane, the storm would be monitored for several days and residents in the path are usually given an evacuation notice. These evacuations often begin as voluntary, but as the threat and risks increase, the evacuation may become mandatory, particularly for those in the direct path of danger.

Your best line of defense is to be ready to take advantage of a noticed evacuation, so you can take as much as you can with you.

Unfortunately, an earthquake usually doesn't give much notice. It normally just shows up uninvited and unexpected. As a result, if you need to evacuate—due to your home not being safe or an earthquake-induced hazard threatening your safety—you will probably have little advance notice. Most likely it'll be a grab-and-go situation. Just hope you can take your vehicle so you can take more than just the basic kit with you.

Evacuation and earthquakes

Unlike many disasters—such as hurricanes, wildfires, or a lava flow—earthquakes rarely provide any kind of warning, which is probably why so many people seem to be afraid of earthquakes.

Here's the reality: Most people survive an earthquake. And, unless you live or work in an older building (pre-1980) or happen to be near the earthquake's epicenter, it's not likely the building will collapse on you. The biggest immediate hazard during an earthquake is an unsecured object falling on you, which is why you need to take cover.

If you're fortunate to live in an area that uses an early warning system and/or app (like those mentioned at the end of chapter 5), you might get as much as 30 or 45 seconds before the real shaking starts. That's enough time to make sure you and your loved ones are in a safe place and maybe to take precautions such as turning off the stove. You may even have time to exit an older building to get to a safe location. But it's unlikely enough time to evacuate. Unless you are completely ready to grab your pack and leave in seconds, you may still want to find a safe place to take cover when the shaking starts.

The real evacuation, if needed, is after the tremor stops. If there is any doubt as to the safety of the building you are in, you need to leave as quickly, and safely, as possible. It may also be that the earthquake has caused other hazards that threaten your location.

Your best plan for an evacuation after an earthquake is a rapid one.

A note about government camps and shelters

Some people figure they will just go to a FEMA camp or emergency shelter in the event of an emergency. Most who end up at these shelters do so because they don't have food. For some, it's lack of water or being unprepared for the emergency, but for most hunger drives them to the shelter.

If possible, you should not be so unprepared that you (or your family) needs to go to one of these shelters. This is not because they're necessarily a bad place. Many of the volunteers who help do a fantastic job.

The problem is the government is not well prepared to handle a large number of people in an emergency. That has been evident in the aftermath of previous large disasters. One of the worst examples was the Louisiana Superdome after Hurricane Katrina. In the case of the Superdome, it became a trap that was poorly prepared to handle the scope of the disaster and large number of people, including the ill and injured.

The reality is these camps and shelters need to be highly controlled based on the number of people. Even with control, there will still be crime within the confines of the camp. Additionally, being near hundreds of others increases the chances of the spread of disease.

And, as was mentioned earlier, if you happen to have pets, they will not be allowed in the camp or shelter.

You and your family will be much better off if you are prepared for the emergency, disaster, or catastrophe by having food, water, shelter, supplies, and a plan.

If you need to evacuate, you need to do so as quickly as you can and, ideally, to a place of your choosing.

Chapter 11
Home Preparedness

Many of us spend about half of our life in our homes, although much of that time is spent sleeping. Our homes are places of refuge and safety. They are where we gather with our families and friends. We take them for granted, and while we may experience emergency preparedness drills at work and school, most people do little at home in preparing for an emergency.

As part of preparing your home for an earthquake, we'll cover the following:

- utilities and securing them;
- actual preparations you should be making for food, water, fuel, shelter, and kits;
- securing items around the home;
- special considerations, such as planning for pets and children;
- other preparations to consider, such as documentation; and
- storage for emergency equipment.

Utilities

If you suspect a leak or problem with one of the utilities (such as gas, water, or electricity) in your home, the safest course of action is to leave and contact the appropriate entity, such as the utility company, a trained professional, or call 911 if the emergency threatens life or property. However, shutting off a utility coming into your home may help prevent further damage if you have time and the know-how to safely do so.

There are two things you need to know about home utilities when it comes to emergencies. First, you need to know where the "mains" are. That is, you need to know where each utility is turned off and on.

The second is related to the first: you need to know how to shut off the utility. It's one thing to know where the gas meter is, and to think that is where you shut off the gas. But, it's another thing to know where and how to shut off the gas. And, in the case of many gas and water meters, you need to have the right tool to do so.

A word of precaution. If you have any doubts about how to shut off a utility, please contact a qualified professional. While many utilities have become standardized, there may be subtle differences. The last thing you want to be doing in an emergency is trying to figure out how to shut something off. In fact, if you can't shut off a utility quickly in an emergency, it is best for you to leave quickly. It's a good idea to practice shutting off a utility in a non-emergency situation and to make sure other adults also know how.

What I am sharing by no means constitutes professional advice. Many utility shut-offs are similar. The three most common utilities—at least in the area I live in—are natural gas, electricity, and water.

If you live in a house, it's useful to know where those utilities are located. Many utilities run underground before they come to your home. If you ever need to dig in your yard, you are required to have the utilities marked prior to digging. Most states offer a free utility marking service by calling 811. In some places, the service is known as Blue Stakes.

In any case, if you get the utilities marked, take a picture of the markings. This is not for future projects, as you are required to get utilities marked before each digging project, and the marking is only good for two weeks. These photos are for emergency reference.

Natural gas

If there is any utility I am most cautious about, it is gas.

Natural gas has no smell. However, the chemical mercaptan is added to create an odor that most people describe as rotten eggs, so a leak can be detected.

While natural gas is a safe and clean fuel, it is highly combustible, and a leak can cause a risk of fire or explosion.

Besides the smell of rotten eggs possibly indicating a gas leak, other potential signs of a leak are good to be aware of:

- The sound of whistling, roaring, or hissing coming from a natural gas appliance.
- Damaged gas lines going to a natural gas appliance.
- Grass or shrubs changing color, looking more brown or rusty, could also indicate gas leaking out of the pipe.
- Unusual bubbling or soil movement, particularly if it's near the natural gas line going to your house (remember the

recommendation to photograph your utility lines; a picture could help you know if the bubbling is near your gas line).

- An exposed gas pipeline after a fire, earthquake, or other disaster.

If you smell a gas leak (rotten eggs), or suspect a leak, follow these recommendations:

- Don't do anything that might cause a spark, such as unplugging an electrical device, turning on/off a light switch, or even using a phone.

Figure 15: An example of a gas shut-off right in front of the meter.

- Immediately extinguish anything that is burning—such as candles and cigarettes—and don't light a match, stove, or cigarette lighter.

- If you can quickly and safely do so, let fresh air inside by opening windows and doors.

- Turn off the main gas supply at the meter, and don't turn it back on until safe to do so.

- Get a safe distance away from your home and then make calls to 911 and your gas provider.

You should call the gas provider about the leak. Most providers recommend calling 911, as a gas leak does constitute an emergency situation that could potentially cause injury or death.

Figure 16: An electric meter.

If you turn off the gas supply to your home, it is strongly advised that you call the gas company to turn it back on, especially if you suspected a leak.

Electric

Electricity is certainly dangerous, but I have a lot more experience with electricity than gas. And electricity (usually) isn't likely to blow up my home, although a spark from an electric source could start a fire or ignite an explosion, particularly if gas has accumulated.

Unless I suspect damaged electrical cables or have reason to suspect possible arcing and sparking (which could cause a fire), the electricity is the last utility I worry about turning off.

If an electronic device or electric appliance has fallen over or been damaged, it's best to unplug it and have it checked for safe operation before plugging it back in.

If electrical damage inside the home is not suspected, a big reason to turn off the electric main would be to prevent a high-voltage surge from going through the home and damaging appliances and electrical devices.

If the power goes out, you may consider unplugging sensitive electronics, particularly if they are not plugged in to a surge protector. A voltage surge is possible when power is restored. Usually the surge isn't too bad, but it doesn't take much to fry a sensitive system.

Your best option for your electronics, so you don't have to worry what should be unplugged, is to invest in a high-quality surge protector. Without going into a chapter about what constitutes a good surge protector, the biggest thing is, generally, the higher the joules rating on the protector, the better.

A joule is a measurement, or unit, of energy. Basically, more joules mean your surge protector should be able to protect your equipment from higher blasts of electricity.

Figure 17: An electric main.

To turn off the electric main, you first need to know where to do so. Most people assume the circuit breakers in the house are where the electricity gets turned off. If you're only wanting to turn off certain parts of the house, then that is true. The place to turn off electricity entirely is, in many homes, at an electric main outside, usually near the electric meter. The electric main frequently looks like a big circuit breaker switch.

Most newer homes (particularly those built in the 1970s and later) will use circuit breakers with similar-looking mains, but there are still plenty of older homes that have older-style breakers, circuits, and even fuses.

If you don't know where your electric main is located, your best option is to get an electrical professional to show you where yours is located.

Water

While water shouldn't be the cause of an explosion or fire, it can cause a lot of damage to a home.

Because water lines are susceptible to freezing, in most homes there is a water main shut-off inside the building, not exposed outside, as the electric and gas mains usually are.

While this main will shut off water throughout the house, it does not prevent water from coming into the house. If there is a break in the main line from the water meter to the house, there is still a chance of water getting into the home. To help prevent this, the real water main would need to be shut off.

The actual main is usually outside, often in the hole where the water meter is located. Most of these mains are a foot or more below ground level and not very easy to shut off. If you want to mitigate the possibility of water from the water main coming to your house, this is where it needs to be shut off. Just be aware that if there's snow piled on the water main access (usually a round metal plate in the ground), you're probably not going to be able to turn it off very easily.

Figure 18: An example of a water main shut-off inside a home.

Other utilities

Some houses have other sources of heat, such as oil or propane gas. Because of the varying nature of these other utilities, I will mention only a few of them briefly.

For houses with external propane tanks, usually found in rural areas, the shut-off is at the main tank, usually next to the gas level gauge.

I have no experience with homes that use heating oil, so I strongly encourage you to talk to your supplier or qualified professional about how to secure the system in the case of an emergency.

Similarly, it is best for you to consult qualified professionals concerning the various utilities in your home and how to secure each one of them in the event of an emergency.

Solar panels

Many people who have solar panels hope to have at least a measure of energy independence. Most assume they will have power when the electrical grid is out. Unfortunately, if the solar panel system doesn't have a battery storage system, it probably won't be a reliable source of power in an electrical grid outage, if it even provides power.

While solar panels are awesome, they aren't a guarantee you'll have electricity in a grid failure after an earthquake or other natural disaster. Solar panels, along with their systems, can be damaged in an earthquake or other natural disaster.

If you have solar panels, I strongly advise you talk to your solar panel professional about what you should check for to ensure safe operation after an earthquake or other disaster. Some of the things you should be looking for include broken panels, loose connections, damaged wires, and fallen or damaged batteries.

If you are considering purchasing solar panels, be sure to ask about what needs to be done and checked in the event of an emergency.

Preparations

There are all kinds of preparations that can be made. Many emergency preparation classes focus on the very short term—usually three days and maybe up to two weeks. More serious preppers will discuss long-term preparations, such as months or even a year or more. For our discussion, we will look more at a short-to-intermediate time frame: longer than 72 hours but not the serious long-term preparations.

This focus should help you prepare for a short-term situation, and it lays the foundation of any long-term plans you may want to start.

Food

Let's face it: a 72-hour emergency kit does not provide enough food. Yes, you can eat for those three days. But, what about beyond that?

We'll later dive more into emergency kits, but let's assume you will be in your home for the duration of the emergency, including the immediate aftermath.

While you need emergency food in your kit and extended kit, in your home you should plan to have a minimum of two weeks' worth of food for each person.

Two weeks is the absolute minimum. Surprisingly, most people have much less than that on hand, many with less than a week's worth of food.

My recommendation is to shoot for a one-month minimum, and then make a goal to get a 90-day supply of food.

As side note, in some countries there are laws against food hoarding, meaning it is illegal have more food than is needed for a specified time period. Even in the United States of America, there is the potential for the government to restrict how much food and other supplies you can have on hand, specifically in the event of a long-term emergency (such as a war) or martial law.

If you have a concern about the legality, make some phone calls to inquire about any food storage laws in the area.

As for the United States, I'm not aware of any laws that would prohibit you from storing food and other supplies. But it is your responsibility to find out for yourself.

Because most disasters are not nationwide, and usually do not affect more than a small region, it is safe to plan on you being able to keep your food and supplies.

However, I also advise you not to talk to others about how much food or other supplies you may have. The best course of action is to downplay your preparations, limiting your discussion to the short-term preparations.

As for your emergency food, the best option is for food requiring minimum preparation. This is because the ability to cook may be limited due to fuel and energy restrictions. For the first few days, you want to minimize your food preparation time because stress will be building, and your physical, mental, and emotional energy will be at their limits. Easy food preparation just makes life a little easier. During those first few days, you'll get a better idea of the situation and can better decide how food preparation will need to occur after the initial aftermath.

Cooking

While there is food that doesn't require cooking or other preparation, most long-term food storage requires some kind of preparation, even if it's just adding water.

If your gas or electric stove isn't working (no electricity), how will you boil the water for your oatmeal or meal that requires you to "just add hot water"?

There are several options—too many to discuss—but they can be summarized into three broad categories: home, camping, and backpacking.

At home, you have the option of propane or charcoal barbecue grills. Some homes have fireplaces, wood stoves, or an outdoor fire pit. These options are generally not portable, but they should not be neglected your preparations for at home. If you have a charcoal stove, you can easily store bags of charcoal—just make sure the charcoal stays dry.

If you have an alternate cooking source at home, such as a wood stove, make sure you have plenty of fuel for it.

Large camping stoves often attach to a twenty-pound propane tank. There are smaller camp stoves, with smaller fuel tanks. The main feature of these stoves is they can be easily packed into a vehicle, but they are too bulky to take with you if you're on foot. These camping stoves are great options for home preparedness and for easy transport if you need something to take in a vehicle during an evacuation.

The backpacking category consists of the smaller, lightweight stoves than can be easily packed into a backpack.

A strong caution: unless a stove is rated for indoor use—most are not—do not use it inside a building or in an enclosed environment. People have died, usually from fire or carbon monoxide poisoning, by misusing camp stoves.

Of course, making a campfire may be possible. However, in the middle of an urban environment, a campfire may not be an easy option.

As you plan your cooking options, keep in mind some of the previously discussed earthquake scenarios. It may be a month or more before your electricity or gas is restored.

Besides fuel-based stoves and ovens, there are alternative fuel stoves/ovens. One popular variety are solar ovens.

While my intent is not to analyze the pros and cons of a bunch of different stoves and ovens, my recommendation is for you to not rely on a single source for cooking. And, I would advise at least three different cooking options.

For us, we have a large two-burner propane camp stove, a multi-fuel stove/oven (it's like a portable fire pit that can use wood and charcoal and has propane tank attachments), and a smaller two-burner propane camp stove. Additionally, I have a variety of options for starting a campfire, should the need arise.

Regarding the use of a campfire, I've read articles about how cooking over a fire will likely be common after a major emergency.

However, unless you are in a rural environment, if everyone is trying to make a fire to cook with, how long will the fuel supply last? And, when readily available wood is gone, what burns next? If you expect to use your wood stove or fire pit, make sure you have plenty of firewood.

Another potential problem with using a cooking fire is it may draw unwanted attention. The smell of smoke, not to mention the smoke itself, can bring unwelcome guests. Not that we should uncharitable towards others, but there are unsavory sorts who might come around. A camp stove is less likely to draw the same attention.

Most important, don't rely on a single source for your cooking.

Fuel

If you have a generator, you will need fuel. My ideal generator (which I have yet to purchase) is a dual fuel generator—one that can run on gasoline or propane. For now, we have a gasoline-powered generator. The fuel source for our camp stoves is propane. Between the two items, we need to store gasoline and propane.

Before you start storing any fuel, you need to know any legal fuel storage limitations your city and/or country have. For example, the city I live in has the following regulations:

- Up to five gallons of gasoline (flammable liquids) may be stored in an attached garage. Up to ten gallons may be stored outside in an unattached building.
- Empty fuel containers are considered fuel when calculating total fuel capacity. That means legally I cannot have a full five-gallon gas container and an empty five-gallon container in my attached garage.
- At least one 2A2BC-rated fire extinguisher is to be within fifty feet of the containers, but not closer than ten feet.
- Diesel, kerosene, lamp oil, and other combustible liquids are limited to a maximum of twenty-five gallons in an attached garage, and up to sixty gallons in an outside building.
- Propane is limited to a total capacity of twenty-five gallons, which is five twenty-pound cylinders.
- Propane is to be stored separate from flammable and combustible liquids.
- It's best to store fuels in an unattached garage, building, or shed.

The advantage of propane is it stores well, meaning that if there are no leaks, it doesn't go bad. Essentially, its only limitation is the container it's stored in.

Gasoline, on the other hand, doesn't store well. Unless you are going to use it quickly, it should have a stabilizer added to it. A good stabilizer should keep the gasoline usable for up to one year. Without the stabilizer, the gasoline should be used within three months, as its octane will substantially decrease (making it less combustible). It can start leaving sludge-like deposits, which can clog small openings.

Water is the enemy of gasoline. Even as little as a single tablespoon of water can contaminate a gallon of gasoline, making it unusable. Of note is ethanol blend gasolines. The ethanol, which is a type of alcohol, has an affinity for water, meaning it likes water and wants to blend with it. Under ideal circumstances ethanol blend fuels (E10) may last 90 days. Most of the time conditions are less than ideal.

Gasoline blends without ethanol have a longer shelf life.

With these limitations of gasoline, you can better understand why propane is the better fuel for long-term storage.

Power

Electricity is what makes our modern civilization possible. The question is, what do we do when the power is out?

For a short-term situation, batteries can be an adequate solution for small devices, like flashlights, radios, or small gaming systems.

However, if you want to run more power-hungry electronics, like a laptop computer, TV, microwave, or power tool, then batteries won't cut it.

While I have yet to invest in a home solar system, we do have some portable solar panels and a couple of small battery banks. It's far from being able to power our home, but it could power some lights and keep electronics (like our phones) charged. And we could even watch a video on a TV or computer to help keep the kids entertained.

Water

Water is essential to survival. However, its importance is often minimized in emergency preparations. It is important that you don't ration water unless you are required to do so. Your body needs water more than food, and water should be a top concern in your preparedness.

After covering some of the earthquake scenarios earlier in the book, you should have an idea of how critical water is and how likely it may become limited or inaccessible in an emergency. You should have also noted how much longer it will take to restore potable water service to an earthquake-devastated area than it will to restore electrical power.

Hence, you should begin to understand that water for three days doesn't cut it. Even a week isn't enough.

The basic rule of thumb for emergency water storage is one gallon of water per person per day. This is just for drinking, for use in food preparation, and for basic sanitation. If you're conservative, you could even use a small amount for brushing your teeth.

My strong recommendation is to have, whenever possible, a minimum of two weeks' worth of emergency water storage. For my family of six, that equates to six gallons per day times fourteen days, or eighty-four gallons, on hand.

The goal should be at least four weeks of water per person—at least 28 gallons per person. Storing that much water is a challenge, especially if you live in limited space.

In addition to the actual water you store, you need water purification filters as well. The stored water will get you through the initial disaster and days or weeks immediately following the disaster. But you will still need to get water after that. You might be able to lug a container to a public water dispensary, but it's best to not count on that.

Just as at least two methods of cooking are recommended, you should have at least two types, ways, or means to filter and purify water to make it suitable for drinking. While you may have actual water storage of a month (or longer), it is vital you have options for long-term drinking water.

Filtration and purification

Remember some of the earthquake scenarios—where culinary water may not be restored for three months or more?

At six gallons a day, for ninety days, my family would need 540 gallons. That would be ten fifty-five-gallon drums, or 108 of the five-gallon containers. I'm not sure where I could even put that many containers.

This is my recommendation: store enough water to get you through a month, and then have several means to make water safe to drink after that. After using the thirty days of water storage, you can use the empty containers to gather and store water, especially if water is unreliable. Your various methods of filtering and purifying water can then be used on the water you've been collecting, as well as new water sources.

As part of our emergency equipment, I have purchased several water filters. Among the filters are water bottles with built-in filters, filter straws, backpacking pump-style filters, and a filter with a UV sanitizer.

The best time of year I've found to purchase water filters has been at Black Friday sales. I have also found great deals at large membership warehouse stores, but these stores do not carry the filters year-round, so it's kind of a hit and miss. Other options are outdoor retail stores (including online options) that have sales during the spring and summer months. I have also found the rare deal in clearance, usually at the beginning of the year.

For us, the biggest water-related post-disaster challenge will be to locate water than can be filtered for use. Near our current home, a small river is less than 500 feet away. Hopefully it will still be running after an earthquake. I suspect it will be, although I've read accounts of springs and streams drying up, or even increasing flow, for a time after a large earthquake.

Most commercial water filters will filter out contaminants from questionable water and make it safe to drink.

Water bottles with built-in filters and filter straws are great for personal use but lousy when it comes to purifying a larger quantity for use in cooking or to share with others. This is where pump-style water filters can be more useful.

Besides commercial filters, there are methods you can use to disinfect water to make it drinkable.

Emergency water disinfection

If you read material from the Red Cross, FEMA, or other disaster assistance organizations, they usually do not mention the use of backpacking-type water filters. From what I can gather, there are a few reasons for this. First, being non-profit and/or government organizations, they are not allowed to endorse a commercial product, so you won't see them recommending any particular filter.

Another factor is that backpacking filters cost money. These organizations want to promote easy, inexpensive methods to obtain clean drinking water.

The United States Environmental Protection Agency has a PDF document about emergency disinfection of drinking water located at https://www.epa.gov/sites/production/files/2017-09/documents/emergency_disinfection_of_drinking_water_sept2017.pdf.

Three methods of emergency water disinfection are generally recommended: boiling, chlorination, and distillation.

Boiling

Boiling water is the most common and probably one of the easiest and safest methods to disinfect water. The downside is it requires a heat source, and, once boiled, you need to wait for the water to cool down. If you're cooking food, make sure you have some water that can be boiled. While boiling water on a propane stove may not be able to happen simultaneously as cooking a meal, you can probably add an extra pot with water on a cooking fire. That way, you're using the same fire to cook your food and provide safer drinking water.

Boiling water will kill most disease-causing biological contaminants, such as viruses, protozoa, and pathogenic bacteria. However, because some of the water leaves as steam, any other contaminants in the water become more concentrated. A good pre-filter can strain out many of the larger particles.

Here are the recommendations for boiling water:

- If the water is cloudy, let it settle first.
- Filter the water through a coffee filter, clean cloth, or other type of homemade filter to remove the larger debris and contaminants from the water.
- Bring the water to a rolling boil for at least one minute—this is a *rolling boil*, not just little bubbles. If you're at high altitude, above 5,000 feet, boil the water for at least three minutes.
- Let the water naturally cool down and then store it in clean containers.

Boiled water will taste flat. A couple options to improve the taste is to add a pinch of salt for each quart of water. Taste can also be improved by aerating the water, by pouring it from one clean container to another several times.

Chlorination

Another method for disinfecting water is to use regular household bleach. If you can't boil the water, this is a good alternative.

This is important: Do not use color safe or scented bleach or bleaches that have added cleaners!

Use only regular, unscented chlorine bleach products. The active ingredient should be 6 or 8.25% of sodium hypochlorite. Some sources will recommend 5.25 to 6%. In any case, it should be no less than 5.25 and no more than 8.25%.

The bleach should be stored at room temperature and be less than a year old because it will degrade over time. Unopened bleach can last longer, but the bleach you should use for chlorination should be from an unopened or newly opened bottle because the potency decreases over time. Even unopened bleach will degrade over time.

Because bleach does lose its potency, boiling water is a better alternative. But, if you choose to include chlorination as an option, be sure to rotate your bleach regularly so none of it is more than a year old.

To treat your water with bleach, the United States Environmental Protection Agency, recommends the following steps, similar to the recommendations for boiling water: https://www.epa.gov/ground-water-and-drinking-water/emergency-disinfection-drinking-water.

First, let cloudy water settle. Filter the water through a coffee filter, clean cloth, paper towel, or other homemade filter to remove larger debris.

Using a clean dropper (you might have one in the medicine cabinet or emergency kit) and fresh bleach (less than one year old), use Table 15 as a guideline for how many drops of bleach should be added.

If the water is cloudy, colored, or very cold, double the amount of bleach.

Stir the bleach into the water and let it sit for thirty minutes. There should be a slight chlorine smell to the water. If there isn't, repeat the dosage and let it sit for another fifteen minutes before drinking. If, after a second treatment, it still doesn't have a bleach smell, discard the water and find another source.

If the chlorine taste is too strong, pour it from one clean container to another and let it sit for a few hours, which allows for some of the chlorine to evaporate and degrade.

Table 15: Amount of bleach per volume of water. Bleach may contain 6 or 8.25% sodium hypochlorite. From https://www.epa.gov/ground-water-and-drinking-water/emergency-disinfection-drinking-water.

Water Volume	Amount of 6% Bleach to Add	Amount of 8.25% Bleach to Add
1 quart/liter	2 drops	2 drops
1 gallon	8 drops	6 drops
2 gallons	16 drops (1/4 tsp)	12 drops (1/8 tsp)
4 gallons	1/3 teaspoon	1/4 teaspoon
8 gallons	2/3 teaspoon	1/2 teaspoon

Distillation

While chlorination and boiling are options for disinfecting water, distillation is the process to get clean water. This process removes biological and other contaminants from the water. It is also the only process that can purify and make saltwater drinkable.

To understand distillation, consider nature's water cycle. Water evaporates into the atmosphere, where it condenses, and then precipitates through rain or snow.

During the evaporation process, which is primarily caused by the sun heating the water (such as the oceans), liquid water turns into vapor. In this process, any contaminants are left behind while the pure water vapor rises into the air.

Eventually the water vapor cools and condenses into clouds, which move over land, and the water falls to the earth in some form of precipitation. Unless the precipitation—such as rain or snow—is falling through polluted air, the water is pure.

The distillation process is similar. In a closed system (meaning water vapor doesn't escape), water is heated up and water vapor forms. The water vapor then condenses on a surface, which is collected as pure water.

The Red Cross and FEMA have produced a pamphlet titled "Food and Water in an Emergency," which describes a simple emergency still. The following image is from page 12 of the pamphlet.

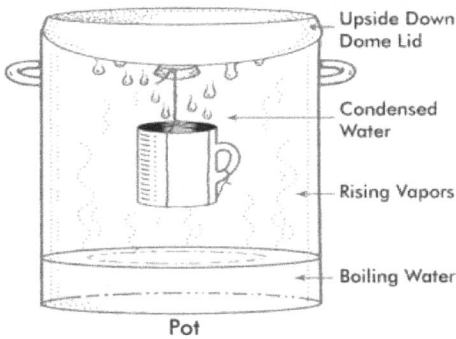

Figure 19: From FEMA and Red Cross pamphlet, "Food and Water in an Emergency."

For the emergency still, you need a heat source, a large pot with a lid, and a cup. Tie the cup to the handle of the lid so that the cup will hang upright with the lid upside down. Fill the pot about halfway with water but not so much that the cup will dangle into the water. Then boil the water for at least twenty minutes.

In this emergency still, water vapor rises and condenses on the lid, runs down to the handle, and drips into the cup.

Ideally, the lid and handle should be as clean as possible, as any contaminants on them could contaminate the condensing water. Using nitrile gloves when handling the lid and prepping the cup can help reduce the likelihood of contamination.

Commercial water distillers are available. If you get one for emergencies, it's better if it doesn't use electricity for the distillation process.

There are also do-it-yourself options for creating solar-powered water distillers.

Water storage

The goal for your water storage is to get you through the emergency, whether it lasts less than a day or for several months.

In the immediate aftermath of a natural disaster, such as an earthquake, the last thing you need to be doing is preparing water to drink. You want ready-to-drink water, at least a few days of it. Commercially bottled water works well, although it costs more than if you were to store water yourself.

After you've gotten through the first several days after the emergency, you will be in a better position to figure out where you can obtain water and what options would be best to make it drinkable. Therefore, it's best to have a few alternatives because one might be better than another in the actual emergency aftermath.

My preferred storage containers are the five-gallon water jugs, with a spout. These food-grade containers are easy to move and transport, if needed. Should I need to evacuate by vehicle, I plan to grab a few of these.

You can also buy huge water storage barrels, even some that stack. These are great, but you won't be able to move them once they're full. In some future year I may purchase a couple of these, although in our current home I'm not sure where I'd put them.

Be aware that an earthquake can knock over tall, or stacked, water storage. Just like the water heater, which we'll talk about later in the chapter, you need to secure water storage. If you can push the top of the empty container and easily cause it to tip over, then, when it's filled with water, the shaking of the earth could cause the weight of the water to rapidly shift inside the container and knock it over.

Since I do a lot of preparations "on the cheap," we also use a lot of juice bottles, and a few soda bottles, for water storage. These bottles and lids need to be cleaned out thoroughly, as sugar residue from juices and sodas give bacteria a great place to grow. Clean the containers using dishwashing soap and water and rinse them well.

Sanitize the bottles by adding a solution of one quart of water and one teaspoon of unscented bleach to the bottle. Swish the solution around the entire inside of the bottle. If you're sanitizing multiple bottles, you can then pour the water-bleach solution into the next bottle or into a pitcher to be used when then next container is ready. After sanitizing the bottle, rinse it thoroughly with clean water.

After getting them cleaned out well, these bottles make easy water storage. Personally, I prefer the juice bottles, as they tend to be a heavier-duty plastic. And most of the juice bottles are more rectangular in shape, which means they fit better on the shelves than round soda bottles.

As a child, I remember seeing some of our water storage in cleaned-out, one-gallon milk jugs. These are not ideal, as the plastic is flimsy and deteriorates easily. I've seen some jugs become brittle and break, and others that get punctured easily. But they are better than nothing, and they will last for a short period of time. Just make sure the bottles and lids are really well cleaned out and sanitized because any milk residue will also become a bacteria breeding ground. If you don't have anything else, at least start your water storage with these. Just plan to start replacing them as soon as you can.

Do not use cardboard-based containers. These are not designed for long-term storage.

And, it's better to not use glass containers, as they can break easily and are much heavier. But, if these are what you have to start with, they are better than nothing.

After you have clean and sterilized containers, you need to make sure you're not going to contaminate the water. Before filling any containers, wash your hands really well. Ideally, use sterile gloves when filling the containers. Any bacteria from your hands can contaminate your water storage.

Fill your bottles with regular tap water. If the water utility company already treats the water with chlorine, you don't need to add anything to the water to keep it clean. If you're using water from a well or other source that is not treated with chlorine, add two drops of unscented liquid bleach to each gallon of water. This is about one drop per two-liter bottle.

Use the original cap to close the container, being careful to not touch the inside of the lid.

Write the date on the container so you know when it was filled. Store the water in a cool, dark place.

The recommendation is to replace your water storage every six to twelve months. Although water does not have an expiration date if it's stored in a clean, sealed container, there are a couple of reasons to replace the water.

First, rotating your water helps keep it tasting fresher. But it will still start to taste stale after a while. If your water tastes stale, aerate it a bit by pouring between a couple of clean containers.

Second, water rotation will keep you aware of what your water storage situation is like. If water is going bad, possibly due to a bad seal or contamination, you will discover the problem before you need to use the water.

When you do rotate the water, try to use the old water where it can do some good, instead of just dumping it down the drain. For example, if you rotate your water during the summer you could empty the old water on your garden beds, trees, or grass. They need to be watered anyway. Then, instead of using fresh water for the plants, you can fill your water containers.

If you forget, or choose not, to rotate your water frequently, be aware that it probably won't taste very good. Aerating it can help improve the taste. A pinch of salt might help. If the container was properly cleaned and sanitized, the lid has a good seal, and the water is still clear, the water should be usable for a long time.

When you do open stored water, check it before you drink or use it for cooking. In my experience, there usually isn't any kind of smell, but if there is, don't drink it. However, it could still be usable. Even if the water does smell bad, or is questionable, you may still be able to filter or sanitize it so it's safe to drink.

As for where to store water, the best place is in a cool location, out of sunlight. There is concern about storing water containers directly on cement because the cement could leach chemicals through the plastic, particularly thinner plastic, into the container. The reality is, while cement can leach chemicals, it's unlikely to do so in a cool environment. The leaching is more likely if the cement heats up, like in a garage. Storing water on the floor of the garage, where temperatures fluctuate, could possibly have the leaching effect. However, in the dark, year-round cool of the basement, the leaching is less of an issue.

You can probably safely store you water containers on a cement floor, provided the location is out of the sunlight and the temperature is constantly cool. But there are other reasons to keep storage containers off the cement (or other) floor. Personally, I prefer to keep my water storage containers off the floor—on a pallet or blocks of wood. If something spills on the floor, it doesn't stick to the containers. Keeping the containers off the floor also allows for more air circulation under them.

You also do not want the water to freeze. Not that freezing is bad for the water. The problem is that water expands when it freezes, and if there is too much water in the container when that happens, the container could burst.

I keep a lot of our water storage in our garage. However, it's on shelves off the ground and against the wall of the house, which is warmer than the other three (exterior) walls of the garage. In the several years of having water stored there, it has never frozen. We used to have a dog kennel in the garage, with an exit to the dog run, and I kept a thermometer near the door. There were times when the dog's water froze, when the temperatures in that part of the garage dropped to single digits, but the water storage remained liquid. This doesn't mean the water won't ever freeze; it just hasn't yet.

A sample water storage plan could be as follows:

- Commercial bottled water for up to three days. This allows you some time to figure things out, get organized after the chaos of the disaster, and consider long-term water options.

- Your own bottled water, enough for up to thirty days. After the commercial water is gone, or mostly gone, you can move on to the other water storage. During this time, you need to really consider and implement long-term options. If the infrastructure was severely damaged, you may be months (or longer) without potable water coming through the pipes to your home.

- Long-term water filtration, disinfection, and sanitation solutions. What water sources are available? How will you disinfect/treat the water?

Hidden water around your home

Even without water storage, which you still need to have, your home will likely have a few places where you can get some water in an emergency. These sources are not enough for a long-term solution, but, depending on the number of people in your home, they could give you several days of water.

In an emergency, like a large earthquake, the ideal is to shut off your water main to prevent any contaminated water from infiltrating your home water system.

Then, you can access water from a few different "sources" in your home. Some are ready-to-drink and other sources need to be treated before using. Two possible ready-to-drink sources are from the water pipes and the water heater tank. I say "possible" because it's also possible contaminated water from the main could have contaminated your home's water system.

Other sources should be treated—filtered and disinfected—before use. These include toilet tanks, pools, and other water sources such as rainwater, streams, ponds, lakes, or springs.

Water pipes

To access the water remaining in your home's pipes, you basically get one chance.

In a multi-level home, open one faucet on the highest level. You may want to place a container (like a pot or bowl) under it to catch any wayward drips, but the primary purpose of opening this faucet is to let air into the system. Then go to the lowest faucet of the home, place a container under it, and open the faucet. Turn it off before the container gets too full.

In a single-level home, there may be a faucet that is a little higher or lower than others. Often the bathtub will be the lowest faucet, and kitchen sinks are higher than bathroom sinks. Sometimes the washing machine water hook-up is highest. But, if you can't identify the highest and lowest faucets, put containers under each and have someone help you turn the faucets on and off.

Water heater

In the event of an emergency, many houses have a built-in emergency water storage: the hot water heater tank. Remember, small tanks are usually thirty to forty gallons, while larger tanks are fifty or more. Here's how to access that water.

You will need to turn the heater off. Even if a power or gas outage has already shut it off, it's good to make sure the water heater is off. For electric water heaters, shut off the water heater's circuit breaker. On gas water heaters, turn the thermostat down and rotate the gas supply knob to the off position.

You should let the water in the tank cool down before you attempt to access it. You don't want to get scalded from hot water. Because water heaters are generally insulated, you should let it cool off for a few hours.

When you're ready to get water from the tank, shut off the water supply going into the tank. The shut-off valve will likely be a quarter-turn ball valve or a gate valve, which needs to be turned several times to shut off the supply. Since your water main should already be off, shutting off the supply is more to preserve the cleanliness of the water in the tank, as contaminated water may come through the lines at first when water service is restored. It can also help prevent siphoning of contaminated water into the tank when you start draining it.

At the bottom of the tank there should be a drain valve. Many valves look like a threaded connector that you can hook a garden hose to, and that's basically what you need to do. You don't need a long hose, and most garden hoses are not sanitary enough to use with drinking water. But, a convenient hose of about the right length is one of the water hoses for your washer. Turn off the washer's water valve and remove the hose. Then thread the hose onto the drain "faucet" of the water tank. The best option is a potable/drinking water hose (often colored blue) but remember the washer hose as an emergency option.

If the drain valve does not have an ordinary handle, but a slot where a handle could attach, you could use a screwdriver or coin to rotate the slot.

Be careful, and work slowly when trying to open the drain valve. These are seldom used (maybe once a year if you get your water heater serviced) and will likely be difficult to open. You don't want to break or damage the valve.

If you've opened the valve, most likely you'll find very little water coming out. For the tank to drain, you will also need to allow air into it. This is easily done by turning on any hot water faucet in the house. This allows air into the pipes, and back into the tank. You will probably hear some strange sucking-like sounds as water drains into your container.

Be aware that sediment does collect at the bottom of the tank. This is typical mineral sediment found in your drinking water. If there is sediment, just allow it to settle to the bottom of your container.

If your tank uses an aluminum anode, you may find a jelly-like aluminum corrosion by-product on the tank bottom. Don't drink that.

While the water should be safe to drink, it wouldn't hurt to boil or filter it before drinking.

Something you may consider doing before an emergency is to replace the factory drain valve with a ball valve. Ball valves allow for a straight water flow and are less likely to get clogged by hard water sediments like a gate valve might. Ball valves are also much easier to turn should someone lacking strength need to access the water.

An important note: be sure to refill the water tank before you turn the water heater back on.

Treat-before-you-drink water around the home

Where the water in the pipes and water heater should be safe to drink, particularly if you shut off the water main, other sources of water around the home should be treated before you drink or use for cooking.

Toilet tanks

First, this is the water in the tank and not the bowl. If you don't add any cleaning chemicals to the tank, this water could be utilized, after being filtered and disinfected. While this water comes directly from the water pipes, the tank itself is usually not clean enough for drinking. If you add any chemicals to the tank, the water is unsafe and should only be used for non-internal use, meaning don't drink it and don't use if for cooking or for personal hygiene.

Pool

There were several times during our years in Chile when the water supply was either contaminated or had failed. Thankfully, my parents kept water storage, so we had water for drinking and cooking.

Remember our pool I mentioned at the beginning of the book?

Whenever there was a water outage, we would get buckets of water from the pool to take to the bathrooms. We'd then use this water to flush the toilets. It's a surprise to some people, but the water system does not need to be running for the sewer to work. The water drains use gravity, so you can flush toilets by dumping water into them.

However, be aware that in an earthquake, the sewer lines could be damaged and prevent proper flow. Most likely there won't be enough usage of the sewage system for this to be noticed, but it is a real possibility that things won't drain as expected and could back up.

Besides using the pool water for sanitary purposes, the pool water can also be filtered and boiled for drinking.

Temperatures were mild enough where we lived (meaning it rarely got below freezing) that we kept water in the pool year-round. This doesn't mean it was always treated and clean enough for swimming, only that we had water in it. Springtime usually came with a serious pool cleaning.

If you live in a temperate climate, you might consider leaving water in your pool. However, leaving water in an above-ground pool year-round is not advisable.

Rainwater collection

Rainwater collection is more of a potential water source than a water storage solution. The problem is not knowing when rain is coming. However, if you have a rainwater collection system, there may be water you can treat and disinfect for other uses.

I'm considering the creation of a rainwater collection system, mostly to catch water from our roof so I could use it on the garden. I plan to modify the rain gutter downspouts to run into a series of barrels, which could then be siphoned to the garden beds. I won't go into details, as there are a wide variety of systems that could be built.

You should also be aware that in some areas, there are laws that govern rainwater collection. Yes, it sounds crazy, but there are places where it's illegal to collect rainwater. In some places it may be frowned upon, while in others it might be encouraged. It's in your best interest to check your local regulations.

A rainwater collection system would be valuable if you are in a post-disaster situation and need an additional source of water for other needs, such as a garden.

Other water sources

As mentioned earlier, there is a small river near our home. It will be convenient if it's still running after a natural disaster, but I'm not counting on it. And there are a lot of people upstream from us, so there may not be much water left, and it may be contaminated. There is a lake a couple miles away, but its distance and occasional algal bloom problems make it an unreliable source.

Before an emergency, consider what your other water sources might be, such as

- rainwater,
- rivers, streams, or other sources of moving water,
- lakes and ponds, and
- natural springs.

Also, be aware of some cautions:

- Don't use water that has an odor, is dark in color, or has floating material (like oil).
- Don't drink flood water.
- Don't use saltwater unless you distill it first.

Shelter

For me, the best-case scenario is if we get to stay in our home. I believe for most people being able to remain in their home is also probably the best option, if they're prepared.

The next best is if your home is still fully functional and safe but maybe the roof has some damage. In this case, a large tarp can help keep the elements from infiltrating and damaging your home's structure.

A good option, but one we and most people I know don't have, is an RV or camp trailer.

If you must evacuate or your home becomes uninhabitable, the issue of shelter comes into play.

If you choose to go to an evacuation center, you will be at the mercy of whatever shelter the center has available. It may be a school, a church, an indoor stadium or arena, or maybe tents.

You should have an emergency shelter, preferably one you could take with you. For most people, their emergency shelter is most likely a tent.

The type of tent you get depends on what you like and what you can afford.

For my family, in the case of an evacuation where we can take the vehicle, we have a large family tent. We also have a couple of smaller tents we can take if we need to leave on foot. And, there are very minimalist shelters (basically a tarp) in some of our emergency packs.

Related to shelter preparations, if you can remain in your home, you need some roof and window supplies as well.

For the roof, you should have a couple of large tarps. Not only could these tarps be used on their own, as shelters, but if your roof has a leak or other damage on it, the tarp(s) can reduce water leakage and roof and structure damage.

Windows play a big part in maintaining the temperature inside your home. If windows are broken during an earthquake, what do you have as a replacement or for repair?

Plastic sheets, with duct tape (or other tape) could be used as a temporary window repair. Plastic sheeting used for painting works.

Various window insulation kits are available to buy. Some are for insulating the interior of the window, and other kits are more for exterior use. You can buy plastic window insulating kits, which are usually a plastic sheet with tape on one end. The kit usually includes two-sided tape for the other sides. You just stick the one side of the plastic sheet to the top frame of the window, then cut the sheet to size and tape the remaining sides.

However, these kits are more expensive than just getting plastic sheets and tape. If you do want to go with the ease and convenience of window insulation kits, the best time to buy them is near the end of the winter season. These items, and similar winterizing items, frequently go on clearance in late February and into March.

As a final note about windows, you should also consider blackout options. The idea is to prevent others from seeing light filtering out your windows if you have electricity and others don't. Of course, if you have a noisy generator, that will give you away. But, light from any source can be a beacon in the night. You goal is to minimize the likelihood of others targeting you.

Personally, I prefer blackout curtains to blinds, as they tend to do a better job at keeping sunlight (and heat) out during the summer and heat in during the winter. They're also better at keeping the windows darker at night than blinds do. Some people plan to use black plastic to cover their windows.

As I've mentioned elsewhere in this book, I am an advocate for helping others in need. However, my highest priority is my family's well-being. I will do what I feel like I can to help others, while minimizing risk and exposure to my own family and our supplies. Those same people who will say it's unfair for you to have food and supplies during an emergency, and who will take food and supplies from you and your family, are often the same who will squander money on entertainment, sports, electronics, lottery tickets, and other items instead of making sure they are prepared for an emergency. I personally feel very sorry for the children of parents who choose to not become prepared. Those parents are failing in providing for the well-being of their children.

Emergency Kits

The old standby was to have a 72-hour (three-day) emergency pack. This is still the norm if you look around the web or shop for emergency supplies. But when you experience the brunt of an earthquake, this won't be enough.

To me, a 72-hour kit always seemed too minimalistic. Most 72-hour kits I've seen look like a joke, often with poor quality items. I suppose the idea is they are one-time use products, and then you throw them away.

Many years ago, I decided I needed to prepare for a longer duration, and I needed equipment that was higher quality but not necessarily top-of-the-line. While I'm all about being prepared for a week or longer, I was interested when I heard in class the term "96-hour kit."

My first encounter of someone teaching and recommending the use of a 96-hour kit was in about 2015. I was helping at the Utah Public Safety Summit and stepped into a class about earthquake preparedness in time to hear the instructors talking about a 96-hour kit. Intrigued that someone "official" wasn't preaching 72-hour kits, I stayed and later asked a couple of questions.

First, I wanted to know why the change from 72-hour to 96-hour. I was told that after a number of studies on response times—how long it actually takes for emergency crews and aid to get into an area ravaged by a natural disaster—it was discovered that it can take four days, or longer, for aid to get into most of the area. This isn't full-on assistance, this is just emergency assistance beyond the local resources and getting basics, such as water, to the worst hit areas.

Since four days seemed to be more of a minimal expected time of arrival for the cavalry, I followed up asking why they weren't pushing for a 7-day kit.

He replied that a 7-day kit would be great, but they found that most people cannot carry more than four days' worth of supplies. So, a 96-hour kit was decided on.

More is better, but realize this kit is something you need to be able to grab and go. These kits are for an evacuation or emergency departure, when there isn't time to grab lots of extras.

My recommendation is a two-tier approach.

The first tier is to have a 96-hour kit. While there are items in the kit that are easily shared and you only really need one of each, there are other items where each person in the family needs their own.

Keep in mind, these kits are for foot evacuation, meaning you can't take a vehicle. Or, if can evacuate by vehicle, it is in a rapid departure scenario.

The second tier is an extended kit, which is a supplement to the 96-hour kit. If you can evacuate by vehicle, you take your 96-hour kit(s) and the extended kit(s).

96-hour kit

The following items are recommendations. Each kit should be personalized to fit individual needs. Parents will need to include items for their children, particularly for infants and small children, in their own packs. It's valuable to let each child have their own pack, with some of their own items, even if they can't carry much. It gives them a sense of ownership, responsibility, and inclusion.

There are those in preparedness and survival who are extreme minimalists, and there is something to be said about reducing the weight you carry by eliminating non-essentials. Personally, I'd prefer to start with too much and drop the non-essentials than wish I hadn't been so stingy on weight. If needed, you might even be able to barter your non-essentials for something you need.

The following lists of items are divided into sub-kits, with two columns. The first column is for "essential" or strongly recommended items. While some of these items may not be essential for survival, they will make life a little more comfortable.

The second column, labeled "consider," includes items that may not be as essential as the first column, but they still could be valuable.

As with all the lists and suggestions, these are recommendations and considerations. You need to personalize your kits.

Each of the kits could be contained in separate small bags and then placed together in a larger bag, suitcase, or tote. You could just think of each kit as a section of preparedness and just pack everything together, which is more of what I do, although I will keep certain items, like first aid stuff, together.

Food and water kit

The main goal for a food and water kit is a four-day supply of non-perishable food, along with four gallons of water per person.

Table 16: Food and water kit recommendations.

Essential	Consider
Energy bars	Water purification—tablets or bleach
Water (refillable bottle)	Just-add-water meals
Protein/energy snacks	Pet food
Water filter	

The simplest approach to food is to get pre-made emergency meal kits. Most of the food in these kits simply require adding water. Some people like to use MRE-style food, but MRE is short for "Meal, Ready to Eat" and that means they don't necessarily require adding water. That means the MRE will weigh more because it's ready to be eaten.

Other types of food that are probably better in an emergency, and which weigh less, are dehydrated or freeze dried. Generally, freeze dried food retains more nutrients and usually tastes better. But it's more expensive. Most emergency food is of the dehydrated variety, which costs less than freeze dried. Normally you just add water (usually heated) to make the meal.

Hygiene kit

Hygiene kits are another kit that can be contained in a smaller bag within a 96-hour kit. Some people think some of the items listed in the hygiene kit are unnecessary—and for pure survival, that may be the case. However, survival does include reducing the chances of infection, whether from injury or disease, and personal sanitation plays a big part.

Table 17: Hygiene kit recommendations.

Essential	Consider
Toilet paper	Lip balm
Soap (liquid)	Sunscreen
Deodorant	Bug repellent
Toothbrush	Metal mirror
Toothpaste	Tweezers
Washcloth	Nail clippers
Comb/brush	Dental floss
Feminine products	Baby powder
Hand sanitizer	Cotton swabs
Eyeglasses/contacts	Contact lens case & contact lens solution

Having toilet paper makes things more comfortable, and cleaner, when nature calls.

Washing your hands with soap and water does a better job at keeping your hands clean than simply using hand sanitizer. But, having the hand sanitizer is a good option if water is unavailable.

A mirror can double for signaling if you need help.

Bug repellent keeps you more comfortable and reduces the chances of a disease-carrying insect bite.

Sun protection is a big issue, so the sunscreen and lip balm are to help protect you from burns.

For a few days, not cleaning your mouth may not be a big issue. Personally, I can hardly go a day without my teeth getting cleaned, and it's a big morale boost to have my mouth feeling clean.

First aid kit

Keep in mind that the listed items are, like for the other kits, just recommendations. You can certainly add more or make changes, as needed.

Table 18: First aid kit recommendations.

Essential	Consider
Adhesive bandages (assorted)	Saline solution
Nitrile gloves	Burn gel/cream
4x4 gauze (4–6)	Pressure dressing
2x2 gauze (4–6)	Splint
4" roller gauze bandage (2)	Instant ice pack
2" roller gauze bandage (2)	Heat pack
Scissors	Anti-diarrheal medication
Cloth tape	Stool softener
Antibiotic ointment	
Triangle bandage	
4" ACE bandage	
2" ACE bandage	
Spare blanket	
Pain killer/anti-inflammatory/fever reducer such as ibuprofen or acetaminophen	
Antihistamine/allergy medication	

Tool kit

When it comes to battery-operated devices, I try to use only one or two types of common batteries, such as AA or AAA. I've seen some nice flashlights, but they use an uncommon battery, which makes them useless when the batteries die, and you can't get a replacement. Whenever possible, I like my electronics to use interchangeable batteries that are easy to replace.

Among my emergency items, I have a small, very portable folding solar cell that came with a battery charger. My plan is to mostly use rechargeable AA and AAA batteries.

Table 19: Possible items for a tool kit.

Essential	Consider
Emergency plan	Multi-tool
Leather gloves	Paracord (100')
Goggles/safety glasses	Duct tape
Dust mask (N95)	Sewing kit
Flashlight/headlamp	Fire starter
Extra batteries	Sleeping bag
Whistle	Tent
Manual can opener*	Small binoculars
Knife	Hand warmers
AM/FM radio, battery operated	Compass/GPS
Pen/pencil, notepad	Glowstick**
Gas shut off tool	Matches in waterproof container

*A great lightweight, manual can opener is the military P-38.
**Glowsticks are good, long-lasting light sources and are fun for kids.

Clothing

If you always wear good shoes, then this item may be unnecessary. However, let's look at this in the case where you need to grab-and-go. If you happen to be wearing, on the rare occasion, less-than-optimal shoes (or none at all), wouldn't it be nice to have something better to wear and protect your feet?

Extra socks come in handy. If your socks get wet and you need to keep walking, it's best to put dry socks on to reduce the chance of getting blisters.

A hat is mainly for sun protection.

Extra underwear is for personal comfort and even hygiene. I'd consider a single extra set of underwear to be minimal.

The items under "Consider" are more for other weather and seasonal conditions. If the emergency happens in the summer, you can easily drop the unneeded items. But, if you're out in the cold, you'll be glad for the layering options.

Table 20: Clothing kit recommendations.

Essential	Consider
Good shoes	Warm gloves
Socks (minimum 2 pair)	Scarf
Underwear (2 pair)	Beanie hat
Hat	Seasonal jacket
Rain poncho	Sunglasses

Other items to consider

The above kits do not include all the items you may want to consider. Depending on your personal needs, there may be others to include:

Backpack or rolling bag—strong and durable enough to meet your needs as well as large enough for your supplies and easy to move

Extra clothing

Extra blanket(s)

Photocopies of identification and other important documents

Cash and coins: small denomination bills, nothing larger than a $20 bill

Special needs items: Prescription medication(s), eyeglasses, hearing aid batteries

Items for infants: formula, diapers, wipes, bottles, pacifiers, sippy cup, burp cloths, infant medication (such as anti-colic, teething, infant dosage acetaminophen, etc.)

Items for children: puzzles, games, coloring books, crayons, books, children's medications

Communication devices and a way to power them

Extended Kit

An extended kit in a large duffle bag can be easily grabbed and tossed into the car, along with your 96-hour kits and a couple other items. It's helpful to have a list attached to the extended kit identifying any other items that should be taken as well. That way you're not trying to remember what else you need to grab.

Ideally, all parts of the kit will be together, but it may be that some of the parts are stored elsewhere. For example, the main kit may be stored in a closet or in the garage—near the car—but you keep an extra thirty-day emergency food pail inside the house, where the temperature is better for food storage. You'll want a note on the extended kit reminding you to grab the other item(s).

Remember, the extended kit supplements the 96-hour kit. So, don't duplicate items unnecessarily or you add extra weight and take space that could be better used with something else.

Besides supplementing the equipment in your 96-hour kit, making your emergency a little more comfortable and manageable, the extended kit should also allow you to extend your emergency for at least another three days (for a minimum of one week).

To create your extended kit, possible items to include could be anything on one of the lists—either the "Essential" or "Consider" lists—that you did not put in your 96-hour kit. Here are other items you should consider including:

- Additional non-perishable food to extend meals for a full week (or more)
- Extra batteries
- Extra flashlight
- Sleeping bags
- Sleeping pads
- Extra blankets
- Tent(s)
- Winter gear
- Cook kit (if you have a family to feed)—these are only a few possibilities:
  - 4-quart (or larger) pot
  - 2-quart pot
  - Frying pan
  - Large bowl (which can double as a plate) for each person
  - Eating utensils for each person
  - Cup for each person
  - Serving utensils—large spoon, ladle, spatula, tongs
  - Knife
- Extra fire-starting items—matches, lighters
- Small camp stove and fuel
- Water storage—additional one gallon per person per day
- Emergency candles (these are 100+ hour candles)
- Additional medications, including prescription medication
- Additional first aid items

- Extra clothing—this is a personal decision, but I'd suggest at least three changes of clothes for each adult and five changes for children. Babies will need more.
- Sanitation Kit—
  o 5- or 6-gallon bucket (to be used as a port-a-potty)
  o Port-a-potty lid
  o Port-a-potty bags
  o Port-a-potty chemicals
  o Latex-free gloves
  o Additional N95 masks
  o Dishwashing detergent
  o Rubber dishwashing/cleaning gloves
  o Scrub brush (for dishes)
  o Cleaning bleach (doubles as water disinfectant and add to dish rinse water for sanitizing

A note on using bleach to sanitize dishes. After washing and rinsing your dishes, soak them for at least two minutes in a water-bleach solution (2 teaspoons bleach per 1 gallon of water, or 2 tablespoons of bleach per 3 gallons of water). Use tongs or rubber dish gloves to remove the dishes from the sanitizer solution and let them air dry. Do not use the sanitizer solution with non-stainless steel, aluminum, silver, or chipped enamel.

A note about your bag/backpack

In an emergency, disaster, or catastrophic event, the last thing you need is to call attention to yourself. You do not want to advertise your preparedness.

So, a word of caution: don't use bags that make others think you are prepared, you have supplies, and you know what you're doing. The simple advice is, don't use bags that are camouflage or red. Too often, pre-made 72-hour kits and emergency kits come in red bags. Think about this. If you're caught unprepared and find yourself (or your children) hungry, who do approach for help—someone with a plain-looking backpack or the person with the red backpack that looks like those advertised emergency packs?

Military packs are great, and camouflage tends to make people think of the military. If, in the same scenario, you see someone with a camo-style tactical-looking backpack and another person with a plain-looking pack, who would you think is more likely to have food and supplies?

I am not suggesting you never help others. On the contrary, we need to be willing to extend a helping hand. But our top priority should be to provide for and protect those in our care—our families. That priority can be jeopardized if the bag you carry makes you a target.

The best color is one that is easily overlooked. Dark blue is a good all-around color. If all you have is a camouflage or red backpack, start with what you have. But, make a note to get something that will make you less of a target.

Vehicle Preparation

First, you should try to always keep your vehicle's fuel tank at least half full. While there is a practical reason—it helps reduce the potential for water condensation to form and cause engine problems—there is also a preparedness reason as well. Most of the vehicles I have owned can drive 250 to 300 miles (or more) on a full tank of gas. Half a tank should, reasonably, get us 100 or more miles down the road.

In an emergency, people will be lining up to get fuel, if it's even available. The last thing you need when trying to leave quickly is to have to stop for gas. Having a half-tank of fuel should get you far enough away that the rush on gas won't be as great.

Additionally, you should, if you can, keep a tank's worth of fuel stored in a safe location. Most cities and/or counties have fuel storage restrictions. It's good to be aware of those local regulations so you don't violate any. Any fuel you do store should be treated with a stabilizer and rotated every six to twelve months.

Taking the extra fuel with you can help ensure you and your family can get out of the immediate danger zone, without having to worry about where to fill up.

You should have a vehicle emergency kit in every vehicle. Table 21 lists potential items:

Table 21: Emergency equipment to keep in your vehicle.

First aid kit & manual	Flashlight & extra batteries
Hazard reflectors & flares	Jumper cables
Waterproof matches	Candles
Fire extinguisher (class ABC)	Radio & batteries
Non-perishable food kit	Bottled water
Bag of sand & shovel	Tool kit
Blanket or sleeping bag	Pen & paper
Map	Tissue
Moist towelettes	Plastic bags
Essential medications	Rain poncho or rain gear
Leather work gloves	Water filter/purifier
Tow rope	Extra clothes & shoes
Tarp	

In a later section, we'll discuss "get-home" equipment. Many of the above-mentioned recommendations to keep in your vehicle could be part of an extended get-home bag for your vehicle.

Securing the home

The most dangerous place to be in an earthquake is inside a building. Not because the building will collapse—which it might, especially if it's an older building or constructed of unreinforced masonry—but because of falling objects.

As you go around your home, the big question to ask about every piece of furnishing is, "Could it fall down?"

If the answer is yes, then you can follow that question with, "Would it hurt if it fell on me (or my child)?" In most cases, the answer is "Yes, it would hurt," and most items can cause injury or even death.

If the object isn't likely to fall on somebody, then could it cause other damage if it fell over?

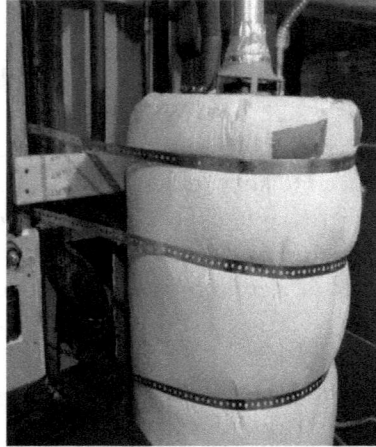

Figure 20: Straps around our old water heater, with backerboard behind water heater and between studs.

Water heater

This is an oft-forgotten item, hidden away somewhere, usually in a utility room. It's very unlikely to fall over on somebody, unless an earthquake happens when it's getting serviced.

Consider this: A gallon of water weighs about 8.34 pounds. A small water heater is 30 gallons, or it holds 250 pounds of water. A larger 50-gallon water tank heater will have 417 pounds of water in it.

If an earthquake can shake a building, a measly 417+ pound water heater is nothing.

What kind of damage would 417 pounds cause if it were knocked over? It could certainly crash through a wall. Since it's attached to water pipes, those pipes would break and cause flooding damage. If it's a gas water heater, the gas line could break and cause a gas leak.

Figure 21: Our new water heater, with actual earthquake straps

So, while the water heater isn't likely to fall on someone, if it falls over, it will very likely cause significant damage. Securing your water heater can help prevent this disaster.

In our home, on the old water heater, I had secured three metal straps to the 2x6 wall studs behind the water heater. I also added a 2x4 behind the water heater, between the studs, to help prevent it from rocking back into the wall. This was easy to do in our house because the walls around the water heater are unfinished.

In late 2020 we replaced the old water heater and got things up to code, including actual earthquake straps. Our plumber told us a top and bottom strap are both required. The top-only strap used to be what was required but in California they found water waters that managed to "walk" under the top strap during tremors.

Figure 22: Flexible water pipe.

The other consideration for your water heater is to make sure it has flexible pipe fittings for both the water and the gas (if your water heater is gas like ours). If the water heater moves, which it will in an earthquake, it will likely break any rigid fittings. The flexible pipe allows for movement.

The flexible pipe should be standard (it's code) with newer construction, but it doesn't hurt to make sure your water heater has it.

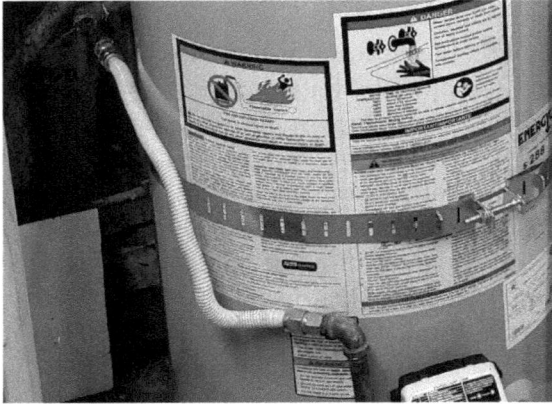

Figure 23: Flexible gas line going to our water heater.

Shelves

It doesn't take much shaking to knock a shelf over. There are securing brackets and straps you can buy that are designed for earthquakes. Most of these straps will allow the shelf to move but not fall over. The advantage of these straps is they are less likely to damage your wall.

I do much of my preparation on the cheap. I have secured most of our shelves to the wall. To secure my shelves, I have used angle brackets; I screw one end into a solid part of the shelf (usually the top, not a loose shelf) and the other side into a stud in the wall. (A stud is a wood board behind the sheetrock or drywall, and to which the sheetrock is attached.)

You could anchor the shelves to the wall using sheetrock anchors, but

Figure 24: Conduit clamp securing shelf.

I don't trust them to hold in an earthquake, and I would expect them to certainly end up causing more damage to the wall when the shelf is ripped out.

It's possible that in an earthquake the attached shelf could end up damaging the wall, particularly to the sheetrock, but my preference is to keep the shelf from falling over.

Figure 25: Angle bracket securing shelf from top.

On one shelf, I used electrical conduit clamps. I screwed them into a stud in the wall and over the vertical rod on the back of the shelf.

Pictures

Personally, the pictures I am most concerned about securing are those near a bed and any my wife wants to make sure aren't damaged.

Like shelf anchor straps, specialty picture hangers are available that will keep your picture frame secured to the wall.

A picture fastener or hook that closes is the best option to hang the picture on. The fastener should, preferably, be screwed into a wall stud.

Without a hanging hook that closes, the next best option is a hook-like fastener that is attached to a wall stud. You can take a normal picture hanger and nail it (or screw it) into a stud. Then use needle-nosed pliers to bend the hanger hook towards the wall so there is barely enough room between the wall and hook for the picture framing wire to slide through.

Figure 26: Another angle bracket securing a shelf to the wall.

Alternatively, instead of making a hook out of a picture hanger, you can use a screw hook (screwed into a stud) as your picture hanger. Just screw the hook in until the hook almost touches the wall, leaving just enough room for the picture wire to slide between the hook and wall.

For large or heavy items, use two hooks, both screwed into studs.

During an earthquake, pictures will bang around, and glass could break. To help keep the frame from moving, secure the bottom two corners to the wall. A good method is to use a commercially available product. Some of these use hook-and-loop fasteners that stick the corners to the wall. If you choose to leave pictures hanging on nails, there is almost a guarantee they will fall.

TVs

Most TVs are now narrow LCD- or LED-style displays, and not the old, bulky CRT televisions. In any case, you don't want a TV to fall.

To secure a TV to a shelf, table, or entertainment center, you can buy TV straps. However, the best option for flat-panel TVs is to mount them to the wall. The wall mount needs to be secured to wall studs to provide the best strength, and all the wall mounts I've installed basically have this as a requirement.

While the wall mount looks great, often giving the TV a picture-like look, they can be expensive, with some common mounts costing well over $100, and others a lot more. There are some cheaper options.

The best time to buy these mounts is on Black Friday, although there are a few other times during the year when prices are a little more reasonable.

Figure 27: Our TV secured to the wall.

Bedrooms

Bedrooms are one of the most likely places in your home for you to be in during an earthquake. If you are getting the recommended average of eight hours of sleep each night (that would be nice…if only that could happen), then one third of your day is in the bedroom. That means there's a 33% chance you will be in the bedroom when an earthquake happens.

Bedrooms often have TVs, shelves, and pictures, but they also have other items such as dressers. If your dresser is tall, it should be secured to the wall. If the dresser is shorter and has a wider or deeper base, then it would still be a good idea to secure it to the wall, but it is less likely to tip over in an earthquake. It is more likely its drawers could be shaken out.

Beds are another consideration. Most are unlikely to fall over, and if they do, you have more serious things to worry about, as the house is probably tipping for the bed to fall over.

I've heard some officials recommend to people to put shoes, flashlight, water, and a few emergency items in a bag and then attach the bag to the leg of the bed. Their reasoning is, if there is a big earthquake and the bed moves you will be able to find the bag, even with the electricity off.

While I agree with having shoes, flashlight, and a few other items easily accessible near your bed, I'm not convinced with the idea of attaching the bag to the leg of the bed. Here's why. Having a bag attached to your bed seems useful only if your bed has the potential to move in an earthquake. My beds have always been on a carpeted floor. Not a rug, but a carpet that is attached to the floor. Moving the bed takes a lot of effort. And, if the wheels aren't working well, the bed end with the bad wheels must be lifted. Additionally, the kind and queen bed frames we've had have a non-wheeled center post, so the bed doesn't move easily even if the corner wheels are working. Our rooms are also not very big, and there is usually nearby furniture, so if my bed were to move it wouldn't go very far. The loft beds in the kids' rooms don't have wheels and are on carpet, so they don't move.

The situation you may want a bag attached to your bed is if your bed is on a wood floor or polished surface, where it can move easily. In this case, some emergency stuff attached to the bed may be good.

If you do decide to attach a bag to your bed, make sure it has a quick-release type mechanism. The last thing you want to do is be fumbling in the dark, trying to untie a knot so you can take the bag with you.

Also, make sure your bed can't roll over onto the bag, pinning it to the floor and making it more difficult for you to grab it and go.

I keep a working flashlight nearby (actually, we have three or four near the bed), so I can flip it on and not fumble around in the dark. If there's broken glass, I don't want to be blindly grabbing at things on the floor, even if what I'm looking for is supposed to be attached to the bed leg.

Additionally, I would rather keep my shoes out of the bag so I can more quickly put them on. If your window breaks, or a glass picture frame shatters on the floor, you don't want to be walking around blindly without shoes on. And it's not just inside where you need to protect your feet. Outside can be just as dangerous with debris on the ground. But other factors as well would warrant wearing shoes.

Shoes were a small part of one account from a cousin who has family near where the July 5, 2019, Ridgecrest earthquake struck. A few minutes before the main earthquake struck, a magnitude 5.0 earthquake shook the house. The father put on his shoes, and a few minutes later, the 7.1 hit at 8:19 PM. Everyone got out of the house.

The problem is, Ridgecrest is close to the Mojave Desert, and temperatures that day reached 102 degrees Fahrenheit (38.9 Celsius). At the time of the earthquake, outside temperatures were still in the mid-90s and the ground was hot. Those without shoes found themselves burning their feet on the asphalt and cement.

Besides shoes, having some clothes ready could also be helpful. Normally, I keep my pants I wore from the previous day ready—with belt, keys, and wallet—so I could put it on quickly if needed. If there wasn't an emergency (as is normally the case), I get a clean pair of pants in the morning. Alternately I could get a clean pair out in the evening and get it ready, but I'm a little lazy that way and would rather wait until after a morning shower to get my clean clothes out.

Another piece of advice I've heard is, if you are in your bed when an earthquake happens, you should cover your head with your pillow to protect your head. Like attaching an emergency bag to the bed, my response is, it depends on your room and your level of earthquake preparation.

If you're in your bed when an earthquake happens, it's best to just stay in your bed, as you're less likely to be injured in the bed during the shaking. You can use a pillow to protect your head; just turn your face to the side so your breathing isn't obstructed. If you've checked your room thoroughly, and done earthquake preparations, you shouldn't have anything heavy or unsecured near the head of your bed. Most likely you're keeping safe from a window breaking in on you.

Keep your bed's headboard cleared of any large, unsecured items. If you have a lamp above you on the headboard, consider securing it or move it to a bedside table. Likewise, any pictures you have hanging on the wall at the head of your bed should be securely fastened to the wall. A falling picture frame doesn't feel good.

The exception is if your pictures have no frames and are just posters taped or stuck to the wall. Falling posters aren't so bad if the earthquake manages to detach them from the wall.

Kitchen

Most of the cabinets in our kitchen have child locks on them. These are great, as they also keep the doors closed in an earthquake. If the cabinet doors don't lock, assume they will open during an earthquake and anything inside could fall out.

Special considerations

Every individual and family are unique in some way. Therefore, lists of suggested items are general. You need to customize your kits and emergency preparations to your specific needs. Two common special considerations are pets and small children.

Pets

As previously mentioned, pets are not allowed at most evacuation centers. In fact, I haven't heard of any accepting pets. Pets are usually sent to other locations that are designated as pet shelters. If you have pets, you need to have other plans.

The two biggest considerations for your pets are making sure you have enough emergency food and water for them and knowing what to do with them in the event of an evacuation.

If you have two weeks of food and water storage for each person, you should store that much for your pets as well.

Ideally you will be able to shelter-in-place at your home. However, if you need to evacuate, you need to also have predetermined what to do with your pet(s). If you can't be at home, where is the next best place? A relative's home?

Small children and babies

Small children and babies have their own special needs and considerations. One of the more obvious is in the diapering department. You need to make sure you have enough diapers and wipes for the entire emergency. That or get cloth diapers and be cleaning diapers through the duration of the event. But, with limited water, the better option is probably disposables.

Small children, and especially babies, require more changes of clothing or at least options to clean and dry clothing.

Medications are also items to consider. These could include children's acetaminophen and/or ibuprofen, teething gel, and medications and ointments for diaper rash.

Children need entertainment so a few games, toys, and books could be brought.

If you need to evacuate, you should plan to grab the favorite blanket and/or animal as you go. These familiar items can help calm a child in an uncertain situation.

Other preparations

A couple other areas to get prepared in are to get copies of all your legal paperwork and to document what is in your home.

Legal papers and documentation

Copies of your legal documents should be kept with your emergency kit. Here are examples of some of the legal documents to include:

- driver's license
- passports
- social security cards
- marriage license

- house mortgage
- home/property ownership
- insurance policies
- automobile ownership
- motorhome and other personal property (trailers, recreational vehicles, etc.) ownership
- wills and trusts
- appraisals for jewelry, instruments, and other valuables

Some people include copies of birth certificates and passports with their legal documents. Others will also include credit card and other financial information.

While all this information is important, it also needs to be protected. Physical copies of your legal identification and documentation should be kept secured in a safe.

Instead of physical copies, I have heard of some people keeping digital copies of these documents, usually on a flash drive. If you do use digital copies, it's safest to encrypt the files or the entire drive. Most flash drives come with encryption software. Encryption uses a password to "lock" your data, so it is unreadable. The password is then required to "unlock" or decrypt the files to read them.

It's also good to keep recent photographs (printed) of those in your household, including pets. These can be helpful for locating a missing family member.

If you have a pet that is microchipped, keep a copy of the microchip tag number with your documents.

Other documentation

In the case of a disaster, especially one which results in property loss, you may want, or need, to file claims. If theft is part of loss, you will need detailed information to provide to law enforcement.

In addition to the legal papers and documents, consider taking the following documentation:

- Take color pictures, from opposing sides, of every room.
- Take color pictures of all valuables, especially anything that has a written appraisal. Multiple angles are helpful, as is a photo of any identification or serial numbers of the valuable.
- Make an inventory of all valuables with their serial numbers.

After you make copies of all the photos, inventory, and legal paperwork, send a copy to a trusted out-of-state contact who can safeguard the information. Again, any documents with personally identifiable information on them must be kept as secure as possible.

Earthquake insurance

As surprising as it is to some people, most homeowner's insurance policies do not cover earthquakes. So, what about earthquake insurance?

The decision is up to you, although it's probably best made with the advice of someone familiar with the risks for your area.

With increased development and expansion into seismically active areas, along with the vulnerability of older structures, there is an increased earthquake risk for many buildings. A 2017 study by the Federal Emergency Management Agency (FEMA) estimates earthquake losses in the United States to eventually average $6.14 billion a year (Insurance Information Institute, 2018).

There are even places in the country that have a low seismic hazard but high risk. For example, New York City and Boston have very low probability of an earthquake striking the area. But, if a catastrophic rupture does occur, the high number of buildings and infrastructure that were built without seismic codes puts the economic cost as very high.

If your home or place of business is in a high-risk area, earthquake insurance may be a valuable addition.

Where to store your emergency equipment?

Once you get your pack(s) together, where is the best place to store it (them)?

The simple answer is, where you can get it in an emergency.

The best option is to have all your packs, including food and water, in the same place, where you can grab and go, if needed. When seconds count, you don't want to be looking around for all the different pieces.

However, space can be a limiting factor. With my wife and four kids, it's almost impossible to find a single location where everything can be stored.

One ex-military and survival expert I've listened to recommends your bug-out bag be kept in a bin in your car because your car will be home if you have to shelter-in-place at home, and it's with you if you're out and can't get back home. I've mentioned a similar strategy about keeping some key equipment in your vehicle.

But there are a couple issues I have with keeping your primary emergency equipment in a vehicle. First is the issue of multiple vehicles. What if you have multiple cars and you and your spouse drive each vehicle at different times? Do you transfer your emergency equipment back and forth to whichever car you are driving? Do you get doubles (or triples) for everyone and just keep full emergency packs in each vehicle?

Personally, I use one vehicle (a small, efficient one) for going to work every day. But we also have a van to transport the family in.

And there is my second issue. The survival expert has himself, his wife, and (I think) one child, who is a teenager. My family is twice that size, with four kids under the age of ten. I don't really want to store emergency/bug-out bags for all six members of my household in both vehicles or even just one. There are too many occasions where that storage space is needed, such as for grocery shopping.

Having all your equipment in your vehicle may certainly be an ideal, but it's not practical for our family.

There is something else to keep in mind. Any food stored in the vehicle will degrade in quality after a hot summer, so you need to remember to rotate it out on a regular basis.

When I was single, I did tend to keep my emergency equipment in the trunk. However, I've had to adapt. That is why I decided a tiered approach would make more sense for our situation.

Chapter 12
Get-Home Preparedness

Most of us spend at least a third of the workday away from home. With lunch and commute times, the eight-hour workday can become ten or more hours away from home.

This means that during a normal workday, there is at least a 33% chance you won't be home in the event of an earthquake.

If an earthquake happens and you're unable to drive your vehicle home (probably because of damaged roads), how will you get home?

Someone in decent physical condition should be able to walk a mile in about twenty minutes. That's on flat, even terrain. If conditions are such that you can't drive home, it will probably take you longer to traverse a mile. Add more time if you're out of shape.

For me, I expect my walk-home time in a post-earthquake environment to take at least twice as long as it would normally. But I'm planning for at least three times as long, just to have the extra time buffer. Thankfully I'm seldom further than six miles from home, a luxury many people don't have.

For an example, let's say the distance from work to home is ten miles. To walk ten miles, a person in decent physical condition should take about three hours and twenty minutes. Double that time, and it's around six hours and forty minutes. That's how long I'd expect the walk to take after an earthquake. However, in my preparations I would plan for a ten-mile trek home taking at least ten hours. The simplified strategy is to plan on one hour of travel time for every mile.

When you take that approach, your preparations should revolve around what you would need to get home in that planned timeframe.

Some things to keep in mind: First, actual travel time could be much quicker. But, it's better to be over-prepared and drop excess weight than to not have a critical item because you wanted your preparations to be light.

Second, during your trek home you need to evaluate your progress. Hopefully you're familiar with landmarks and can determine when you are around the halfway point. No later than this point, you need to evaluate your progress. Your evaluation should include how long it's taken to get halfway, the time of day, and weather conditions. Should you find a place to take shelter for the night?

Third, most people—unless they are in good condition—have a difficult time travelling on foot for more than twenty miles on level terrain in a single day in good conditions. If you work more than fifteen miles away from your home, it is a good idea to plan on spending the night somewhere on your journey home.

Even if you're only ten miles from home, depending on the time of day and season of the year that an earthquake (or other major disaster) strikes, you may have to spend the night somewhere.

For example, the big earthquake happens just as you're finishing work at 5:00 PM. It's winter, so the sun is setting in 30 minutes. While most people might just consider walking home in the dark, remember that the earthquake will have caused extensive damage, and it may not be safe to walk if you can't see well. What if there's a snowstorm? Or maybe there's just a lot of snow to contend with?

Get-Home bag

The various preparations you make for a trek home on foot can be assembled into a "Get-Home" bag. The further away from home you are, the more items you will probably have in your get-home bag.

To discuss get-home bag considerations, I've divided the items into three categories: basic, expanded, and vehicle expanded.

If you take public transportation to get to work or school, you may find it useful to add items from the expanded list to the basic kit.

For me, it is more practical to have my get-home items organized into separate kits. In the backpack I take to work, I keep the basic kit plus some additional items from the expanded kit.

In some ways I tend to over-prepare, because I know I can always leave something behind. It's more difficult to get something that I need but don't have. An example of this are the instant heat packs I have. If an earthquake strikes in the summer, even if I have to trek home overnight on foot, nighttime temperatures rarely drop below 60 degrees Fahrenheit, so I won't be taking the heat packs with me.

On the other hand, if an earthquake results in me walking home in the middle of winter, I may be using some of the heat packs on my two-mile walk home.

For those who just want a single pack get-home kit, I have created the "10 Get-Home Kit Essential Systems." I will go over what I consider the ten essential areas for building your own get-home kit. First, let's look at the get-home bag and expansion kits I've created.

Basic get-home bag

For those who are familiar with the ten essentials you should take with you whenever you head into the backcountry, even for a day hike, you will note some similarities. However, a few of the essentials I have put into the expanded sections.

The idea with the absolute basics is to minimize the number of items to a point where they could be carried in a small bag, or even put into pockets.

Table 22: Basic get-home items.

Walking shoes (if you don't already wear them)	Whistle
	Flashlight (headlamp)
1 quart/liter of water (metal or unbreakable container)	Matches/fire starter
	Adhesive bandages
3–6 granola or protein bars	Moleskin
Emergency blanket	Acetaminophen or ibuprofen
Rain poncho	Bandana

Here's a brief explanation of each item in the basic list:

Walking shoes are an absolute necessity. If you don't wear good walking shoes to work, you should keep some in a desk drawer, your vehicle, or somewhere you can easily get to them. Without comfortable shoes, you will likely get blisters before you get far.

A quart, or liter, of water is also needed. The stress of the situation and time it takes to walk home will dehydrate you. Having the water in a metal container is useful should you need to boil water during your trek home. Ideally your water bottle should have its own bag/case with a shoulder strap, or you can keep it in a backpack.

Granola and/or protein bars will help boost your energy and keep you going.

A cheap emergency blanket takes up minimal room and can be a lifesaver if you're stuck outside overnight. It can also help protect you from adverse elements. You don't need an expensive emergency blanket because this will likely be a one-time use. I have higher quality emergency blankets in my 96-hour kit and in my vehicles.

Cheap rain ponchos also don't take up much room, although I prefer slightly higher quality ones. Having worked at high adventure camps, I have seen how quickly a cheap rain poncho can get torn up. You may consider a cheap poncho in the basic kit; then have a better quality one in your vehicle kit.

A whistle is helpful for calling for assistance. It will save your voice. The international call sign for distress is S.O.S., which in Morse code would be three short blasts on the whistle, followed by three longer ones, and then three short blasts.

A flashlight is extremely useful if you need to walk in the dark. A headlamp is preferred, as it keeps your hands free. While most flashlights are now LEDs, there are still some which are not. The LED lights are preferable. Extra batteries should be kept in the extended kit.

The matches/fire starter are in case you need to make a fire for warmth or protection or just to boil some water. Ideally the matches should be waterproof and strike anywhere. However, these can be difficult to come by. Matches can be made (mostly) waterproof by dipping them in melted wax or coating them with a light coat of fingernail polish. Just remember that if the matches are not strike anywhere, they will need something abrasive to strike against, such as the matchbox or a piece of sandpaper.

The list includes three first aid items: adhesive bandages, moleskin, and a painkiller such as ibuprofen or acetaminophen. You could certainly add other items, but this is the minimum. The bandages are to help stop any bleeding injury. Use the moleskin if you start getting any pre-blister hotspots on your feet. And, the pain killer is if you need it to help control inflammation or pain.

The final item is a bandana. This multi-function item has various uses:

- sun protection—use it to cover your head and neck
- dust mask
- tie hair back
- emergency bandage or sling
- washcloth
- pre-filter for water you plan to boil

Expanded bag items

Table 23 lists items that expand on the basic list. Some of these could be included in the small bag with the basics.

Table 23: Expanded get-home items to add to your basic kit or keep in your vehicle.

Quality multi-tool	Lip balm
Toilet paper	Pepper spray?
Hand sanitizer	Prescription medication?
N95 face mask	Expanded first aid—
Cash	-Gauze pads
Water purification tablets	-Medical tape
Straw-type water filter	-Tweezers
Extra batteries (for flashlight)	-Allergy/antihistamine
Duct tape	medication
Sunglasses	-Antibiotic ointment

There are a couple of items in the expanded list with a question mark. The first is pepper spray. Some people feel that a method of self-defense should be included. The safest method is probably pepper spray. The safest alternative is to avoid needing any defense by not marking yourself as a target.

While I'm a proponent of firearms, firearms shouldn't be needed in the initial aftermath of a natural disaster. There are preppers who include firearms with their lists and promote them as being essential. Here's the reality. Most people believe the government will be coming in quickly to save the day and provide assistance. Most people are more readily willing to serve and help others during those first few days.

After about three days, when supplies and water have become scarce and the government and other aid still hasn't arrived or is scarce, that is when means of protection may be needed. Hopefully you are home by that time.

The other question-marked item is prescription medication. This could be described more broadly as special medical needs. You should keep at least a day's worth of any prescription medication you need on hand.

A quality multi-tool provides you with a knife as well as several other tools that could be useful in an emergency. Don't get a cheap multi-tool. The blades on the few cheap ones I've had have not held an edge well, and the tools tend to break easier.

You should not need a full roll of toilet paper. For a small get-home bag, I include a partial roll of toilet paper in a zippered plastic bag. The idea is to get you home, so you probably don't need more than one- or two-days' worth of toilet paper.

Hand sanitizer is not as good as thoroughly washing with soap. But, when you're short of water for cleaning, sanitizer is a good alternative. A small travel-size bottle is sufficient. If it's alcohol-based, you could potentially use it to help clean a wound as well. I have gotten several free sanitizers from various vendor shows and conferences.

Most emergency references will include a N95 respiration mask. These masks filter the air you breathe and give some protection against airborne contagions. You can buy regular R95 or surgical N95 masks. The "95" indicates that it blocks at least 95% of the very small (0.3 micron) test particles, which is better than a regular face mask. These masks aren't designed for children or for use with facial hair, as they cannot be properly fitted. That said, they'd still be better than nothing.

You can get these masks as N95, R95, or P95. The "N" means it is not resistant to oil. Oil in aerosols or industrial environments can degrade the mask's efficiency. The "R" designation indicates the mask is somewhat resistant to oil. A "P" indicates strong resistance to oil. The "R" masks are certified for up to eight hours of service. A "P" mask is certified for forty hours or thirty days of use, whichever happens first.

While the longer life may be enticing, the "R" and "P" masks are increasingly dense, making them harder to breathe in. The "N"-rated masks are cheaper and better if you expect more strenuous or physical activity because they're easier to breathe through. However, price isn't always a factor, as I found some R95 masks at a hardware store that were less expensive than N95 masks at an emergency supply store.

Having some cash can be helpful. With cash, you can purchase something even if the electricity is out, which means credit card and other electronic purchase processing means won't be working. The cash should be smaller bills, as you don't want to be paying $20 for something that costs less than $5.

Next on the list is water purification methods. In my get-home equipment, I have two means for purifying water. The first is water purification tablets. These take a while to work, so it's a good idea to be treating some water while you're walking.

The second is a filter straw. This straw is lightweight and useful for drinking from a practically any water source. The type I have can attach to a regular water bottle, so I could fill a bottle and then use the straw to drink the water. But it doesn't fit my metal water bottle, although I could stick the straw down inside the bottle's mouth.

This expanded kit should include extra batteries for your flashlight. I did not include extra batteries as part of the basic get-home bag for weight reasons.

Next is duct tape. I do not include a full roll of duct tape in the expanded items. Instead I either have a partial roll or I roll a bunch of duct tape around another item in the bag. Duct tape is useful for repairing items such as a rain poncho or clothing; I've even seen duct tape used as a temporary shoe repair. If you need other ideas, just do an internet search on "uses for duct tape."

Sunglasses will be beneficial if you must walk for any length of time with the sun glaring at you. Not only can they help protect your eyes, they will help reduce the eye strain.

Related to sun protection, you should have lip balm, ideally with sunscreen. Besides keeping lips from getting chapped, I've used lip balm on my knuckles if they start getting dried and cracked. If I'm desperate, I could even use the lip balm with sunscreen as a sunscreen for my nose, ears, and cheeks—places where I'm most likely to experience a sunburn without protection.

Your expanded bag items should also expand your first aid options:

- gauze pads
- medical tape
- tweezers
- allergy/antihistamine medication
- antibiotic ointment

The common gauze pads I include are two-inch square pads. I do have some three-inch pads. Recently I've added a few larger pads that have adhesive edges.

The most common first aid antibiotic ointment is a triple antibiotic. Because of a mild allergic reaction in our family, we use bacitracin—one of the antibiotics in the triple version—and I've included it in most of our first aid kits.

Alternatively, you can also apply petroleum jelly to minor cuts. While a bit greasy, I often apply petroleum jelly to my hands, especially the knuckles, if they get too dry and the skin starts cracking.

Vehicle—extended bag

A word of caution: If your vehicle becomes inaccessible—maybe it's crushed in the parking garage or under a tree or collapsed building façade—you will most likely not be able to retrieve the items from your car.

Even with that remote possibility, it's best to have additional emergency items in your vehicle.

Table 24: Emergency kit in vehicle—get-home kit additions.

Walking shoes/hiking boots	Blanket (wool)
Water, 2 quarts/liters	Small shovel
Water filter	Power bank (for phone)
Rain gear	Extra socks
Leather gloves	Paracord (50–100 ft)
Lighter/waterproof matches	Emergency radio
Additional food (min. 24 hrs.)	Flashlight & extra batteries
Insect repellant	Tarp (5 ft x 7 ft)
First aid kit	Quality emergency blanket
Sunscreen	Toilet paper
Hat (sun protection)	Other hygiene items
Glasses (if you wear contacts)	(feminine products)
Cash	Instant heat packs

If you don't wear good walking shoes as part of your regular everyday dress, you need to have some in your vehicle. If you don't have a vehicle, keep a pair at work. Most dress shoes are not made for more than casual walks, and they could give your feet blisters.

From personal experience, you don't want to keep going when you get a big blister. The best option is prevention.

Two quarts of water is the recommended minimum. Yes, a large hydration pack works well. However, here's the advantage of two separate water containers. After the first is empty, you can fill it with water from another source and be treating it (with water purification tablets) while you drink from the second. Water purification tablets usually take some time to work, so you don't want to be waiting for water.

Rain gear can be a simple rain poncho or raincoat and pants. If you opted to have a cheaper poncho in your basic kit, you should keep a better-quality poncho in the vehicle.

Leather gloves are included primarily as a safety item, although they can help keep your hands warm. While their main purpose is to help keep your hands from getting cut up if you need to scramble over debris, they can also keep your hands from getting dried up if the wind is blowing.

The lighter and waterproof matches are to help start a fire to keep warm or to boil water.

You should keep extra food in your vehicle as well. My recommendation is at least a day's worth of food, primarily in the form of granola bars, protein bars, and other quick and easy-to-eat forms. The goal of your get-home kit is to get home, not spend extra time preparing food during your journey home. Food should be replaced regularly in your vehicle due to the high temperatures that can affect the food quality.

Including insect repellant in your kit is better than constantly using your hands to swat at pesky critters. If you need to sleep outdoors without a tent, it can also help reduce the number of bites you might get.

If you are out in the sun, you need protection from being burned. The hat can help cut down some glare, and you can put a bandana, or small towel, under it to help cover your ears and neck.

If you wear contacts, keep a pair of your prescription glasses in the car. The biggest reason is to give your eyes an option if the contacts start irritating them, due to being in too long or having dust or debris getting into your eyes. Most likely you will not have suitable conditions for swapping out contacts.

For those who wear glasses, a backup pair in the vehicle could be useful if the pair you are wearing gets damaged, such as from a fall.

While you should have some cash with your expanded items, having additional cash in the vehicle to supplement what you already have can be helpful.

A wool blanket is listed because wool can still retain heat when it's wet, and it usually doesn't cost too much. However, any blanket could work, particularly if it doesn't get wet. The idea is to provide some warmth if you need to sleep outdoors.

The small shovel is for digging a hole, should the need arise.

A spare power bank for the phone will help prolong its life should it be usable. However, I would not plan on my phone working.

Extra socks are included for two reasons. First, after I walk for a while in the heat, my feet get sweaty, and a change of socks is helpful. The other reason is a second pair of socks could be worn either for warmth or to help reduce the likelihood of getting blisters. If you wear two pairs of socks, a lighter, thinner pair should be worn first, with the thicker pair over them. I have also heard of some people using knee-high nylon stockings as the thinner pair. Socks can also be worn on the hands for additional warmth.

The paracord is to have some lightweight, but strong, rope on hand. Some uses include tying up a tarp, securing items to a pack, and using it as a line to dry wet clothes.

The emergency radio is a battery-operated radio that can get regular radio stations. Most news radio stations will try to continue to operate for as long as possible during an emergency or disaster. Having the radio will help you know what is happening.

Although this is not listed, a two-way radio is a valuable emergency communication device. It doesn't rely on cellular towers or networks. There are several options, but the ones with the best range and power require licensing to use.

Having a second flashlight, along with extra batteries, in the vehicle provides you with a backup light. The best option is for the flashlight in your expanded kit and in the vehicle to use the same size batteries.

The tarp is a lightweight shelter option. The smallest recommendation is a 5 ft x 7 ft tarp. Personally, I would not go bigger than a 10 ft x 12 ft, as the increase in size isn't worth the extra weight. The goal is to help keep you dry. The smaller tarp could be held over the head or wrapped around the body to help you stay dry while you walk.

A cheap emergency blanket should be part of your basic kit, but a higher quality one should be in your vehicle. While an emergency blanket can be used as a tarp, I'd prefer both the blanket and tarp. My plan, if I must sleep outdoors without a tent and sleeping bag, is to have the tarp as a shelter, a blanket around me, and an emergency blanket over that.

The toilet paper in the vehicle kit is to supplement (and replace) what you should already have.

Other personal hygiene items, such as feminine products, should also be included. They may or may not be needed, but they can be left or even discarded if they aren't needed. It's better to have the option and not need it than to wish you had it.

An item I started adding a couple of years ago was instant heat packs. These packs can last up to eight hours. Some are small enough to put inside gloves. Others are for putting in shoes/socks. I also have some larger ones for warming the body. I have a package of these in the vehicles and in our emergency kits.

The first aid kit in your vehicle should be much more complete than the smaller ones of your basic and expanded get-home kits.

Table 25 is a recommended list from the Red Cross for a first aid kit for a family of four.

Table 25: Red Cross suggested first aid kit, retrieved from http://www.redcross.org/get-help/how-to-prepare-for-emergencies/anatomy-of-a-first-aid-kit.

2 absorbent compress dressings (5 x 9 inches)	25 adhesive bandages (assorted sizes)
1 adhesive cloth tape (10 yards x 1 inch)	Antibiotic ointment
5 antiseptic wipe packets	2 packets of aspirin (81 mg each)
1 breathing barrier (for rescue breathing)	1 instant cold pack
2 pairs of nonlatex gloves	2 hydrocortisone ointment packets (1 gram each)
Scissors	1 roller bandage, 3 inches wide
1 roller bandage, 4 inches wide	5 sterile gauze pads (3 x 3 inches)
5 sterile gauze pads (4 x 4 inches)	Oral thermometer (non-mercury/non-glass)
2 triangular bandages	Tweezers
First aid instruction booklet	Emergency blanket

Personally, I would not limit quantities to the amounts listed here but would use those amounts as minimums.

Other items you should consider for your first aid kit are listed in table 26.

Table 26: Possible additions to the first aid kit.

Butterfly bandages/adhesive wound closures	Ibuprofen and/or acetaminophen
Elastic wrap	Antihistamine
Finger splints	Insect sting/bite relief treatment
Hemostatic (blood-stopping) gauze	Safety pins
Oval eye pads	Lubricating eye drops
Benzalkonium chloride (BZK) antiseptic wipes	Cotton-tipped swabs
Liquid bandage	Splints
Blister treatment (e.g., moleskin)	Duct tape
Petroleum jelly	Breathing barrier (surgical mask)
Calamine lotion	Anti-diarrhea medication
Turkey baster or bulb syringe for flushing wounds	Eyewash solution
Super glue	Aloe vera gel

It should be apparent that if you include all the listed first aid items, your kit would add considerable mass to your get-home equipment. Keeping a comprehensive first aid kit in your car is a good idea but depending on the distance you need to walk and terrain you'll be covering, you may not need everything.

Some additional items, listed in table 27, are worth considering for keeping in a vehicle. These are particularly useful if you expect to not get home for a few days or you can't leave your current location.

Table 27: Possible additions for the emergency kit in your vehicle.

72-hour kit Change of clothes Sleeping bag Small axe and/or survival knife Paper map (& compass) Small tent	Cold weather gear (e.g., beanie-type hat, gloves, sweater/pullover, waterproof jacket) Small towel Toothbrush/toothpaste Mouthwash Soap

These additions are, like everything in the lists, suggestions. Some of the suggestions may raise questions, so let's go through these items.

A 72-hour kit could be useful as a get-home supplement. You could have a 96-hour kit, but the focus of the vehicle kit is for a vehicle emergency and getting home, which hopefully shouldn't take more than a day or two. As with other food items, be aware that the extreme heat that can build up in your vehicle could affect the nutritional quality of food. To mitigate against this, replace the emergency food in your vehicle regularly.

While a change of clothes isn't usually a necessity, if you wear dress clothes to work (skirts, dresses, or dress pants), these are not the most comfortable, or practical, for a trek home on foot. Good, comfortable hiking-type clothes will make your walk home more bearable, especially in inclement weather.

If you expect your trek home to be overnight, a sleeping bag will help you through the night. Alternatively, you could stick with an emergency blanket and rough it for the night. I keep a sleeping bag in my car more so if I need to sleep overnight in the car, or nearby, I have a more comfortable option.

A small axe and/or a survival knife is a valuable tool for getting wood cut for a fire. Besides other tool-oriented uses, these can also be useful in a defensive situation.

A paper map and compass are the old-school method of finding your way. If the GPS on your phone, or other device, isn't working, what's your backup? The downside is you need to know how to use a map and compass, otherwise it may not be useful to you. Unless you're a long way from home, a compass may not be necessary, as you can probably find your way home. The map is helpful in identifying landmarks if you need help knowing where you are and locating alternate roads if the primary roads are unusable.

Like a sleeping bag, a small tent is useful if you need to spend the night outdoors. It does add weight if you need to walk a long distance, so you might just stick with the emergency blanket and maybe a tarp or tube tent for some shelter.

Cold weather gear should include a beanie-type hat, gloves, sweater or pullover, and a waterproof jacket. The sweater or pullover should be a non-cotton material, such as fleece or wool, which can help keep you warm even if it gets wet. The jacket doesn't need to be a heavy winter coat. The pullover and jacket combine as layered clothing, so you can use one or the other if you get too warm.

The small towel, toothbrush, toothpaste, and mouthwash are more for personal hygiene. The towel could be used for other purposes, such as a sling, bandage, or for covering and protecting your head and neck from sunburn. Not cleaning your mouth for a few days won't kill you, but a clean mouth can help boost your morale. If I haven't brushed my teeth for a day, my mouth, especially the teeth, start to bother me.

Soap is a much better option for cleaning your hands than hand sanitizer, but it requires water, which may not be available. If there is water, my hands prefer soap, as sanitizer tends to dry them out more.

The 10 Get-Home Kit Essential Systems

For those who just want a single get-home bag/kit instead of multiple parts, you may want to use my 10 Get-Home Kit Essential Systems as a guide.

The original 10 Essentials list, which is geared towards being outdoors, appeared in print in the third edition of *Mountaineering: The Freedom of the Hills* (January 1974). The original list included a map, a compass, sunglasses and sunscreen, extra clothing, a headlamp/flashlight, first aid supplies, a fire starter, matches, a knife, and extra food.

Over the years, the list has been modified and updated by various outdoor organizations, and in 2003 the list was updated to a "systems" approach to keep up with newer equipment. The 10 systems you should have with you when you're out in nature are:

1. Navigation—topographic and assorted maps and magnetic compass, optional GPS and altimeter
2. Sun protection—sunglasses, sunscreen for skin and lips, hat, clothing for sun protection

3. Insulation—hat, gloves, jacket, extra clothing for coldest possible weather for the current season
4. Illumination—Flashlight, headlamp, extra batteries; LED bulb is preferred for extended battery life
5. First aid supplies—also includes insect repellent
6. Fire—matches in a waterproof container, lighter
7. Repair kit and tools—multi-tool, knife, scissors, pliers, screwdriver, duct tape, trowel/shovel, cable ties
8. Nutrition—1 extra day of emergency food
9. Hydration—2 extra quarts for an extra (emergency) day
10. Emergency shelter—bivouac sack, space blanket, plastic tube tent, insulated sleeping pad, tarp, jumbo trash bags

In addition to these items, some recommended supplements include portable water purification and signaling devices (such as a whistle, mobile phone, satellite phone, two-way radio, and unbreakable signal mirror).

All these 10 essential systems, along with the recommended supplements, could be useful in a get-home bag. However, some may not be needed. Remember, you should be traversing terrain that is at least a little familiar, even if you have probably never walked it, and you may not be in a wilderness environment.

Take into consideration what terrain and environment you will most likely need to trek through on your way home, and factor in the time it will take to make the journey, remembering to at least double your expected time.

Combining items from the earlier get-home bag lists and using the 10 Essentials list for outdoors as a guide, we can create a 10 Get-Home Kit Essential Systems.

Table 28: The 10 Get-Home Kit Essential Systems.

1.	Insulation—walking shoes or hiking boots, extra socks, jacket and/or pullover, rain poncho, beanie hat, gloves
2.	Emergency shelter—emergency blanket, small tarp
3.	Illumination—LED flashlight (headlamp is best) and extra batteries
4.	First aid kit—adhesive bandages, moleskin, acetaminophen and/or ibuprofen, hand sanitizer, gauze pads, antibiotic ointment, tweezers, prescription medication, N95 face mask, nitrile (non-latex) gloves, medical tape, disinfecting ointment, insect repellent
5.	Fire—matches, lighter, fire starter
6.	Nutrition—at least one extra day's worth: granola, energy bars, MRE-type food
7.	Hydration—2 quart (min.) of water, purification tablets, purification/filter
8.	Navigation—map and compass, optional GPS
9.	Sun protection—hat, sunglasses, bandana, lip balm, sunscreen
10.	Tools and other items—whistle, multi-tool, duct tape, cash, paracord (50–100 ft), toilet paper, small trowel/shovel

Like other lists, this list is all recommendations. Add or replace items to meet your needs.

Let's go through each system.

Insulation

Insulation is the protection your body needs from the elements. Walking shoes or hiking boots are listed for those who do not normally wear shoes conducive to long walks or hiking. For most people who will be traversing urban or fairly flat rural areas, walking shoes should be sufficient.

The extra socks can be used if the ones you're using get wet. Or, you could use them as extra insulation for your feet in a cold environment. They could even be used for your hands if fingers start getting cold, but hopefully you have gloves for that. You could even use them as a water filter—to filter out debris—prior to boiling. And, if you don't usually wear socks, your feet will probably thank you if you need to walk a long distance.

The jacket and/or pullover, rain poncho, beanie hat, and gloves are for inclement weather. Having both the jacket and pullover allows you to layer your clothing as well. The beanie hat will help keep your head warm, which will help the rest of your body feel warmer as well.

On the topic of hats and keeping your body warm, it is a myth that we "lose 40 to 45 percent of body heat" through the head. Several studies, including an article from 2008 on the *British Medical Journal* website (Collins, 2008), prove that body heat is lost fairly proportionately across the entire body's surface area. The reality is, we only lose 7–10% of our body heat through the head.

However, due to the concentration of blood vessels in the head, we are generally more susceptible to sensing temperature changes in our head than in other parts of the body. Blood vessels in our ears, nose, cheeks, hands, and feet also help control the cooling and warming of the body. So, while heat loss may be fairly proportionate across the body, our ability to feel warmer or cooler can be greatly affected by these areas of the body.

Emergency shelter

In the event of adverse weather, it may be better to hunker down under some protection. While a rain poncho may work, staying dry under a tarp might be better.

A good quality emergency blanket can act as a small tarp or can help you keep warm.

Illumination

Headlamps are the best source of light, as they allow you to keep your hands free. At night, lights can also act as signaling devices.

First aid kit

The items in table 28 are what I would start with in assembling a basic first aid kit. Modify this as you need to.

Insect repellent is included in this system, as it has the potential to help keep you from getting sick from an insect bite.

Fire

Warmth, protection, and boiling water are the three biggest reasons to have a fire. Some of your food may require adding heated water.

Nutrition

You should have at least one extra day's worth of food, in addition to what you anticipate for travel. If you estimate on ten hours of travel, it would be wise to have food for two days: one for the anticipated day of travel plus one extra day's worth.

Examples of this food can be freeze-dried or dehydrated meals, or non-cook items such as extra granola and energy bars, dried nuts and fruits, or jerky. Food that requires cooking will require extra time to prepare.

Remember, if you keep your get-home bag in a place that can get hot (such as your vehicle in the summer) you will need to replace your food regularly.

Hydration

Ideally, we should have one gallon of water available for each day. But, carrying a gallon of water adds weight, not to mention two gallons. Hydration packs make it easier to carry large amounts of water. I have a couple that carry about three quarts each. But these may not be as practical as having at least one water bottle.

As mentioned earlier, I like to have at least one of my water bottles be metal so I can boil water in it, if the need arises.

Since it may not be practical to carry enough water for the trek home, you should have a couple of options to disinfect and/or purify water along the way. Besides boiling as an option, I have water purification tablets and a lightweight water purification/filter straw in my get-home kit.

With purification tablets, I can refill and treat one bottle of water while drinking out of the other. This worked for me on a 25-plus-mile hike I did in one day many years ago.

Navigation

Don't plan on your cell phone, with its GPS, to be working—at least not reliably. Depending on the phone, the GPS may or may not work accurately without a data connection. Even if the GPS does work, it's likely that the maps on your phone won't (unless you keep a cached, offline copy of the map).

A compass is useful if you're disoriented and need your bearings. But, to be of real use, you also need a topographical map.

However, if you are primarily in an urban and suburban environment, a topographical map may not be as useful as a good street map, something where you can identify alternate routes to your destination. Even with a street map, which are usually oriented with "north" at the top, a compass can help you identify which direction you're looking at and where to look for landmarks.

Sun protection

Getting sunburned can ruin your day, especially when it's a second-degree burn. The hat, sunglasses, lip balm, and sunscreen are all to help you avoid that misery. Besides burn protection, a hat and sunglasses also help reduce eye strain as a result of the sun's glare. The bandana can be used to help cover your neck and ears, but it also has a lot of other uses, some of which we previously discussed.

When it comes to sun protection, most people only consider sunburns as the hazard you're trying to protect yourself from. However, while a sunburn can be serious, a more serious threat is heat exhaustion, followed by the life-threatening condition of heat stroke. It is vitally important that you do everything you can to not get overheated and to keep hydrated.

Keeping hydrated involves drinking enough water. If you feel thirsty, you are already getting dehydrated.

Preventing overheating involves protecting yourself from the heat of the sun, drinking plenty of water, and not overexerting your physical capacities.

Tools and other items

The 10 Essentials identifies this system as the Repair Kit and Tools. I decided to call it "Tools and Other Items" because it's the catch-all system. A good multi-tool should have a knife, pliers, and screwdrivers. Duct tape is the universal repair tool. Additional items I would add are a whistle (for signaling), cash, paracord, toilet paper, and a small folding shovel.

Some may balk at including cash, but it may be the "tool" you need to purchase additional supplies during your trek home.

School

For this discussion, school refers to elementary and secondary schools.

A college or university environment can be treated more like a work scenario if you travel to attend your classes. Keeping the very basics with you can help you in an emergency. If you have a vehicle, you can keep more equipment and supplies in the car instead of dragging them to all your classes.

Most public school districts have the policy to keep children, especially young children, at the school in the event of an emergency, until a parent or authorized adult can pick them up.

However, policies vary among schools and school districts, so it's best to contact your child's school to find out what their policy is.

Young children should not walk home alone, particularly in the aftermath of an emergency or disaster. You, or an authorized adult, should expect to go and pick up the child from their school.

Depending on the school, as well as the age and maturity of the youth, an older child may be permitted to walk home. However, there are various factors to consider, such as the distance to home and the child's ability to navigate home in the stressful aftermath of an emergency or disaster.

Whenever possible, it is always best for a parent, or trusted adult, to pick up the child to bring him/her home.

Another consideration is that in many communities, a school will become a designated emergency center. If this is the case, it may be best for the child to remain at the school until it is determined safe to return home.

If you are unable to pick up your child soon after an emergency or natural disaster, and he/she needs to remain at the school for an extended time, you need to have a plan. Some questions should be considered when coming up with an emergency/disaster plan:

- If it takes you a day or longer to get home, who will get the child?
- How are you going to communicate with the school regarding your situation and the child's?
- Does your spouse also have a long trek home?
- Is there a trusted adult who can pick up the child and take him/her to their home until you can return?
- Would the child be better off at the school, especially if it will be an emergency center?
- Does your child have any special medical, physical, or dietary needs?
- Should the child have any kind of emergency or get-home kit?

The biggest problem with having any kind of emergency or get-home kit in your child's backpack, or with them, is it probably won't be there when it's needed. Kids, especially younger ones, have the tendency to get into things. They're curious and are learning, but they have a harder time understanding why something, such as emergency preparedness, may be important.

Do you try to train them to not get into something unless it's an emergency? Then you need to clearly define what an "emergency" is. Even then, you may discover the child's interpretation of an emergency is not what you thought you clearly explained. Do you make the kit "child resistant" so only an adult can open it?

If you do opt to have any kind of emergency kit with the child, it will need to be checked regularly, at least monthly. Any emergency food will be likely be eaten. Adhesive bandages will get used. Water will get drunk. Flashlights will get lost or won't work.

Like adults, emergencies are stressors for children. But children often take emotional cues from adults, especially trusted adults. If the adults are stressed, children will likely be stressed as well. However, if the adults are calm and collected, the children usually won't be as stressed.

Teaching your children about emergencies, disasters, and what to do can give them confidence when their normal is suddenly turned upside down with an earthquake or other disaster. Having a small emergency kit with them can help boost their confidence, particularly if you've worked with them on what to do.

Chapter 13
Where to Get Emergency Stuff

I like to consider myself a practical and frugal prepper. I'm reluctant to spend money. Sometimes it takes months before I actually make a certain purchase. Over the years there have been several sources I generally go to for equipment.

The obvious: retailers

I don't like to pay full price if I can avoid it. If I suspect something will go on sale in the next month or two, and I don't need the item now, it's not unusual for me to put off a purchase.

That said, sometimes items don't go on sale, and sometimes you just need the item now.

I have made purchases online and in traditional brick-and-mortar stores. Generally, I prefer the traditional stores so I can touch the item(s) and take them home immediately, if I'm ready to make the purchase.

Don't overlook freebies and clearance

At least three or four times a year, I attend either a conference or some type of "fair" where there is a vendor area. Many vendors give away various freebies. The truth is most of these freebies are cheap advertisements. Some are just gimmicks. However, there are some that are not just worth taking home but getting extras to add to your get-home and/or emergency kits.

Here's a list of some of the free stuff I've gotten from various vendors and that I've added to get-home bags, vehicle kits, and emergency kits:

- Beanie hat
- USB battery charger/power bank
- Sanitizer wipes
- Hand sanitizer in small bottles and spray bottles

- Anti-diarrheal medication (two tablets per pack)
- Acetaminophen packets (two tablets per pack)
- Ibuprofen packets (two tablets per pack)
- Insect repellent wipes
- Small carabiners (useful for clipping various objects)
- Lip balm
- Sunscreen
- Sunglasses (these are cheap, but they'd be better than nothing, and I got some for the kids)
- Playing cards (keep kids or adults from getting bored)
- Colored pencils
- Notepads
- Pens
- Adhesive bandages (in a small dispenser)
- Face mask (for rescue breathing)
- Baseball-style cap
- T-shirts
- Socks
- Metal water bottles
- Small blanket (throw)
- Flashlights
- Granola bars and other snack foods
- Bottles of water
- Toothbrush
- Flossers

Using just what I've gotten for free, I can easily assemble most of the basics of a get-home bag. The rest of the items of a basic kit wouldn't cost too much.

Sometimes local retail merchants have marketing promotions to bring people into their stores. With these promotions I've gotten a couple of small first aid kits. Granted, these kits would've been overpriced had I paid for them, but they're certainly worth "free."

I've also taken advantage of occasional promotions for emergency supplies. For example, I got another free first aid kit and whistle/combination device. I would not have paid for any of these items, but they're better than nothing. The only way they'd be better is if I were paid to take them.

Regarding the whistle/combination device. It was marketed as a "survival tool" and has a whistle, temperature gauge, compass, flashlight, matches, mirror, and magnifying glass (plastic). While several of the items on the tool are useful (whistle, mirror, magnifying glass, matches), this is a perfect example of why cheap is not always good. Here are a few problems with the tool:

- The flashlight stopped working and uses a button battery, which is not easy to replace.
- The temperature gauge is inaccurate.
- The magnetic compass is unreliable.

Be wary of any small magnetic compass—sometimes referred to as a button compass—especially those attached to another device. I have yet to see one that is accurate, at least on any consistent basis. The following image (figure 28) shows a small compass (part of a "survival tool") compared to a higher-quality (and much more expensive) compass. This particular compass isn't even consistently inaccurate. It not only fails to point to magnetic north on a regular basis but also varies from 20 to 90 degrees off. Even if it were accurate, these small compasses are lousy for navigating. The only thing they do is make you think you're prepared, but they could make things worse for you if you were to trust them for navigation.

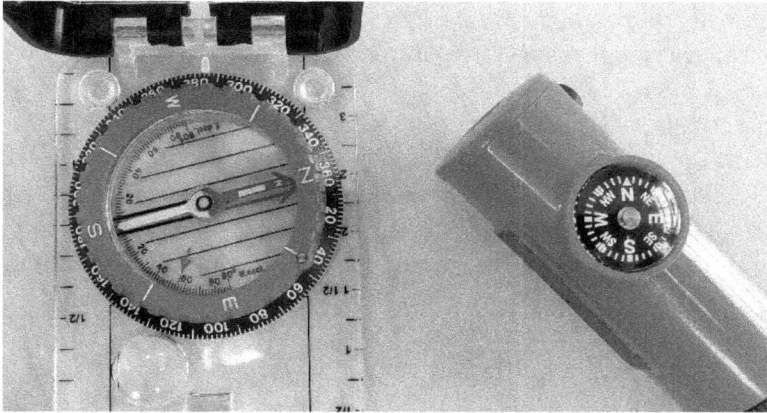

Figure 28: Compass comparison. You can see how far off the small compass is compared to the higher quality one by looking at where the "N" is pointing.

If I shake the "survival tool" compass several times and then lay it completely flat, it sometimes will almost point to magnetic north. But you wouldn't know when it was accurate if you don't have another compass to compare it to.

Unless you have money to burn (and if you do, you can send some my way), be mindful when you shop for emergency equipment. I like to review, upgrade, add, and/or replace winter items when retail stores start clearing out winter gear. Depending on how the weather and season behaves, I've seen winter items (headbands, balaclavas, gloves, etc.) start getting marked down by the end of January. By March I can often find items marked down 50 percent or more. Sizes and types are usually limited, but in an emergency, I'm not going to care about the latest model or a trendy-looking item.

At the local retailers I frequent, from December into January (and possibly February) I can sometimes find camping and hunting items marked down. Choices are limited, but the prices are often better than Black Friday specials.

And that's another time to look: Black Friday and other holiday specials. I've gotten some great discounts on water purification pumps and straws from Black Friday specials.

A "source" for some hygiene items

Another thing I do is when I stay at a hotel (which I usually do a couple times a year), I'll take the small bottles of shampoo, conditioner, lotion, mouthwash, and bars of soap. I think some people look down on this, but I paid for the room. Plus, room service will end up throwing these items out, so I might as well keep them. My preference is to have unopened items in my emergency supplies. Opened and partially used items will be kept in my overnight bags or camping supplies until I either throw them out or use them up.

If I have a multi-night hotel stay, I will open the items to use on the first day and then put them in my bags before I leave for my meetings in the morning. Room service usually replenishes the items, and I'll then take the unopened items for my kits, while I continue to use the items from the first day.

Used but still useful

While I certainly don't recommend getting everything used, don't overlook thrift stores, yard sales, and classified ads for acquiring good, gently used, or nearly new equipment.

We have gotten some free clothing from yard sales just wanting to get rid of stuff, usually after several hours of slow sales. In an emergency evacuation (or just as extra clothing in a vehicle), I'm more interested in comfort and functionality than wearing something fashionable or trendy.

Are you buying new clothes? Consider the clothing you are replacing and whether the "old" clothes would be suitable for an emergency or vehicle kit.

The trick is to keep in mind what items you need and would like to get. You also need to know what you have and what you would like to replace it with, if you get the chance. This is part of a preparation mindset and understanding that preparation is not a once-and-you're-done deal. It doesn't require a lot of time, but it does require some effort, a little bit of time, and at least some awareness of what you have, need, and would like to improve.

Chapter 14
Emergency Plans

Plans are needed so you have an idea of what to do or what needs to be done. Rehearsing the plan does two things. First, it provides a type of "muscle memory," where you learn to act without thinking about what you need to do.

Second, it provides a psychological benefit in that, while the emergency/disaster is real, the action is not new. This is part of mental preparedness.

Here are some of the considerations emergency plans should cover:

- home evacuation, such as in the event of a fire
- shelter-in-place options
- safe places in the home
- what to do if you can't get home immediately after a disaster
- types of disasters, focusing on the ones most likely for your area
- emergency communications, including calling 911 on the phone and alternative communications, like a two-way radio.
- how to use emergency items

Practice drills with family

Why do sports teams practice formation drills or plays? Why do martial artists repeat katas? It is because rehearsal and practice develop muscle memory, a response that is almost subconscious. Musicians similarly rehearse music so they can play without thinking about where every note is.

This same kind of muscle memory is why you need to practice emergency drills with your household.

Most likely the children have fire drills and other simulated exercises at school. Your employer may have drills as well. But what about your home? We are doing a disservice to our families, and others in our home, if we don't create, review, and practice what should be done in various emergencies.

Besides giving everyone an opportunity to review and physically execute what should be done, this type of practice does a couple of other things.

First, with small children, practice creates familiarity. So, in the case of an actual event, they will know what to do, and they will feel more comfortable and confident when things aren't normal.

Second, emergency drills also help psychologically. Kind of like getting your mind prepared.

When planning and practicing these drills at home, make sure everyone has access to flashlights, just like they would need in the event of a true emergency. In our home, I've replaced a few outlet covers with emergency LED nightlights. Normally they are nightlights. In the case of a power outage, the nightlights turn on.

Home evacuation

If you home is multiple stories, consider how those on the higher floors will get out if the main exits are impassable. Emergency chain ladders can be bought for the upper-story bedrooms.

What about basements? What are the windows and window wells like? How would you get out if the main exit (up the stairs and out of the house) is unusable? I've seen some older homes with such small basement windows that I doubt many people would be able to get out through them.

Draw up a plan and go through it with those in your home. Designate safe places outside of the home to gather and account for everyone.

Shelter-in-place plan

This scenario probably doesn't need to rehearsed, but it does need to be discussed. Some of the items to talk about:

- What is expected, such as tasks that will need to be performed on a regular basis, of each person?
- What will be done without specific utilities?
- How will water be treated?
- How will food be prepared?

Safe places

Where are the safe places in and around the home? Emergency plans and drills should identify these safe places.

Types of disasters

Part of your preparations needs to include discussions about the various types of natural disasters and emergencies that are most likely for your area.

For our home, the main disasters we focus on are

- fire;
- storms, such as thunderstorms, excessive rain, hail, blizzards;
- flooding; and
- earthquakes.

Some disasters are unlikely, or even just an extremely rare occurrence. For example, we are far enough inland that if a hurricane reached us, nearly half the nation would be in trouble. Similarly, a tsunami would inundate half the continent if it reached us. So, these aren't disasters we prepare for. Tornados are an extremely rare occurrence in my area, so they aren't a normal disaster topic for us. We are also far enough from the mountains that landslides aren't a consideration. There are also no volcanoes that are an immediate threat to us.

However, while we may not have certain disaster threats, many of the preparations we make are easily transferable to other disasters. And we will talk about other disasters.

When an earthquake happens

Since this book is primarily about earthquakes and earthquake preparedness, the three things to do when an earthquake happens are

- drop,
- cover, and
- hold on.

In a truly violent earthquake, you could easily get knocked down, and injured, so dropping to your hands and knees is the first thing to do. Having been in a big earthquake and exited the house during the quake, and having seen lots of earthquake videos, I know it is possible to walk when the earth is shaking. But it is safer to not be moving when the ground is moving under you. If you're in bed, it's safer to stay put.

Cover is to protect your head, neck, and entire body, if possible. Normally the recommendation is to get under a sturdy table or desk. Without this cover, get down near an interior wall or low-lying furniture that won't fall over, and use your arms and hands to cover your head and neck the best you can.

Hold on to your shelter. If it moves, move with it.

If you can, particularly during the early moments of the shaking, move away from glass (windows), hanging objects, shelves, bookcases, and other large furniture that could fall. Be aware of potentially falling objects from light fixtures, ceilings, cabinets that could swing open, and bricks from fireplaces or chimneys.

If you're in the kitchen when an earthquake happens, and the stove is on, quickly turn the stove off and then take cover.

If you are outside when an earthquake happens, move away from buildings, trees, power lines, or anything else might fall on you, if it's possible. Generally speaking, outside is safer than being indoors during an earthquake, if you're away from buildings and anything that might fall on you.

If you're driving when an earthquake strikes, pull over to a clear location, stop, and stay in your car (with your seatbelt on) until the shaking stops. When the shaking stops, continue driving with extreme caution and avoid bridges or ramps that may have been damaged.

Great ShakeOut

The Great ShakeOut drills are state- or region-wide drills designed to get the population involved with an earthquake drill. For more information, including how to register yourself or your organization for participation, go to www.shakeout.org.

The main purpose of a Great ShakeOut is to remind you, along with a lot of other people, what to do in an earthquake.

Communication

How are you going to communicate with your family, whether it's with those who live in the same home as you or in another location? For most, the answer is their cell phone. But in a natural disaster, cell phones may not work. Sometimes text messaging works, but what if cell towers and electricity are out?

Normal landline phones (the normal phones, not the internet/VOIP phones) use power over the phone lines, so they may still work even if the electricity to the rest of the house is out. But, if your landline phone requires power, probably because it's a cordless phone and its base needs to be plugged in, then the phone probably won't be working.

Internet may not be working. While the internet may be through the phone line (DSL), cable, or fiber and those lines may be good, routers and modems require electricity to run. No power, no VOIP phone, no internet.

If you're at work and can't contact anyone through your cell phone, landline phone, email, or other messaging service, how do you communicate with your family?

Radio is the alternative most people turn to. Some will get an amateur radio license and radio. Others will use cheaper two-way radios, if the distance isn't too far.

If you use two-way radios, be aware that some channels (frequencies) require a license to use.

Another option is a satellite phone, although the high cost keeps these out of most people's supplies.

Use of emergency items

While you do not need to use anything from your emergency packs during a practice drill, you and those in your household need to be familiar with the contents of the emergency packs and how to use the various items. An actual emergency is not the time to be reading instructions.

Take time with your family, and other members of your household, to regularly (at least twice a year) go through your emergency packs and equipment.

As you go through the items, be sure to do the following:

- Make sure everyone knows what each item is and how it is used. If someone doesn't know how to use something, take time to do some training. If you're not sure how to use something, ask someone who does. The internet is great for how-to videos, but personal, hands-on training is more valuable.

- Check expiration dates of perishable items, like foods and medicines. Replace as needed.

- Check that flashlights, generators, and other items are working.

- Check fire extinguishers to make sure they do not need to be replaced or recharged.

- Check that clothing and size-dependent items still fit. For example, we have a toddler who needs diapers, so we need to check that we have the right size in the kit (I like to have the next size up until the child is wearing size 5, which is about the time the kids are getting potty-trained).

- If you store any fuel, it may need to be replaced.

Chapter 15
What to Do Now?

If you're feeling a little overwhelmed, that's natural. Remember, preparedness is not a one-time act. While you can, if you have time and money, get all the supplies you might need in a single push, you really can't be prepared without continual effort. It takes time and a little regular effort to really become prepared.

The good news is, if you make little efforts, over time you will become better prepared.

And, the best time to begin those efforts is well before you expect an emergency or disaster.

Preparing for an earthquake: some ideas

Obviously, the sooner you are prepared with food, water, and other supplies, the better. However, time and money are limiting factors for most of us.

Again, being prepared is not a once-and-you're-done thing. Even if you can purchase everything you could possibly need, you still need to regularly evaluate what you have, determine what you need and what should be replaced, consider better options and other additions, and implement changes appropriate to your situation.

A great example of the need to regularly re-evaluate your preparation is children. As they grow, you need to make sure clothing is updated. When all our kids get out of diapers, diapering items will be removed from our kits.

The next few sections give some suggested actions to help you get started over the next weeks and months. Keep in mind that these are not complete lists, but they're meant to be a springboard towards becoming better prepared.

In the next week

These are the minimum goals to accomplish during the next seven days:

- Get water storage for three days.

- Get easy-to-prepare food for three days.
- Identify utilities and learn how to shut off all utilities—gas, water, and electricity.
- Assemble a basic get-home kit.
- Secure pictures, shelves, and other potential hazards that could fall onto beds.

The water storage is water for drinking, use in food prep, and basic hygiene. You need about one gallon per person per day. This is ready-to-drink water, not water that you need to disinfect/purify before using.

In the next four weeks

During the first week, work on the previous list. Then, over the next three weeks, the following should be included in your preparedness goals:

- Increase water storage to one week's worth.
- Add at least one option for water purification/disinfection. The easiest option is either boiling or chlorination.
- Expand your get-home kit by adding an expanded kit and/or a vehicle kit.
- Build up your food supply to one week of easy-to-prepare/minimal cooking food.
- Start assembling 96-hour kits for everyone in the household, focusing first on a food and water kit.
- Start getting copies of important/vital documentation.
- Create a basic emergency plan for your home.

Goals for ninety days

For the first month, the previous two lists should be completed. Then over the following two months, work on the following preparations:

- Increase your food storage to a two-week food supply.
- Increase your water to a two-week storage.
- Assemble vehicle emergency items, including those to supplement your get-home bag.

- Secure other shelves, pictures, and items in your home that may fall in an earthquake. Week one was focused on the bedrooms; now secure the rest of the house.
- Gather copies of all-important identification and vital documentation.
- Complete 96-hour kits for everyone in the household, including:
    o All sub-kits: Food and Water Kit, Hygiene Kit, First Aid Kit, Tool Kit, Clothing.
    o Some items in the sub-kits are easily shared among the household, so only one of those items would be needed for everyone. For example, one radio could be shared among four people, but each person should have their own N95 dust mask.

Remember, you should already have a week's worth of food and water by the end of the first month. By adding at least one additional day's worth of food and water each week over the next two months, you should have added at least another week's worth of food and water by day 90.

Additional preparations over the next year

After only three months, you should have a good start on some preparations. Keep it up, slowly expanding and improving your preparations. By the end of a year, you should have the following additional preparation goals met:

- 30-day food storage
- 30-day water storage
- a second (or third) water purification (filter, tablets, etc.) and disinfecting option
- secured water heater
- completed a first aid & CPR class (certification is great, but at least get some training)

There are a lot of other areas you can work on, but the big focus is to make sure you've got all the basics covered.

Don't forget specific needs/considerations

During your preparations, don't forget to consider any special needs that you and/or those in your household require, such as the following:

- prescription medication(s) and/or allergy medications
- small children—diapers & wipes, games, toys, special toy/blanket/stuffed animal
- infants—diapers, wipes, changes of clothes, burp cloths, bibs, sippy cups, formula
- older children—games, toys, give them responsibilities/assignments
- pets—food, water

Involving others and a caution

One of the problems I have with a lot of "prepper" sites and information is the assumption that you will be on your own. While I am not discounting the possibility of a survivalist situation, where you are on your own, it is more likely that others will be involved.

It would be great to be able to be ready for anything and to know how to do everything. But the reality is, that isn't a practical possibility. There is a greater chance of survival if you have joined forces with others who are similarly prepared and who have other experience and knowledge you don't.

However, you should not share details about your preparations with anybody outside of your own household. Even within your home, you may need to limit what is shared. Young children tend to not think, and some are too willing to share information that shouldn't be public knowledge. It's not that it should be a secret, but it can be difficult to know who you can really trust in a long-term emergency or disaster situation. You also don't want to be labelled as a "prepper" or "doomsday prepper," as that could give you unwanted attention.

Before I go on, I am not suggesting you share supplies. I am a believer in every family being ready and prepared to take care of their own. You need to have food, water, shelter, and whatever other supplies you will need. In the event of an emergency, you don't want to be trying to decide who gets what.

Let's imagine that you, through hard work, diligence, and sacrifice, manage to scrounge, gather, and store enough food and supplies to last a year. At some point, you (or someone in your household) freely shares this information with others in the neighborhood. Maybe you're proud of what you're accomplishing and the sense of satisfaction and peace that comes with being prepared, and you want to share that accomplishment and/or encourage others to get better prepared. What can happen?

Two things come to mind. First, your neighbors, who may not be as preparedness minded as you, will immediately realize they could go to you (since you're a good neighbor) and ask for food should the need arise, which means they won't feel the need to prepare for themselves. Or, maybe an unintended person overhears your conversation and makes a mental note that you're a source for food.

The other thing is, in today's world you need to be careful who knows the extent and details of the preparations you make. While your neighbors may be good people, if they happen to talk to the wrong person (especially in an emergency or disaster, where food is scarce), it could put you and your family in danger. Not just the potential theft of your food but also the lives of those in your home should someone come to forcefully take what you have.

In both cases, others are taking advantage of you and the sacrifices you made in time, money, and effort to become prepared. In an emergency or disaster, the unprepared think it's not fair for you to be prepared and that you need to share with them. It doesn't matter if they squandered their time and money and didn't prioritize getting prepared, they will want what you have and believe they deserve it.

I am not telling you to turn people away who need help in the event of an emergency or catastrophe. Being prepared puts you in a place where you can help others, particularly if you can store more than you need. Those of us who are prepared should be willing to help. However, we need to be cautious in exposing our preparations to those who will take advantage of our efforts, and even put our lives at risk.

Now consider a slightly different scenario. What if you, your neighbors, and others have worked together to become better prepared? You have an idea of the various skills and expertise each person has. In the event of emergency, there is already a sense of common purpose. You know who to go to for help with a repair, who can fix things, who has first aid skills, etc. While you might be able to survive on your own, your chances of survival increase when more people are prepared and work together.

It is during the preparing stage that we need to cautiously involve others.

Casual questions can help you identify whether someone is open to preparedness. Maybe a comment about some recent disaster or a recent preparedness initiative.

If they're receptive, you might ask non-probing questions about how they're preparing. You might share some of your short-term preparations but not everything. If the option for further discussion is open, it may be worth pursuing. I've noticed that when someone is prepared, and realizes you're trying to get better prepared and aren't looking for someone to depend on, they are often willing to share their knowledge, experience, and offer advice.

You'll want to identify whether someone is open to preparing and if they've done anything. If they haven't done anything, you might find out why. If they aren't interested and/or haven't done anything towards preparedness, you're not likely to change their mind. It's probably not a good idea to talk to them about all your preparedness efforts.

Sometimes the uninterested person is a spouse or family member. Realize that you probably won't change his or her mind. You may convince them of the need for some minor preparedness if your area is prone to certain hazards. Most people will accept the idea of 72-hour kits, even if they don't have one, but they may not be convinced of the need for long-term preparation efforts or survival situations. Just be ready and have something ready for them as well. When the emergency happens, they will look to you to know what to do.

In a shelter-in-place scenario, it would be most beneficial if you are able to work with others who are similarly prepared.

In an evacuation, you may not have others in your neighborhood, but your evacuation plan should include options of places you could go. Some of those places may be relatives or friends living in a nearby state. Make sure you have already involved those people in your plans before you need to follow your plan.

Chapter 16
The Time to Prepare Is Now

By this point, you should, hopefully, have a better idea of what earthquakes and their related hazards are, along with some examples of where and how destructive a big earthquake can be.

The good news is most people survive an earthquake. Very few are killed by the actual tremor. Most injuries and fatalities are from falling objects and other hazards caused by the earthquake.

The scariest thing about an earthquake is it can strike without warning. And, based on lots of past ruptures, quakes can happen even if a fault isn't visible.

But preparedness helps mitigate fear. I have found that the better prepared you are, especially if you are regularly reviewing and improving your preparations, the less anxiety and fear play a role.

As we've discussed many of the preparations that can be made, I have primarily focused on what I have done in my home and with my family. This doesn't mean I don't have more work to do. Preparation is a continual process. It's a mindset; you are never completely done because being prepared means you try to be ready for whatever life throws at you. And circumstances change. Sometimes change is slow. Other times it's instant. A big part of preparedness is adaptability and flexibility, and you can't be either if you're not continually working to improve, and re-evaluating what you have and what is needed.

It doesn't need to take a lot of time and work. Simple and regular efforts will pay big dividends towards preparedness. Spend a little time every week in preparedness efforts. At times it may feel like you're not getting anywhere very fast, and it may be frustrating to not get prepared quicker. But, look back after a month, then three months, and after a year, and you will see a big difference in your preparedness.

It should also be clear that the preparations in this book are not all-inclusive. That would require an extensive multi-volume series dedicated to preparations, and it would require frequent updates and additions.

Start today with improving your preparations. Remember, while it'd be nice to do, you don't have to get completely prepared immediately. Start small and keep working at it.

Remember, it's better to start getting prepared years in advance than one second too late.

When an earthquake strikes, it's too late to get prepared. There are no early warnings. You don't get a three or more days' notice like you might for a hurricane. If you're lucky and have an early warning system in your area, you might get a 20–30 second heads up—or heads down and covered. Or, you may get a foreshock to wake you up, although the odds are slim you'll get that warning. And you won't know it's a foreshock until the bigger one strikes.

A big problem with procrastinating preparations until the lucky foreshock shakes you to reality is others will be thinking the same thing. It's like the stores before a hurricane strikes. Food and supplies are quickly depleted when people suddenly realize there's an impending disaster and they're not ready.

Savvy people will be prepared before the need arises. That way they can customize their preparations, and they often get better deals. They also have time to become more familiar with their equipment and supplies.

Earthquake risks vary across the country, but the reality is, most places have the risk. And, in most places a Big One is overdue.

The time to get prepared is now.

Appendix A: Kit Lists

The following lists are only suggested items, but they make a good starting point. Items in your kits should be customized to fit your needs and your circumstances.

Basic Get-Home Kit

Walking shoes (if you don't already wear them)
1 quart/liter of water (metal or unbreakable container)
3–6 granola or protein bars
Emergency blanket
Rain poncho
Whistle
Flashlight (headlamp)
Matches/fire starter
Adhesive bandages
Moleskin
Tylenol or ibuprofen
Bandana

Expanded Get-Home Items
(add to your basic kit or keep in a vehicle)

Quality multi-tool
Toilet paper
Hand sanitizer
N95 face mask
Cash
Water purification tablets
Straw-type water filter
Extra batteries (for flashlight)
Duct tape
Sunglasses
Lip balm
Pepper spray?
Prescription medication?
Expanded first aid—
-Gauze pads
-Medical tape
-Tweezers
-Allergy/antihistamine medication
-Antibiotic ointment

Emergency Kit in Vehicle
(additional Get-Home Kit items)

Walking shoes/hiking boots
Water, 2 quarts/liters
Water filter
Rain gear
Leather gloves
Lighter/waterproof matches
Additional food (min. 24 hrs.)
Insect repellant
First aid kit
Sunscreen
Hat (sun protection)
Glasses (if you wear contacts)
Cash

Blanket (wool)
Small shovel
Power bank (for phone)
Extra socks
Paracord (50–100 ft)
Emergency radio
Flashlight & extra batteries
Tarp (5 ft x 7 ft)
Quality emergency blanket
Toilet paper
Other hygiene items
(feminine products)
Instant heat packs

Possible Vehicle Emergency Kit Additions

72-hour kit
Change of clothes
Sleeping bag
Small axe and/or survival
knife
Paper map (& compass)
Small tent

Cold weather gear (e.g.,
beanie-type hat, gloves,
sweater/pullover, waterproof
jacket)
Small towel
Toothbrush/toothpaste
Mouthwash
Soap

First Aid Kit

2 absorbent compress dressings (5 x 9 inches)
1 adhesive cloth tape (10 yards x 1 inch)
5 antiseptic wipe packets

1 breathing barrier (for rescue breathing)
2 pairs of nonlatex gloves

Scissors

1 roller bandage, 4 inches wide
5 sterile gauze pads (4 x 4 inches)
2 triangular bandages
First aid instruction booklet

25 adhesive bandages (assorted sizes)
Antibiotic ointment

2 packets of aspirin (81 mg each)
1 instant cold pack

2 hydrocortisone ointment packets (1 gram each)
1 roller bandage, 3 inches wide
5 sterile gauze pads (3 x 3 inches)
Oral thermometer (non-mercury/non-glass)
Tweezers
Emergency blanket

Additional First Aid Kit Items

Butterfly bandages/adhesive wound closures

Elastic wrap

Finger splints

Hemostatic (blood-stopping) gauze

Oval eye pads

Benzalkonium chloride (BZK) antiseptic wipes

Liquid bandage

Blister treatment (e.g., moleskin)

Petroleum jelly

Calamine lotion

Turkey baster or bulb syringe for flushing wounds

Super glue

Ibuprofen and/or acetaminophen

Antihistamine

Insect sting/bite relief treatment

Safety pins

Lubricating eye drops

Cotton-tipped swabs

Splints

Duct tape

Breathing barrier (surgical mask)

Anti-diarrhea medication

Eyewash solution

Aloe vera gel

The 10 Get-Home Kit Essential Systems

1. Insulation—walking shoes, extra socks, jacket and/or pullover, rain poncho, beanie hat, gloves
2. Emergency Shelter—emergency blanket, small tarp
3. Illumination—LED flashlight (headlamp is best) and extra batteries
4. First aid kit—adhesive bandages, moleskin, acetaminophen and/or ibuprofen, hand sanitizer, gauze pads, antibiotic ointment, tweezers, prescription medication, N95 face mask, nitrile (non-latex) gloves, medical tape, disinfecting ointment, insect repellent
5. Fire—matches, lighter, fire starter
6. Nutrition—at least one extra day's worth: granola, energy bars, MRE-type food.
7. Hydration—2 quarts (min.) of water, purification tablets, purification/filter
8. Navigation—map and compass, optional GPS
9. Sun protection—hat, sunglasses, bandana, lip balm, sunscreen
10. Tools and other items—whistle, multi-tool, duct tape, cash, paracord (50–100 ft), toilet paper, small trowel/shovel

Emergency Equipment in the Vehicle

First aid kit & manual
Hazard reflectors & flares
Waterproof matches
Fire extinguisher (class ABC)
Non-perishable food kit
Bag of sand & shovel
Blanket or sleeping bag
Map
Moist towelettes
Essential medications
Leather work gloves
Tow rope
Tarp

Flashlight & extra batteries
Jumper cables
Candles
Radio & batteries
Bottled water
Tool kit
Pen & paper
Tissue
Plastic bags
Rain poncho or rain gear
Water filter/purifier
Extra clothes & shoes

Appendix B: Earthquake Lists

The following lists are modified from lists on the following Wikipedia pages:
https://en.wikipedia.org/wiki/Lists_of_earthquakes
https://en.wikipedia.org/wiki/List_of_earthquakes_in_the_United_States

Table 29: Largest earthquakes in recorded history.

Rank	Magnitude	Location	Date
1	9.4–9.6	Valdivia, Chile	May 22, 1960
2	9.2	Prince William Sound, Alaska, United States	March 27, 1964
3	9.1–9.3	Indian Ocean, Sumatra, Indonesia	December 26, 2004
4	9.1	Pacific Ocean, Tōhoku region, Japan	March 11, 2011
5	9	Kamchatka, Russian SFSR, Soviet Union	November 4, 1952
6	8.5–9.0 *	Arica, Chile (then Peru)	August 13, 1868
7	8.7–9.2 *	Pacific Ocean, USA and Canada (then claimed by the Spanish Empire and the British Empire)	January 26, 1700
8	8.8 *	Chittagong, Bangladesh (then Kingdom of Mrauk U)	April 2, 1762
9	8.8 *	Sumatra, Indonesia (then part of the Dutch East Indies)	November 25, 1833
10	8.8	Ecuador – Colombia	January 31, 1906
11	8.8	Offshore Maule, Chile	February 27, 2010
12	8.7	Assam, India – Tibet, China	August 15, 1950
13	8.7–9.3 *	Pacific Ocean, Shikoku region, Japan	October 28, 1707

Rank	Magnitude	Location	Date
14	8.7 *	Valparaiso, Chile (then part of the Spanish Empire)	July 8, 1730
15	8.5–9.0	Atlantic Ocean, Lisbon, Portugal	November 1, 1755
16	8.7	Rat Islands, Alaska, United States	February 4, 1965
17	8.6 *	Lima, Peru (then part of the Spanish Empire)	October 28, 1746
18	8.6 *	Oaxaca, Mexico (then part of the Spanish Empire)	March 28, 1787
19	8.6	Andreanof Islands, Alaska, United States	March 9, 1957
20	8.6	Sumatra, Indonesia	March 28, 2005
21	8.6	Indian Ocean, Sumatra, Indonesia	April 11, 2012
22	8.5 *	Valdivia, Chile (then part of the Spanish Empire)	December 16, 1575
23	8.5 *	Arica, Chile (then part of the Spanish Empire)	November 24, 1604
24	8.5 *	Santiago, Chile (then part of the Spanish Empire)	May 13, 1647
25	8.5 *	Concepción, Chile (then part of the Spanish Empire)	May 24, 1751
26	8.5 *	Valparaíso, Chile	November 19, 1822
27	8.5 *	Concepción, Chile	February 20, 1835
28	8.5	Sumatra, Indonesia	February 16, 1861
29	8.5 *	Iquique, Chile (then Peru)	May 9, 1877
30	8.5	Atacama Región, Chile Catamarca Province, Argentina	November 10, 1922
31	8.5	Banda Sea, Indonesia (then part of the Dutch East Indies)	February 1, 1938
32	8.5	Kuril Islands, Russia (USSR)	October 13, 1963

Rank	Magnitude	Location	Date
33	8.5	Sumatra, Indonesia	September 12, 2007
34	8.5 *	Lima, Peru (then part of the Spanish Empire)	October 20, 1687
35	8.5 *	Kamchatka, Russia	October 17, 1737
36	8.5 *	Pacific Ocean, Tōhoku region, Japan	June 15, 1896

* Indicates an estimated magnitude.

It is interesting that the magnitude 7.8 Great Earthquake of San Francisco happened on April 18, 1906, and the Ecuador 8.8 rupture happened on January 31 of that year.

Table 30: Largest earthquakes since the year 2000.

Year	Day-Month	Magnitude	Deaths	Location
2018	23-Jan	7.9	0	United States—Alaska
2017	8-Sep	8.2	98	Mexico
2016	16-Apr	7.8	676	Ecuador
2015	16-Sep	8.3	14	Chile
2014	1-Apr	8.2	6	Chile
2013	24-May	8.3	0	Russia
2012	11-Apr	8.6	10	Indonesia, Indian Ocean
2011	11-Mar	9.1	20,896	Japan
2010	27-Feb	8.8	525	Chile
2009	29-Sep	8.1	192	Samoa
2008	12-May	7.9	87,587	China
2007	12-Sep	8.5	23	Indonesia
2006	15-Nov	8.3	0	Russia
2005	28-Mar	8.6	1,300	Indonesia
2004	26-Dec	9.2	227,898	Indonesia, Indian Ocean
2003	25-Sep	8.3	0	Japan
2002	3-Nov	7.9	0	United States—Alaska

Year	Day-Month	Magnitude	Deaths	Location
2001	23-Jun	8.4	100	Peru

Table 31: List of major earthquakes in the United States of America.

Magnitude	Date	State(s) Affected	Deaths
9.2	March 27, 1964	Alaska	143
8.7–9.2	January 26, 1700	Washington, Oregon, California	Unknown
8.7	February 4, 1965	Alaska	0
8.6	April 1, 1946	Alaska	165
8.6	March 9, 1957	Alaska	0
7.9	January 9, 1857	California	2
7.9	April 2, 1868	Hawaii	77
7.9	April 18, 1906	California	3,000+
7.9	November 3, 2002	Alaska	0
7.9	June 23, 2014	Alaska	0
7.9	January 23, 2018	Alaska	0
7.8	July 9, 1958	Alaska	5 (tsunami)
7.6	February 2, 1975	Alaska	0
7.5–8.0	December 16, 1811	Missouri	Unknown
7.4–7.9	March 26, 1872	California	27
7.3–7.5	August 17, 1959	Montana, Wyoming, Idaho	28+
7.3	July 21, 1952	California	14
7.3	October 28, 1983	Idaho	2

Magnitude	Date	State(s) Affected	Deaths
7.3	June 28, 1992	California	3
7.2	November 29, 1975	Hawaii	2
7.1	October 3, 1915	Nevada	0
7.1	October 16, 1999	California	0
7.1	January 24, 2016	Alaska	0
7.1	November 30, 2018	Alaska	0
7.1	July 5, 2019	California	1
6.9–7.5	December 8, 1812	California	40+
6.9–7.3	August 31, 1886	South Carolina	60
6.9	May 18, 1940	California	9
6.9	October 17, 1989	California	63
6.8	June 29, 1925	California	13
6.8	February 28, 2001	Washington	1
6.7	April 13, 1949	Washington	8
6.7	April 29, 1965	Washington	7
6.7	January 17, 1994	California	57
6.7	October 15, 2006	Hawaii	0
6.5–7.2	April 25–26, 1992	California	0
6.5–7.0	December 14, 1872	Washington	0
6.5–6.7	February 9, 1971	California	58–65
6.5	May 2, 1983	California	0

Magnitude	Date	State(s) Affected	Deaths
6.5	June 28, 1992	California	0
6.5	December 22, 2003	California	2
6.5	January 9, 2010	California	0
6.4	March 10, 1933	California	120
6.3–6.7	October 21, 1868	California	30
6.3	December 4, 1948	California	0
6.2	October 18, 1935	Montana	4
6.2	April 24, 1984	California	0

Appendix C: Websites Referenced

https://en.wikipedia.org/wiki/Richter_magnitude_scale
https://en.wikipedia.org/wiki/Mercalli_intensity_scale
https://en.wikipedia.org/wiki/Fault_(geology)
https://en.wikipedia.org/wiki/Ring_of_Fire
https://en.wikipedia.org/wiki/List_of_volcanoes_in_the_United_States
https://oceanservice.noaa.gov/facts/seiche.html
https://en.wikipedia.org/wiki/Seiche
https://en.wikipedia.org/wiki/Tsunami
https://en.wikipedia.org/wiki/2004_Indian_Ocean_earthquake_and_tsunami
https://en.wikipedia.org/wiki/Teton_Dam
https://en.wikipedia.org/wiki/1983_Borah_Peak_earthquake
https://pnsn.org/outreach/earthquakehazards/surface-rupture
https://www.gns.cri.nz/Home/Learning/Science-Topics/Earthquakes/Earthquake-Hazards
http://www.geo.mtu.edu/UPSeis/hazards.html
https://geomaps.wr.usgs.gov/sfgeo/liquefaction/aboutliq.html
https://depts.washington.edu/liquefy/html/what/what1.html
https://www.shakeout.org/index.html
https://earthquake.usgs.gov
https://www.fema.gov/pdf/library/f&web.pdf
https://en.wikipedia.org/wiki/1935_Helena_earthquake
https://en.wikipedia.org/wiki/1959_Hebgen_Lake_earthquake
https://www.cheatsheet.com/culture/american-cities-sitting-ducks-giant-earthquakes.html/
https://news.nationalgeographic.com/news/2014/07/140717-usgs-earthquake-maps-disaster-risk-science/
https://www.iii.org/article/background-on-earthquake-insurance-and-risk
https://www.kansas.com/news/local/article68729847.html
https://en.wikipedia.org/wiki/Soil_liquefaction
https://pnsn.org/outreach/earthquakehazards/flooding
https://www.hazardouswasteexperts.com/hazardous-materials-in-earthquakes/

http://apps.who.int/iris/bitstream/handle/10665/272391/WHO-CED-PHE-EPE-18.01-eng.pdf?ua=1
https://www.researchgate.net/publication/227958736_Hazardous_Materials_Releases_in_the_Northridge_Earthquake_Implications_for_Seismic_Risk_Assessment
https://d3n8a8pro7vhmx.cloudfront.net/mayorofla/pages/16797/attachments/original/1418064797/Earthquake_report_FINAL_Dec_8_full_report_compressed.pdf?1418064797
https://en.wikipedia.org/wiki/2017_Chiapas_earthquake
https://en.wikipedia.org/wiki/Coulomb_stress_transfer
https://en.wikipedia.org/wiki/2010_Haiti_earthquake
https://www.oxfam.org/en/pressroom/pressreleases/2011-01-06/year-indecision-leaves-haitis-recovery-standstill
https://en.wikipedia.org/wiki/2015_Illapel_earthquake
https://web.archive.org/web/20130513233043/http://www.nationalgeographic.co.jp/news/news_article.php?file_id=20110317002&expand&source=gnews (This page needs to be translated)
https://en.wikipedia.org/wiki/2011_T%C5%8Dhoku_earthquake_and_tsunami
http://www.data.jma.go.jp/svd/eqev/data/2011_03_11_tohoku/aftershock/
https://en.wikipedia.org/wiki/1960_Valdivia_earthquake
https://en.wikipedia.org/wiki/Megathrust_earthquake
https://en.wikipedia.org/wiki/Subduction
https://en.wikipedia.org/wiki/Remotely_triggered_earthquakes
http://www.cnn.com/2004/WORLD/asiapcf/12/27/quake.facts/
https://en.wikipedia.org/wiki/2002_Sumatra_earthquake
https://en.wikipedia.org/wiki/Tsar_Bomba
https://en.wikipedia.org/wiki/Chandler_wobble
https://en.wikipedia.org/wiki/Apung_1
https://en.wikipedia.org/wiki/August_2016_Central_Italy_earthquake
https://en.wikipedia.org/wiki/October_2016_Central_Italy_earthquakes
https://en.wikipedia.org/wiki/2016_Kaikōura_earthquake
https://www.bbc.co.uk/news/science-environment-39373846
https://www.stuff.co.nz/national/90444877/Kaikōura-earthquake-ruptured-21-faults--possibly-a-world-record
https://www.geonet.org.nz/earthquake/story/2016p858000

http://science.sciencemag.org/content/early/2017/03/22/science.a
am7194.full
https://earthquake.usgs.gov/learn/facts.php
https://phys.org/news/2016-08-difference-shallow-deep-
earthquakes.html
https://topex.ucsd.edu/es10/es10.1997/lectures/lecture20/secs.text.
only/node10.html
https://en.wikipedia.org/wiki/Quake_Lake
https://cusec.org/
https://www.geonet.org.nz/earthquake/forecast/Kaikōura
https://quakewatch.net/
http://cses.roma2.infn.it/
https://news.nationalgeographic.com/news/2014/01/140106-
earthquake-lights-earthquake-prediction-geology-science/
https://www.usgs.gov/faqs/what-are-earthquake-lights?qt-
news_science_products=0#qt-news_science_products
https://www.forbes.com/sites/davidbressan/2017/09/10/mysterio
us-green-flashes-filmed-during-mexico-quake-are-neither-earthquake-
lights-nor-ufos/#51a6b8e7e206
https://www.newscientist.com/article/2147401-mysterious-lights-in-
the-sky-seen-after-mexicos-huge-earthquake/
https://www.usgs.gov/faqs/can-position-moon-or-planets-affect-
seismicity-are-there-more-earthquakes-morningin-eveningat-a?qt-
news_science_products=0#qt-news_science_products
https://www.forbes.com/sites/davidbressan/2017/08/19/can-sun-
and-moon-trigger-quakes-on-earth/#41a34241e484
https://earlywarninglabs.com/mobile-app/
https://www.shakealert.org/
http://earthquakes.berkeley.edu/myquake/
https://myshake.berkeley.edu/
https://earthquake.usgs.gov/hazards/induced/index.php#2018
https://en.wikipedia.org/wiki/2008_Sichuan_earthquake
https://web.archive.org/web/20080528082900/http://earthobserva
tory.nasa.gov/Newsroom/NewImages/images.php3?img_id=18034
&rc=3
https://en.wikipedia.org/wiki/List_of_earthquakes_in_the_United_
States
https://en.wikipedia.org/wiki/Lists_of_earthquakes
https://earthquake.usgs.gov/learn/topics/mercalli.php

San Andreas Earthquake Scenario Information
http://www.conservation.ca.gov/cgs/rghm/loss/Pages/shakeout.aspx
http://www.conservation.ca.gov/cgs/rghm/loss/Pages/scenarios.aspx
https://earthquake.usgs.gov/learn/topics/shakingsimulations/shakeout/
https://pubs.usgs.gov/circ/1324/c1324.pdf

San Francisco Scenario Related Web Pages
https://www.fema.gov/media-library/assets/documents/5673
https://www.fema.gov/media-library/assets/documents/19621
https://www.fema.gov/media-library-data/20130726-1742-25045-9381/dl_sfeqlosses.pdf
https://www.fema.gov/media-library-data/20130726-1742-25045-4546/sfeglosses.pdf

Cascadia Scenario Related Web Pages
https://www.seismosoc.org/news/reinforced-concrete-damage-may-be-larger-than-expected-in-seattle-quake/
https://www.seattlepi.com/local/environment/article/Here-s-how-a-9-0-earthquake-would-affect-12788336.php
https://washingtonstategeology.wordpress.com/2018/03/26/newly-published-southwest-washington-tsunami-inundation-hazard-maps/
https://www.oregongeology.org/pubs/ofr/p-O-18-02.htm
https://www.newyorker.com/magazine/2015/07/20/the-really-big-one

New Madrid Scenario Related Web Pages
https://pubs.usgs.gov/fs/2006/3125/pdf/FS06-3125_508.pdf
http://www.cusec.org/documents/aar/NMSZ_CAT_PLANNING_SCENARIO.pdf
http://www.cusec.org/documents/aar/cusec_aar.pdf
http://www.cusec.org/documents/aar/NMSZ_CAT_PLANNING_SCENARIO.pdf
https://pubs.usgs.gov/fs/2006/3125/pdf/FS06-3125_508.pdf
http://www.cusec.org/documents/aar/cusec_aar.pdf
http://cusec.org/new-madrid-seismic-zone/new-madrid-seismic-zone-catastrophic-planning-project/

http://www.cusec.org/documents/aar/NMSZ_CAT_PLANNING_SCENARIO.pdf
https://www.memphis.edu/ceri/compendium/
https://pubs.usgs.gov/fs/2006/3125/pdf/FS06-3125_508.pdf
http://www.eas.slu.edu/eqc/eqcquakes.html
https://adem.arkansas.gov/earthquake
https://www.jacksongov.org/249/Earthquake-Threat
https://fox17.com/news/local/tennessee-earthquakes-what-to-know-and-the-probability-of-the-big-one-hitting

Wasatch Fault Scenario Related Web Pages
https://www.beprepared.com/blog/29491/the-biggest-reason-to-worry-about-recent-utah-earthquakes-and-how-to-prepare-for-it/
https://dem.utah.gov/wp-content/uploads/sites/18/2015/03/RS1058_EERI_SLC_EQ_Scenario.pdf
https://www.shakeout.org/utah/scenarios/
https://www.deseretnews.com/article/865626220/The-startling-projections-of-a-quake-in-Salt-Lake-City-What-you-need-to-know.html
https://utahearthquakesafety.org/what-should-i-know/what-is-utahs-earthquake-risk/
https://www.wsspc.org/resources-reports/earthquake-center/eq-scenarios/

USGS Hazard Maps
https://earthquake.usgs.gov/hazards/hazmaps/conterminous/index.php#2014
2008 Seismic Hazard Maps https://pubs.usgs.gov/fs/2008/3017/

ShakeMap Earthquake Scenarios
https://earthquake.usgs.gov/scenarios/catalog/
https://earthquake.usgs.gov/scenarios/
https://earthquake.usgs.gov/scenarios/related.php
https://earthquake.usgs.gov/hazards/urban/memphis/
https://pubs.usgs.gov/fs/2005/3142/pdf/FS05-3142_508.pdf

Preparedness-Related Sites
http://ugienergylink.com/smell-natural-gas-house/

https://www.wikihow.com/Get-Emergency-Drinking-Water-from-a-Water-Heater

http://www.fuel-testers.com/expiration_of_ethanol_gas.html

https://obamawhitehouse.archives.gov/the-press-office/2012/03/16/executive-order-national-defense-resources-preparedness

https://www.epa.gov/ground-water-and-drinking-water/emergency-disinfection-drinking-water

https://www.fda.gov/medicaldevices/productsandmedicalprocedures/generalhospitaldevicesandsupplies/personalprotectiveequipment/ucm055977.htm

http://trainandcert.com/articles/osha-safety-articles/n95-and-r95-respirators-whats-the-difference/

https://www.artofmanliness.com/articles/hydration-for-the-apocalypse-how-to-store-water-for-long-term-emergencies/

https://beprepared.com/blog/9182/5-myths-about-water-storage/

https://en.wikipedia.org/wiki/Solar_still

https://www.thereadystore.com/water-storage/3106/rotating-your-water-storage/

http://www.redcross.org/get-help/how-to-prepare-for-emergencies/anatomy-of-a-first-aid-kit

https://www.rei.com/learn/expert-advice/first-aid-checklist.html

https://www.mayoclinic.org/first-aid/first-aid-kits/basics/art-20056673

http://princetoninnovation.org/magazine/2015/05/05/heat-loss-head-myth-debunked/

https://www.nytimes.com/2004/10/26/health/the-claim-you-lose-most-of-your-body-heat-through-your-head.html

https://www.livescience.com/34411-body-heat-loss-head.html

http://www.bmj.com/rapid-response/2011/11/02/head-cover-cold

http://ucfoodsafety.ucdavis.edu/files/26437.pdf

https://www.clorox.com/how-to/disinfecting-sanitizing/disinfecting-with-bleach/sanitizing-dishes-using-bleach/

https://www.ksbw.com/article/east-texas-county-tells-residents-get-out-or-die/12142731

https://ftw.usatoday.com/2015/08/refuge-of-last-resort-five-days-inside-the-superdome-for-hurricane-katrina

https://www.seattletimes.com/nation-world/trapped-in-the-superdome-refuge-becomes-a-hellhole/

https://www.ready.gov/water

https://www.who.int/water_sanitation_health/dwq/Boiling_water_01_15.pdf?ua=1&ua=1

https://www.epa.gov/sites/production/files/2017-09/documents/emergency_disinfection_of_drinking_water_sept2017.pdf

References

Aguilera, M. (2016, October 4). *New Fault Discovered in Earthquake-Prone Southern California Region*. Retrieved from https://scripps.ucsd.edu: https://scripps.ucsd.edu/news/new-fault-discovered-earthquake-prone-southern-california-region

Alaska Earthquake Center. (2019). *Assess your risk*. Retrieved from https://earthquake.alaska.edu: https://earthquake.alaska.edu/assess-risk

Amos, J. (2017, March 23). *Most comples quake ever studied*. Retrieved from www.bbc.co.uk: https://www.bbc.co.uk/news/science-environment-39373846

Antczak, J. (2019, January 16). *Northridge quake thrashed Los Angeles 25 years ago this week*. Retrieved from www.apnews.com: https://www.apnews.com/9ff84d752439468494aaf8916424522b

Arkansas Department of Emergency Management. (2019). *Earthquake*. Retrieved from https://adem.arkansas.gov: https://adem.arkansas.gov/earthquake

Arkansas Geological Survey. (2018). *Earthquakes*. Retrieved from https://www.geology.arkansas.gov: https://www.geology.arkansas.gov/geohazards/earthquakes-in-arkansas.html

Aster, R. (2018, February 1). *Earthquake Watch: California Is Overdue for a 'Big One'*. Retrieved from https://www.livescience.com: https://www.livescience.com/61601-california-overdue-earthquake.html

Bauer, J. M., Burns, W. J., & Madin, I. P. (2018). *Open-File Report O-18-02, Earthquake regional impact analysis for Clackamas, Multnomah, and Washington counties, Oregon*. Retrieved from https://www.oregongeology.org: https://www.oregongeology.org/pubs/ofr/p-O-18-02.htm

Baumgaertner, E. (2019, July 15). *L.A.'s ShakeAlert earthquake warning app worked exactly as planned. That's the problem*. Retrieved from https://www.latimes.com: https://www.latimes.com/science/story/2019-07-14/earthquake-warning-shakealert-app-worked

Be Ready Utah. (2019). *Earthquake Scenarios*. Retrieved from ShakeOut.org: https://www.shakeout.org/utah/scenarios/

Becker, S. (2018, June 21). *These Major American Cities are Sitting Ducks for Giant Earthquakes.* Retrieved from https://www.cheatsheet.com: https://www.cheatsheet.com/culture/american-cities-sitting-ducks-giant-earthquakes.html/

Biasi, G. P., & Scharer, K. M. (2019, April 3). The Current Unlikely Earthquake Hiatus at California's Transform Boundary Paleoseismic Sites. *Seismological Research Letters, 90*(3), 1168-1176. doi:https://doi.org/10.1785/0220180244

Borenstein, S. (2016, March 28). *Risk of quakes on the rise in Oklahoma, North Texas.* Retrieved from https://www.star-telegram.com: https://www.star-telegram.com/news/local/article68704062.html

Brannen, P. (2016, June 23). *Is Middle America Due for a Huge Earthquake.* Retrieved from https://www.theatlantic.com: https://www.theatlantic.com/science/archive/2016/06/the-great-middle-american-earthquake/486623/

CBS News. (2019, April 3). *California is overdue for a huge earthquake, seismologists say.* Retrieved from https://www.cbsnews.com: https://www.cbsnews.com/news/california-earthquake-drought-overdue-for-major-quake-today-2019-04-03/

Chang, A. (2016, August 26). *How shallow, deep earthquakes differ.* Retrieved from www.Phys.org: https://phys.org/news/2016-08-difference-shallow-deep-earthquakes.html

Chang, A. (n.d.). *Experts: Expect big Calif. quake by 2037.* Retrieved August 28, 2018, from ABC News: https://abcnews.go.com/Technology/story?id=4652305&page=1

Chao, K., Peng, Z., Hsu, Y.-J., Obara, K., Wu, C., Ching, K.-E., . . . Wech, A. (2017, June 27). Temporal variation of tectonic tremor activity in southern Taiwan around the 2010 ML6.4 Jiashian earthquake. *JGR: Solid Earth, 122*(7), 5417-5434. doi:https://doi.org/10.1002/2016JB013925

Clark, K. J., Nissen, E. K., Howarth, J. D., Hamling, I. J., Mountjoy, J. J., Ries, W. F., . . . Strong, D. T. (2017, September 15). Highly variable coastal deformation in the 2016 MW7.8 Kaikōura earthquake reflects rupture complexity along a transpressional plate boundary. *Earth and Planetary Science Letters, 474*, 334-344. doi:https://doi.org/10.1016/j.epsl.2017.06.048

Collins, K. J. (2008, December 18). *Heat loss from the head in cold weather.* doi:https://doi.org/10.1136/bmj.a2769

Contoyiannis, Y., Potirakis, S. M., Eftaxias, K., Hayakawa, M., & Schekotov, A. (2016, June 15). Intermittent criticality revealed in ULF magnetic fields prior to the 11 March 2011 Tohoku earthquake (Mw = 9). *Physica A: Statistical Mechanics and its Applications, 452*, 19-28. doi:https://doi.org/10.1016/j.physa.2016.01.065

Cooke, M. L., & Beyer, J. L. (2018, August 30). Off-Fault Focal Mechanisms Not Representative of Interseismic Fault Loading Suggest Deep Creep on the Northern San Jacinto Fault. *Geophysical Research Letters, 45*, 8976-8984. doi: https://doi.org/10.1029/2018GL078932

CUSEC. (2011, December). *CUSEC After-Action Report (AAR).* Retrieved from http://www.cusec.org: http://www.cusec.org/documents/aar/cusec_aar.pdf

CUSEC. (n.d.). *New Madrid Seismic Zone.* Retrieved from http://cusec.org: http://cusec.org/new-madrid-seismic-zone/

CUSEC. (n.d.). *New Madrid Seismic Zone Catastrophic Planning Project.* Retrieved from http://cusec.org: http://cusec.org/new-madrid-seismic-zone/new-madrid-seismic-zone-catastrophic-planning-project/

CUSEC. (n.d.). *Our Earthquake Risk.* Retrieved from https://cusec.org: https://cusec.org/our-earthquake-risk/

Daly, M. (2017, Mar 15). *Kaikoura earthquake ruptured 21 faults - that's possibly a world record.* Retrieved from https://www.stuff.co.nz: https://www.stuff.co.nz/national/90444877/kaikoura-earthquake-ruptured-21-faults--possibly-a-world-record

Davidson, B. (2015, September). A Surge and Short-term Peak in Northern Solar Polar Field Magmetism Prior to the M8.3 Earthquake Near Chile on September 16, 2015. *New Concepts in Global Tectonics Journal, 3*(3), 391-393. Retrieved from http://suspicious0bservers.org/wp-content/uploads/2016/04/Paper-2.pdf

Davidson, B. (n.d.). *Forecasting M6+ 'Significant' Earthquakes(I): The First 100 Days.* Retrieved July 17, 2019, from https://quakewatch.net: https://quakewatch.net/wp-content/uploads/2017/04/Forecasting-Significant-Earthquakes-I.pdf

Davidson, B., & Yelverton, Jr., B. (n.d.). *Forecasting M6+ 'Significant' Earthquakes (II): Global Electric Circuit Hypothesis*. Retrieved July 17, 2019, from https://quakewatch.net: https://quakewatch.net/wp-content/uploads/2017/04/Forecasting-M6-%E2%80%98Significant%E2%80%99-Earthquakes-II.pdf

Davidson, B., U-Yen, K., & Holloman, C. (2015, September). Relationship Between M8+ Earthquake Occurences and the Solar Polar Magnetic Fields. *New Concepts in Global Tectonics Journal, 3*(3), 310-322. Retrieved from http://suspicious0bservers.org/wp-content/uploads/2016/04/Paper-1.pdf

de Liso, G. (2018, November). Some Tonal and Rhythmical Sequences in the Vocal Language of Dogs as Significant Earthquake Precursors. *Open Journal of Earthquake Research, 7*(4), 221-268. doi:https://doi.org/10.4236/ojer.2018.74013

Doughton, S. (2018, March 17). *How to survive the Cascadia Earthquake? Tips from seismologist Lucy Jones, 'the Beyoncé of earthquakes'*. Retrieved from https://www.seattletimes.com: https://www.seattletimes.com/seattle-news/science/californias-celeb-quake-expert-says-preventing-damage-is-key-to-quick-recovery/

Dvorsky, G. (2018, September 19). *Something Unexpected and Weird Is Happening Beneath California's Deadliest Faults*. Retrieved from https://gizmodo.com: https://gizmodo.com/something-unexpected-and-weird-is-happening-beneath-cal-1829177182

Early Warning Labs. (2019). *It's Coming Soon*. Retrieved from https://earlywarninglabs.com: https://earlywarninglabs.com/mobile-app/#download-page

Earthquake Engineering Research Institute, Utah Chapter. (2015, June 4). *Scenario for a Magnitude 7.0 Earthquake on the Wasatch Fault–Salt Lake City Segment -- Hazards and Loss Estimates*. Retrieved from https://dem.utah.gov: https://dem.utah.gov/wp-content/uploads/sites/18/2015/03/RS1058_EERI_SLC_EQ_Scenario.pdf

Earthquakes and Faults. (n.d.). Retrieved from https://www.dnr.wa.gov: https://www.dnr.wa.gov/programs-and-services/geology/geologic-hazards/earthquakes-and-faults

Eldredge, S. N. (1996). *The Wasatch Fault.* Retrieved from https://ugspub.nr.utah.gov: https://ugspub.nr.utah.gov/publications/public_information/pi-40.pdf

Elnashai, A. S., Cleveland, L. J., Jefferson, T., & Harrald, J. (2008, September). *Impact of Earthquakes on the Central USA.* Retrieved from http://www.cusec.org: http://www.cusec.org/documents/aar/NMSZ_CAT_PLANNING_SCENARIO.pdf

Eungard, D. W., Forson, C., Walsh, T. J., Gica, E., & Arcas, D. (2018, March 26). *Newly Published: Southwest Washington Tsunami Inundation Hazard Maps.* Retrieved from https://washingtonstategeology.wordpress.com: https://washingtonstategeology.wordpress.com/2018/03/26/newly-published-southwest-washington-tsunami-inundation-hazard-maps/

Farley, G. (2018, July 8). *Why you should be prepared: 3 big earthquake threats in PNW.* Retrieved from https://www.king5.com: https://www.king5.com/article/news/local/disaster/why-you-should-be-prepared-3-big-earthquake-threats-in-pnw/281-457421137

FEMA. (2005, June). *HAZUS-MH Used to Support San Francisco Bay Area Earthquake Exercise.* Retrieved from https://www.fema.gov: https://www.fema.gov/media-library-data/20130726-1742-25045-4546/sfeglosses.pdf

FEMA. (2006, April 20). *Emergency Response: HAZUS-MH Used to Support San Francisco Bay Area Earthquake Exercse.* Retrieved from https://www.fema.gov: https://www.fema.gov/media-library-data/20130726-1742-25045-9381/dl_sfeqlosses.pdf

FEMA. (2010, October 13). *Presentation: HAZUS-MH Used to Support San Francisco Bay Area Earthquake Exercise.* Retrieved from https://www.fema.gov: https://www.fema.gov/media-library/assets/documents/19621

FEMA. (2014, July 21). *Hazus Evaluation of 1906 Magnitude Earthquake in Today's Environment- Economic Loss.* Retrieved from https://www.fema.gov: https://www.fema.gov/media-library/assets/documents/5673

Field, E. H., & and members of 2014 WGCEP. (2015, March). *UCERF3: A new earthquake forecast for California's complex fault*

system: U.S. Geological Survey 2015–3009.
doi:https://dx.doi.org/10.3133/fs20153009

Field, E. H., & Milner, K. R. (2008). *Forecasting California's Earthquakes—What Can We Expect in the Next 30 Years?* Retrieved from https://pubs.usgs.gov: https://pubs.usgs.gov/fs/2008/3027/fs2008-3027.pdf

Field, E. H., Biasi, G. P., Bird, P., Dawson, T. E., Felzer, K. R., Jackson, D. D., . . . Zeng, Y. (2013). *The Uniform California Earthquake Rupture Forecast, Version 3 (UCERF3)--The Time-Independent Model.* U.S. Geological Survey Open-File Report 2013-1165, U.S. Geological Survey, U.S. Department of the Interior. Retrieved from https://pubs.usgs.gov/of/2013/1165/pdf/ofr2013-1165.pdf

Gabuchian, V., Rosakis, A. J., Bhat, H. S., Madariaga, R., & Kanamori, H. (2017, May 18). Experimental evidence that thrust earthquake ruptures might open faults. *Nature, 545,* 336-339. doi:https://dx.doi.org/10.1038/nature22045

Geologists and Engineers for Earthquake Safety. (n.d.). *My Risk?* Retrieved from https://utahearthquakesafety.org: https://utahearthquakesafety.org/my-risk/

Geologists and Engineers for Earthquake Safety. (n.d.). *Utah's Earthquake Risk?* Retrieved from https://utahearthquakesafety.org: https://utahearthquakesafety.org/what-should-i-know/what-is-utahs-earthquake-risk/

GeoNet. (2016, December 2). *Landslides and Landslide dams caused by the Kaikoura Earthquake.* Retrieved from Geological hazard information for New Zealand: https://www.geonet.org.nz/news/oFR6qI4ipaWYYqOUsmYWC

GeoNet. (n.d.). *M 7.8 Kaikōura Mon, Nov 14 2016.* Retrieved from Geological hazard information for New Zealand: https://www.geonet.org.nz/earthquake/story/2016p858000

Grant, R. A., Raulin, J. P., & Freund, F. (2015, March 17). Changes in animal activity prior to a major (M = 7) earthquake in the Peruvian Andes. *Physics and Chemistry of the Earth, Parts A/B/C, 85-86,* 69-77. doi:https://doi.org/10.1016/j.pce.2015.02.012

Grimes, S. (2015, May 22). *8 biggest earthquakes in Nevada history.* Retrieved from https://www.reviewjournal.com:

https://www.reviewjournal.com/news/nation-and-world/8-biggest-earthquakes-in-nevada-history/

Ham, B. (2019, April 24). *Reinforced Concrete Damage May Be Larger Than Expected in Seattle Quake.* Retrieved from https://www.seismosoc.org: https://www.seismosoc.org/news/reinforced-concrete-damage-may-be-larger-than-expected-in-seattle-quake/

Hamling, I. J., Hreinsdóttir, S., Clark, K., Elliott, J., Liang, C., Fielding, E., . . . Stirling, M. (2017, April 14). Complex multifault rupture during the 2016 Mw 7.8 Kaikōura earthquake, New Zealand. *Science, 356*(6334). doi:10.1126/science.aam7194

Hampson, R. (2018, September 9). *Will growing scenes of hurricanes, wildfires and volcanoes make us a go-bag people?* Retrieved from https://www.usatoday.com: https://www.usatoday.com/story/news/2018/09/09/hurricanes-wildfires-and-volcanoes-why-arent-we-better-prepared/984963002/

Harris, S. (2017, May 11). *Study: Massive earthquake likely to strike S.E. Idaho in next 50 years.* Retrieved from https://www.idahostatejournal.com: https://www.idahostatejournal.com/outdoors/xtreme_idaho/study-massive-earthquake-likely-to-strike-s-e-idaho-in/article_8e4da495-125f-5f5e-b4da-7a5b20061ea0.html

Hawaii, the Earthquake State? (n.d.). Retrieved from https://www.lovebigisland.com: https://www.lovebigisland.com/hawaii-blog/hawaii-earthquake-state/

Heid, J. (2016, March 29). *Dallas-Fort Worth Earthquake Risk Has Increased 10-Fold.* Retrieved from https://www.dmagazine.com: https://www.dmagazine.com/frontburner/2016/03/dallas-fort-worth-earthquake-risk-has-increased-10-fold/

Hickey, H. (2017, October 23). *50 simulations of the 'Really Big One' show how a 9.0 Cascadia earthquake could play out .* Retrieved from http://www.washington.edu: http://www.washington.edu/news/2017/10/23/50-simulations-of-the-really-big-one-show-how-a-9-0-cascadia-earthquake-could-play-out/

HNN staff. (2019, April 15). *HVO: Quake that rocked Big Island wasn't caused by magma moving underground.* Retrieved from https://www.hawaiinewsnow.com: https://www.hawaiinewsnow.com/2019/04/15/quake-that-rocked-big-island-wasnt-caused-by-magma-moving-underground/

Holden, C. (2013, October 15). *1959 Earthquake forms Quake Lake West of Yellowstone.* Retrieved from https://www.yellowstonepark.com: https://www.yellowstonepark.com/park/yellowstone-earthquake-of-1959

Howard, B. C. (2014, January 7). *Bizarre Earthquake Lights Finally Explained.* Retrieved from https://news.nationalgeographic.com: https://news.nationalgeographic.com/news/2014/01/140106-earthquake-lights-earthquake-prediction-geology-science/

Hurley, A. K. (2019, January 7). *L.A.'s Public Earthquake-Warning App Is the First in the U.S.* Retrieved from https://www.citylab.com/: https://www.citylab.com/environment/2019/01/earthquake-early-warning-los-angeles-app-shakealertla/579418/

Ide, S., Yabe, S., & Tanaka, Y. (2016, September 12). Earthquake potential revealed by tidal influence on earthquake size–frequency statistics. *Nature Geoscience, 9*, 834-837. doi:https://doi.org/10.1038/ngeo2796

Il, R.-G. L. (2017, March 1). *Oklahoma's earthquake threat now equals California's because of man-made temblors, USGS says.* Retrieved from https://www.latimes.com: https://www.latimes.com/local/lanow/la-me-ln-oklahome-earthquake-20170301-story.html

Illinois Emergency Management Agency. (2019). *Earthquake.* Retrieved from https://www2.illinois.gov: https://www2.illinois.gov/ready/hazards/Pages/Earthquake.aspx

Insurance Information Institute. (2018, October 10). *Background on: Earthquake insurance and risk.* Retrieved from https://www.iii.org: https://www.iii.org/article/background-on-earthquake-insurance-and-risk

Insurance Information Institute. (2019). *Facts + Statistics: Earthquakes and tsunamis.* Retrieved from https://www.iii.org:

https://www.iii.org/fact-statistic/facts-statistics-earthquakes-
and-
tsunamis#Top%2010%20Costliest%20U.S.%20Earthquakes
%20By%20Inflation-Adjusted%20Insured%20Losses%20(1)

Jackson County. (n.d.). *Earthquake Threat*. Retrieved from
https://www.jacksongov.org:
https://www.jacksongov.org/249/Earthquake-Threat

Jackson School of Geosciences. (2019, July 23). *Many Dallas-Fort
Worth Area Faults Have the Potential to Host Earthquakes, New
Study Finds*. Retrieved from http://www.jsg.utexas.edu:
http://www.jsg.utexas.edu/news/2019/07/many-dallas-fort-
worth-area-faults-have-the-potential-to-host-earthquakes-
new-study-finds/

Jacobson, D. (2018, July 14). *New findings clarify the seismic risk in the
Pacific Northwest*. Retrieved from http://temblor.net:
http://temblor.net/earthquake-insights/new-findings-clarify-
the-seismic-risk-in-the-pacific-northwest-7443/

Jacobson, D., & Sevilgen, V. (2017, September 13). *Earthquake swarm
continues to rattle southeastern Idaho*. Retrieved from
http://temblor.net: http://temblor.net/earthquake-
insights/earthquake-swarm-continues-to-rattle-southeastern-
idaho-5079/

Jones, C. (2016, December 8). *Oklahoma 'almost certain' for another
damaging earthquake; risks to be elevated for next decade*. Retrieved
from https://www.tulsaworld.com:
https://www.tulsaworld.com/earthquakes/oklahoma-almost-
certain-for-another-damaging-earthquake-risks-to-
be/article_74cbbc8c-0ba1-510c-8c67-53ac18d3b2b3.html

Jones, L. M., Bernknopf, R., Cox, D., Goltz, J., Hudnut, K., Mileti,
D., . . . Wein, A. (2008). *The ShakeOut Scenario*. Retrieved from
https://pubs.usgs.gov:
https://pubs.usgs.gov/of/2008/1150/

Kentucky Geological Survey. (2019). *Why Earthquake Research Matters*.
Retrieved from http://www.uky.edu:
http://www.uky.edu/KGS/earthquake/earthquake_matters.
php

Kerr, R. A., & Stone, R. (2009, January 16). A Human Trigger for the
Great Quake of Sichuan? *Science, 323*(5912), 332.
doi:10.1126/science.323.5912.322

Klemetti, E. (2018, November 19). *Are Big Earthquakes a Concern for the Eastern United States?* Retrieved from http://blogs.discovermagazine.com: http://blogs.discovermagazine.com/rockyplanet/2018/11/19/are-big-earthquakes-concern-eastern-united-states

Knox, A., & Thatcher, G. (2018, April 18). *1 in 3 Salt Lake County homes at greater risk of crumbling in earthquake.* Retrieved from https://www.deseretnews.com: https://www.deseretnews.com/article/900016237/1-in-3-salt-lake-county-homes-at-greater-risk-of-crumbling-in-earthquake.html

Lefler, D. (2016, March 28). *Survey: Risk of damaging quake greater in southern Kansas than southern Calif.* Retrieved from https://www.kansas.com: https://www.kansas.com/news/local/article68729847.html

Lindell, M., & Perry, R. (2006, May 29). Hazardous Materials Releases in the Northridge Earthquake: Implications for Seismic Risk Assessment. *Risk Analysis, 17*, 147-156. doi:https://doi.org/10.1111/j.1539-6924.1997.tb00854.x

Liu, J., Wan, W., Zhou, C., Zhang, X., Liu, Y., & Shen, X. (2019, March). A study of the ionospheric disturbances associated with strong earthquakes using the empirical orthogonal function analysis. *Journal of Asian Earth Sciences, 171*, 225-232. doi:https://doi.org/10.1016/j.jseaes.2018.10.007

Lundeberg, S. (2018, August 1). *Research finds quakes can systematically trigger other ones on opposite side of Earth* . Retrieved from https://today.oregonstate.edu: https://today.oregonstate.edu/news/research-finds-quakes-can-systematically-trigger-other-ones-opposite-side-earth

MacDonald, C. (2019, May 25). *Damage from the August 1959 Hebgen Lake earthquake.* Retrieved from www.ksl.com: https://www.ksl.com/article/46559572/aftershocks-from-1959-earthquake-sent-tremors-through-yellowstone-in-2018

Mahmoudian, A., & Kalaee, M. J. (2019, June 15). Study of ULF-VLF wave propagation in the near-Earth environment for earthquake prediction. *Advances in Space Research, 63*(12), 4015-4024. doi:Study of ULF-VLF wave propagation in the near-Earth environment for earthquake prediction

Manchir, M. (2015, February 6). *Illinois officials urge earthquake awareness.* Retrieved from https://www.chicagotribune.com:

https://www.chicagotribune.com/news/ct-earthquake-illinois-0206-20150206-story.html

McKellar, K. (2015, April 11). *The startling projections of a quake in Salt Lake City: What you need to know.* Retrieved from https://www.deseretnews.com: https://www.deseretnews.com/article/865626220/The-startling-projections-of-a-quake-in-Salt-Lake-City-What-you-need-to-know.html

Meyer, R. (2016, August 11). *A Major Earthquake in the Pacific Northwest Looks Even Likelier.* Retrieved from https://www.theatlantic.com: https://www.theatlantic.com/science/archive/2016/08/a-major-earthquake-in-the-pacific-northwest-just-got-more-likely/495407/

Meyer, R. (2016, December 1). *In a Decade, Oklahoma's Earthquakes Will Be Normal Again.* Retrieved from https://www.theatlantic.com: https://www.theatlantic.com/science/archive/2016/12/in-a-decade-oklahomas-earthquakes-will-be-normal-again/509297/

Miles, K. (2017, September 9). *New York City is overdue for a major earthquake.* Retrieved from https://nypost.com: https://nypost.com/2017/09/09/new-york-city-is-overdue-for-a-major-earthquake/

Millman, Z. (2019, July 11). *Here's how a 9.0 earthquake would affect Washington's coast.* Retrieved from https://www.seattlepi.com: https://www.seattlepi.com/local/environment/article/Here-s-how-a-9-0-earthquake-would-affect-12788336.php

Mojica, A. (2018, December 12). *Tennessee Earthquakes: What to know and the probability of 'The Big One' hitting.* Retrieved from https://fox17.com: https://fox17.com/news/local/tennessee-earthquakes-what-to-know-and-the-probability-of-the-big-one-hitting

Moore, S. W. (n.d.). *The Borah Peak Earthquake.* Retrieved from https://digitalatlas.cose.isu.edu: https://digitalatlas.cose.isu.edu/geo/quakes/borahEQ/boraheq.htm

Morris, A. (2017, October 5). *Do Earthquakes Have a 'Tell'?* Retrieved from https://www.mccormick.northwestern.edu:

https://www.mccormick.northwestern.edu/news/articles/20 17/10/do-earthquakes-have-a-tell.html

NASA. (n.d.). *Massive Earthquake Along the Sunda Trench.* Retrieved from https://earthobservatory.nasa.gov: https://earthobservatory.nasa.gov/images/5375/massive-earthquake-along-the-sunda-trench

New Zealand Geographic. (2017, March 15). *Kaikoura quake's 21 faultlines could be world record.* Retrieved from New Zealand Geographic: https://www.nzgeo.com/audio/kaikoura-quakes-21-faultlines-could-be-world-record/

Nissen, E., Elliott, J. R., Sloan, R. A., Craig, T. J., Funning, G. J., Hutko, A., . . . Wright, T. J. (2016, February 8). Limitations of rupture forecasting exposed by instantaneously triggered earthquake doublet. *Nature Geoscience, 9*, 330-336. Retrieved from https://www.nature.com/articles/ngeo2653

NZ Herald. (2016, November 20). *Risk of gastro outbreak in Kaikoura under control.* Retrieved from https://www.nzherald.co.nz: https://www.nzherald.co.nz/nz/news/article.cfm?c_id=1&objectid=11751575

O'Malley, R. T., Mondal, D., Goldfinger, C., & Behrenfeld, M. J. (2018, August 2). Evidence of Systematic Triggering at Teleseismic Distances Following Large Earthquakes. *Scientific Reports, 8.* doi:DOI:10.1038/s41598-018-30019-2

Osborne, H. (2017, August 1). *Alaska at Risk of a Massive Earthquake and Tsunami Similar to Devastating 2011 Japan Event.* Retrieved from https://www.newsweek.com: https://www.newsweek.com/earthquake-tsunami-alaska-japan-2011-644942

Oskin, B. (2014, July 3). *Strongest Link: Wastewater Wells Triggered Oklahoma Earthquake Surge.* Retrieved from https://www.livescience.com: https://www.livescience.com/46660-oklahoma-earthquakes-from-injection-wells.html

Oskin, B. (2015, January 5). *Fracking Led to Ohio Earthquakes.* Retrieved from https://www.livescience.com: https://www.livescience.com/49326-fracking-caused-ohio-earthquakes.html

Oyama, K. I., Chen, C. H., Bankov, L., Minakshi, D., Ryu, K., Liu, J. Y., & Liu, H. (2019, April 15). Precursor effect of March 11, 2011 off the coast of Tohoku earthquake on high and low

latitude ionospheres and its possible disturbing mechanism.
Advances in Space Research, 63(8), 2623-2637.
doi:https://doi.org/10.1016/j.asr.2018.12.042

Pang, G., Koper, K. D., Hale, J. M., Burlacu, R., Farrell, J., & Smith,
R. B. (2019, May 16). The 2017–2018 Maple Creek
Earthquake Sequence in Yellowstone National Park, USA.
Geophysical Research Letters, 46(9), pp. 4653-4663.
doi:https://doi.org/10.1029/2019GL082376

Pappas, S. (2018, April 25). *Oklahoma Suffers Its 2,724th Earthquake
Since 2010*. Retrieved from https://www.livescience.com:
https://www.livescience.com/62410-oklahoma-earthquakes-
wastewater-injection.html

Pappas, S. (2019, April 5). *California's Eerie 'Earthquake Pause' Is
Unprecedented*. Retrieved from https://www.livescience.com:
https://www.livescience.com/65163-california-earthquake-
pause-uncanny.html

Penrod, E. (2016, April 18). *New earthquake study says Utah is ripe for
devastation*. Retrieved from https://archive.sltrib.com:
https://archive.sltrib.com/article.php?id=3791904&itype=C
MSID

Perkins, J. P., Roering, J. J., Burns, W. J., Struble, W., Black, B. A.,
Schmidt, K. A., . . . Calhoun, N. (2018, August 8). *Hunting for
Landslides from Cascadia's Great Earthquakes*.
doi:https://doi.org/10.1029/2018EO103689

Perkins, R. (2017, May 1). *Earthquakes Can Make Thrust Faults Open
Violently and Snap Shut*. Retrieved from
https://www.caltech.edu:
https://www.caltech.edu/about/news/earthquakes-can-
make-thrust-faults-open-violently-and-snap-shut-56641

Perkins, R. (2019, March 4). *Fast, Simple New Assessment of Earthquake
Hazard*. Retrieved from
https://www.caltech.edu/about/news/fast-simple-new-
assessment-earthquake-hazard

Perkins, R. (2019, April 18). *Scientists Identify Almost 2 Million Previously
"Hidden" Earthquakes*. Retrieved from
https://www.caltech.edu:
https://www.caltech.edu/about/news/scientists-identify-
almost-2-million-previously-hidden-earthquakes

Perkins, S. (2012, November 7). Seismic Risk in Eastern U.S. May Be
Higher Than Previously Thought. *Nature*. Retrieved from

https://www.scientificamerican.com/article/seismic-risk-in-eastern-us-may-be-higher-than-previously-thought/

Perkins, S. (2012, November 7). *Virginia earthquake wins by a landslide.* doi:doi:10.1038/nature.2012.11763

Perry, S., Cox, D., Jones, L., Bernknopf, R., Goltz, J., Hudnut, K., . . . Wein, A. (2008). *The ShakeOut Earthquake Scenario—A Story That Southern Californians Are Writing.* Retrieved from https://pubs.usgs.gov: https://pubs.usgs.gov/circ/1324/c1324.pdf

Perry, T. S. (2019, June 25). *A 30-Second Earthquake Warning Gives a Menlo Park Fire Station a Chance to Protect Itself.* Retrieved from https://spectrum.ieee.org: https://spectrum.ieee.org/view-from-the-valley/at-work/start-ups/a-30-second-earthquake-warning-gives-a-menlo-park-fire-station

Petersen, M. D., Mueller, C. S., Moschetti, M. P., Hoover, S. M., Shumway, A. M., McNamara, D. E., . . . Rukstales, K. S. (2017, March 1). 2017 One-Year Seismic-Hazard Forecast for the Central and Eastern United States from Induced and Natural Earthquakes. *Seismological Research Letters, 88*(3), pp. 772-783. doi:https://doi.org/10.1785/0220170005

Pipkin, C. (2019, February 24). *The Biggest Reason to Worry about Recent Utah Earthquakes (and How to Prepare for It).* Retrieved from Emergency Essenstials - Blog: https://www.beprepared.com/blog/29491/the-biggest-reason-to-worry-about-recent-utah-earthquakes-and-how-to-prepare-for-it/

Price, J. (n.d.). *Earthquakes in Nevada.* Retrieved from http://www.nbmg.unr.edu: http://www.nbmg.unr.edu/nhmpc/presentations/earthquakesinnevada.pdf

Ramirez, A. (1994, January 18). *THE EARTHQUAKE: Phones and Power; Gas and Electric Services Are Disrupted for Millions of Customers.* Retrieved from https://www.nytimes.com/1994/01/18/us/earthquake-phones-power-gas-electric-services-are-disrupted-for-millions.html

Ramirez, F. (2017, August 30). *East Texas county tells residents 'GET OUT OR DIE!'.* Retrieved from https://www.ksbw.com: https://www.ksbw.com/article/east-texas-county-tells-residents-get-out-or-die/12142731

Rindge, B. (2014, July 16). *We are the bull's-eye' Future events might shake us up, according to quake maps that put Charleston in a high-risk zone, but area is prepared.* Retrieved from https://www.postandcourier.com: https://www.postandcourier.com/archives/we-are-the-bull-s-eye-future-events-might-shake/article_dde5d19d-9637-5e5e-8f1d-c0b918d94074.html

Rokityansky, I. I., Babak, V. I., Terehyns, A. V., & Hayakawa, M. (2019, May). Variations of Geomagnetic Response Functions before the 2011 Tohoku Earthquake. *Open Journal of Earthquake Research, 8*(2), 70-84. doi:http://dx.doi.org/10.4236/ojer.2019.82005

Rusch, E. (2011, December). The Great Midwest Earthquake of 1811. *Smithsonian Magazine.* Retrieved from https://www.smithsonianmag.com: https://www.smithsonianmag.com/science-nature/the-great-midwest-earthquake-of-1811-46342/

Sahakian, V., Kell, A., Harding, A., Driscoll, N., & Kent, G. (2016, September 13). Geophysical Evidence for a San Andreas Subparallel Transtensional Fault along the Northeastern Shore of the Salton Sea. *Bulletin of the Seismological Society of America*, 1963-1978. doi:https://doi.org/10.1785/0120150350

Schulz, K. (2015, July 20). *The Really Big One.* Retrieved from https://www.newyorker.com: https://www.newyorker.com/magazine/2015/07/20/the-really-big-one

Schuske, K. (2013, August 1). Earthquake Risk in the Salt Lake Valley. *Science and Society.* Retrieved from http://www.exploreutahscience.org: http://www.exploreutahscience.org/science-topics/science-and-society/item/126-earthquake-risk-in-the-salt-lake-valley

Seattle Emergency Management. (2019). *Earthquake.* Retrieved from https://www.seattle.gov: https://www.seattle.gov/emergency-management/hazards/earthquake

Seismological Society of America. (2017, April 13). *Forecasting large earthquakes along the Wasatch Front, Utah.* Retrieved from https://www.sciencedaily.com: www.sciencedaily.com/releases/2017/04/170413120048.htm

Seismological Society of America. (2017, September 28). *Large earthquakes along Olympic Mountain faults, Washington State, USA*. Retrieved from https://www.sciencedaily.com: https://www.sciencedaily.com/releases/2017/09/170928094201.htm

Seismological Society of America. (2017, September 28). *Large earthquakes along Olympic Mountain faults, Washington State, USA*. Retrieved from https://www.sciencedaily.com: www.sciencedaily.com/releases/2017/09/170928094201.htm

Seismological Society of America. (2017, April 12). *Seismologists offer detailed look at New Zealand's Kaikoura earthquake*. Retrieved from https://www.sciencedaily.com: http://www.sciencedaily.com/releases/2017/04/170412111125.htm

Shah, M., Tariq, M. A., & Naqvi, N. A. (2019, June 4). Atmospheric anomalies associated with Mw>6.0 earthquakes in Pakistan and Iran during 2010–2017. *Journal of Atmospheric and Solar-Terrestrial Physics, 191*(15 September 2019). doi:https://doi.org/10.1016/j.jastp.2019.06.003

Shallow, intermediate, and deep foci. (n.d.). Retrieved from www.britannica.com: https://www.britannica.com/science/earthquake-geology/Shallow-intermediate-and-deep-foci

Silver, M. (2019, May 3). *Study suggests earthquakes are triggered well beyond fluid injection zones*. Retrieved from https://now.tufts.edu: https://now.tufts.edu/news-releases/study-suggests-earthquakes-are-triggered-well-beyond-fluid-injection-zones

South Carolina Earthquake Education and Preparedness. (n.d.). *Earthquake Regions in South Carolina*. Retrieved from https://scearthquakes.cofc.edu: https://scearthquakes.cofc.edu/?page=sceqregions

St. Louis University Earthquake Center. (n.d.). *Earthquakes*. Retrieved from http://www.eas.slu.edu: http://www.eas.slu.edu/eqc/eqcquakes.html

State of Alaska. (2019). *Earthquake Risk in Alaska*. Retrieved from http://seismic.alaska.gov: http://seismic.alaska.gov/earthquake_risk.html

Suppasri, A., Shuto, N., Imamura, F., Koshimura, S., Mas, E., & Yalciner, A. C. (2013, June). Lessons Learned from the 2011 Great East Japan Tsunami: Performance of Tsunami

Countermeasures, Coastal Buildings, and Tsunami Evacuation in Japan. *Pure and Applied Geophysics, 170*(6-8), 993-1017. doi:https://doi.org/10.1007/s00024-012-0511-7

Tennessee Emergency Management Agency. (2018). *State of Tennessee Hazard Mitigation Plan.* Retrieved from https://www.scribd.com: https://www.scribd.com/document/395554899/Tennessee-Hazard-Mitigation-Plan-2018-FINAL

Than, K. (2010, MArch 3). *Chile Earthquake Altered Earth Axis, Shortened Day.* Retrieved from https://www.nationalgeographic.com: https://www.nationalgeographic.com/news/2010/3/100302-chile-earthquake-earth-axis-shortened-day/

Theriault, R., St-Laurent, F., Freund, F., & Derr, J. (2014, January). Prevalence of Earthquake Lights Associated with Rift Environments. *Seismological Research Letters, 85*(1), 159-178. doi:DOI: 10.1785/0220130059

Thuermer, J. A. (2017, August 1). *Earthquake bigger risk than Yellowstone supervolcano.* Retrieved from https://www.wyofile.com: https://www.wyofile.com/earthquake-bigger-risk-yellowstone-supervolcano/

U.S. Department of the Interior, U.S. Geological Survey. (2015, March). doi:http://dx.doi.org/10.3133/fs20153009

U.S. Department of the Interior; U.S. Geological Survey. (1997). *Volcanic and Seismic Hazards on the Island of Hawaii.* Retrieved from https://pubs.usgs.gov: https://pubs.usgs.gov/gip/7000036/report.pdf

U.S. Geological Survey. (2007, January). *Earthquake Hazard in the Heart of the Homeland.* Retrieved from https://pubs.usgs.gov: https://pubs.usgs.gov/fs/2006/3125/pdf/FS06-3125_508.pdf

U.S. Geological Survey. (n.d.). *Memphis Earthquake Hazard Mapping Project.* Retrieved from https://earthquake.usgs.gov: https://earthquake.usgs.gov/hazards/urban/memphis/

U.S. Geological Survey. (n.d.). *UULEGACY (Scenario Catalog) -- Utah Legacy Catalog.* Retrieved from https://earthquake.usgs.gov: https://earthquake.usgs.gov/scenarios/catalog/uulegacy/

United States Geological Survey. (n.d.). *AKLEGACY (Scenario Catalog).* Retrieved from https://earthquake.usgs.gov: https://earthquake.usgs.gov/scenarios/catalog/aklegacy/

United States Geological Survey. (n.d.). *Earthquake Hazards in Hawaii -- USGS*. Retrieved from https://www.google.com/url?sa=t&rct=j&q=&esrc=s&sour ce=web&cd=2&cad=rja&uact=8&ved=2ahUKEwie4LKb57 7iAhWKoJ4KHW9CC58QFjABegQICxAG&url=http%3A %2F%2Fwww.umsl.edu%2F~naumannj%2FGeography%25 201001%2520articles%2Fch%25203%2520landforms%2520 %26%2520soil%2FEarthq

United States Geological Survey. (n.d.). *HVLEGACY (Scenario Catalog) -- Hawaii Legacy Catalog*. Retrieved from https://earthquake.usgs.gov: https://earthquake.usgs.gov/scenarios/catalog/hvlegacy/

United States Geological Survey. (n.d.). *MT2016 (Scenario Catalog) -- 2016 Montana Scenarios*. Retrieved from https://earthquake.usgs.gov/scenarios/catalog/mt2016/

United States Geological Survey. (n.d.). *NCLEGACY (Scenario Catalog)*. Retrieved from https://earthquake.usgs.gov/scenarios/catalog/nclegacy/

United States Geological Survey. (n.d.). *NNLEGACY (Scenario Catalog) - Nevada Legacy Catalog*. Retrieved from https://earthquake.usgs.gov: https://earthquake.usgs.gov/scenarios/catalog/nnlegacy/

United States Geological Survey. (n.d.). *SCLEGACY (Scenario Catalog)*. Retrieved from https://earthquake.usgs.gov: https://earthquake.usgs.gov/scenarios/catalog/sclegacy/

United States Geological Survey. (n.d.). *What is the probability that an earthquake will occur in the Los Angeles Area? In the San Francisco Bay area?* Retrieved from https://www.usgs.gov: https://www.usgs.gov/faqs/what-probability-earthquake-will-occur-los-angeles-area-san-francisco-bay-area?qt-news_science_products=0#qt-news_science_products

University of Idaho. (n.d.). *Earthquake Hazards*. Retrieved from https://www.idahogeology.org: https://www.idahogeology.org/earthquake-hazards

University of Illinois. (n.d.). *Earthquake Hazard and Impact in the New Madrid Region*. Retrieved from https://www.in.gov: https://www.in.gov/dhs/files/NMSZ_threats_flyer.pdf

University of Memphis. (n.d.). *New Madrid Compendium*. Retrieved from https://www.memphis.edu: https://www.memphis.edu/ceri/compendium/

Urata, N., Duma, G., & Freund, F. (2018, February). Geomagnetic Kp Index and Earthquakes. *Open Journal of Earthquake Research, 7*(1), 39-52. doi:https://doi.org/10.4236/ojer.2018.71003

Utah Geological Survey. (1997). *Earthquakes and Utah*. Retrieved from https://ugspub.nr.utah.gov: https://ugspub.nr.utah.gov/publications/public_information/pi-48.pdf

Warrell, K. F., Cox, R. T., Hatcher, Jr., R. D., Vaughn, J. D., & Counts, R. (2017, June 27). Paleoseismic Evidence for Multiple Mw≥6. *Bulletin of the Seismological Society of America, 107*(4), pp. 1610-1624. doi:https://doi.org/10.1785/0120160161

Waters, D. (2018, March 28). *Expectations for Charleston's next great unexpected disaster*. Retrieved from https://www.charlestoncitypaper.com: https://www.charlestoncitypaper.com/charleston/expectations-for-charlestons-next-great-unexpected-disaster/Content?oid=16875956

Weisberger, M. (2018, May 18). *The Next Cascadian Megaquake May Be Sooner Than You Think*. Retrieved from https://www.livescience.com: https://www.livescience.com/62608-cascadia-megaquakes-more-frequent.html

Weisberger, M. (2018, December 18). *The Weird Reason 'Tsunami Fires' Broke Out After Japan Earthquake*. Retrieved from www.livescience.com: https://www.livescience.com/64334-why-tsunami-fires-after-japan-earthquake.html

Wilcox, C. (2016, April 25). *Researchers say Nevadans are not prepared if a major earthquake occurs*. Retrieved from https://news3lv.com: https://news3lv.com/news/local/researchers-say-nevadans-are-not-prepared-if-a-major-earthquake-occurs

Williams, K. (2018, March 15). *When the 'Big One' hits, Portland faces mass casualties, widespread destruction: Study*. Retrieved from https://www.oregonlive.com: https://www.oregonlive.com/pacific-northwest-news/2018/03/when_the_big_one_hits_portland.html

Working Group on Utah Earthquake Probabilities. (2016). *Earthquake Probabilities for the Wasatch Front Region in Utah, Idaho, and Wyoming*. Retrieved from

https://ugspub.nr.utah.gov:
https://ugspub.nr.utah.gov/publications/misc_pubs/mp-16-3/mp-16-3.pdf

Wyoming State Geological Survey. (2000). *Earthquakes in Wyoming*. Retrieved from http://www.wrds.uwyo.edu: http://www.wrds.uwyo.edu/wrds/wsgs/hazards/quakes/eq_brochure.pdf

Wyoming State Geological Survey. (2019). *Earthquakes*. Retrieved from https://www.wsgs.wyo.gov: https://www.wsgs.wyo.gov/hazards/earthquakes

Thank You

I really appreciate you reading my book about earthquakes and preparedness. Hopefully you can tell that both are topics I'm very interested in.

Besides being informative, I hope you've gotten some ideas and insights to become better prepared as I've shared some things I've done with my family and in our home. Too many people aren't prepared, or think they are, but they're barely prepared for a minor emergency.

The website is being built up, but you can still visit it at www.Prep4Quake.com.

If you've found my book informative and helpful, please refer it to others. I'd appreciate it if you'd submit a review on Amazon.

Best wishes in your preparedness efforts and the peace that comes with knowing you can provide for your loved ones in an emergency.

Thank you,

Christopher K. Cox

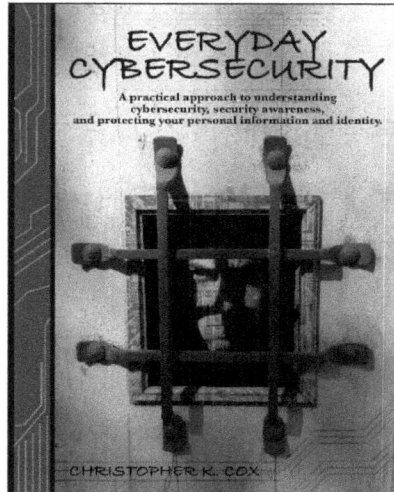

P.S. If you'd like to know how to secure your personal information and identity, better protect yourself against identity theft, and increase your security awareness in an easy-to-understand format, please check out *Everyday Cybersecurity: A practical approach to understanding cybersecurity, security awareness, and protecting your personal information and identity*.

I wrote the book with everyday users in mind, so it's light on technical explanations, geared towards the technology challenged.

About the Author

Chris's interest in earthquakes began as a young teenager when he and his family lived in Santiago, Chile. Living on the Ring of Fire exposed him to many smaller quakes, as well as a very big one.

Being involved with an international troop of the Boy Scouts of America, and having parents who tried to be prepared, laid a foundation for Chris's preparedness mindset.

As a single adult, Chris kept himself prepared. But after being married for a few years, and adding kids to the family, he didn't realize how unprepared he had become due to life getting busy with work, returning to school, kids, church service, and never-ending projects. Preparedness had not only gone to the back burner, but the burner had been turned off.

In 2015 his preparedness consciousness was pricked, and he renewed preparedness efforts and involved his family as well.

He started giving a few earthquake preparedness presentations, and his research led him to want to share more of the information he was learning. He also wanted to provide a preparedness resource for those wanting to help their families get prepared. After two years of compiling research and writing, this book is the result.

Chris lives with his beautiful wife, four children, and dog near the Wasatch Fault in Utah. He has a bachelor's degree in recreation management and youth leadership and another in information systems. He also has a master's degree in cybersecurity.

Past experiences include working in the mountains at high adventure camps, installing security systems, working as an extra and stand-in for films and TV shows, and substitute teaching. Although he hasn't flown in many years, he has a helicopter pilot certificate, and he'd love to take his family flying some year, after getting his skills refreshed.

Earthquake: What, Where, and How to Prepare is Chris's second published book. His first was *Everyday Cybersecurity: A practical approach to understanding cybersecurity, security awareness, and protecting your personal information and identity*. He is currently writing a sci-fi fantasy book.

Facebook facebook.com/christopherkcoxauthor
Instagram instagram.com/christopherkcoxauthor/

www.ingramcontent.com/pod-product-compliance
Lightning Source LLC
Chambersburg PA
CBHW060838280326
41934CB00007B/835